MANAGE IT RIGHT!

More Praise for *Manage It Right!*

"amazingly useful"

"*Manage It Right!* is an amazingly useful book on how managers can make organizations effective. The Zoreas' book is full of usable knowledge that is easy to read, understand and assimilate. Like the consultant that I respect and appreciate from our years of working together and adding value for our stakeholders, I found *Manage It Right!* to be well organized, insightful, hitting on the key topics and associated lessons."

> **—Bob Buckler**
> President (retired)
> DTE Energy

"beyond my greatest expectations"

"*Manage It Right!* is one of the most valuable books a manager or executive could ever have the pleasure of reading. As CEO of a Nasdaq traded company, I found Carlos and Dee's creative way to teach complex business management as explained in this unique book to be invaluable. Having personally witnessed these management methods at work, the Zoreas truly delivered beyond my greatest expectations."

> **—Paul Rosenbaum**
> Former CEO and Chairman of the Board
> Rentrak Corporation

"legendary"

"Manage It Right! helps managers succeed. In my 30 years of business reporting for the *Detroit Free Press, Detroit News,* and *Crain's Detroit Business,* Carlos Zorea is the savviest person I've met. His observations are always spot-on, and he is legendary in the Detroit area for entrepreneurs who became successes because they were smart enough to listen to him."

— **Tom Henderson**
Crain's Detroit Business

"secrets to be harvested"

"Manage It Right! is a comprehensive and highly readable guide to dealing with organizational challenges that require understanding emotions, politics, skill levels and techniques – along with highly organized hard work and a commitment to succeed. It is an amazing encapsulation of the clear logic and highly disciplined methodology that made its authors the successful and sought after consultants they are.

"The commitment Carlos Zorea and Dee Zorea have demonstrated in sharing their methodology, developed through years of successful engagements, is typical of my experience with them as they guided us through very complicated business situations to ultimate strategic and operational success. Reading *Manage It Right!* brings back exciting memories of several engagements: complicated; intense; business saving; difficult; and with brilliant results. Here are the Zoreas' 'secrets' to be harvested."

— **George H. Kuper**
Chairman
Council of Great Lakes Industries

"powerful insights"

"With *Manage It Right!* everyone can gain the same powerful insights we've enjoyed. Carlos Zorea and his team helped us organize for growth and focus sharply on what matters. Every day, we still use the lessons he taught us to drive sales and profitability."

> —**Jeff Padden**
> CEO
> Public Policy Associates, Inc.

"practical management lessons"

"*Manage It Right!* is an engaging story about a realistic business situation and its protagonists. The short chapters teach practical management lessons, not just abstract principles. As a former manager who benefited from Dr. Zorea's mentoring, I can heartily recommend this book, and the man who shares his life lessons in building a sound business."

> —**Ed Waltz**
> Distinguished Member of the Technical Staff
> Virginia Tech

"uniquely different"

"*Manage It Right!* is different from anything I have encountered before and it's worth it. Unlike most 'how to manage' books, this book actually deals with the niche of turnaround situations. Carlos Zorea and Dee Zorea tell a great story that teaches managers the secrets to management success. I witnessed Carlos Zorea apply those same secrets to take control of a business spiraling out of control, stabilize it, and turn it into a success by mentoring middle managers and radically changing the culture."

> —**Kenneth Augustyn**
> Director (former)
> ERIM International, Inc.

"propel any business to success"

"*Manage It Right!* is an engaging compendium of practical and extremely valuable business management lessons embedded within a hypothetical, but realistic, business success story. Carlos Zorea and Dee Zorea successfully introduce a new element of business discipline in each chapter, culminating in an overall business management construct that can propel any business to success. From personal experience, I can testify that Dr. Zorea's management methods deliver. I strongly recommend that every business manager adds *Manage It Right!* to his or her library."

—**Ralph H. Mitchel**
　　Distinguished Member of the Technical Staff
　　General Dynamics

MANAGE IT RIGHT!

Intrapreneurial Skills to Succeed in Any Organization

Carlos Zorea

and

Dee Zorea

For more information on the concepts presented in this book or additional copies, please contact:

Carlos Zorea
Chicago, IL
Email: info@zoreaconsulting.com

ISBN-10: 0991392701
ISBN-13: 9780991392704

Library of Congress Control Number: 2013914067
Manage It Right! Press
Chicago, IL

To my wife, Silvia, who inspired me to learn new things, understand life, and always help others. Her support made writing this book possible.

To my sons, for your continuous support and encouragement.

—Carlos Zorea

To my parents, Carlos and Silvia. You constantly inspire me.

—Dee Zorea

TABLE OF CONTENTS

Exhibits List

Section 4

FOREWORD

"take this book to heart"

I finished reading *Manage It Right!* and congratulate its authors, Carlos Zorea and Dee Zorea, on a job well done. Most management books with this depth of knowledge are rather dry and difficult to read. In contrast, the authors have done a fine job of writing in a narrative style that makes reading it a joy. Its valuable tools and insights are relevant to managers at any stage of their careers.

As I read the book, I couldn't help but think of all the things I could and should have done better as a manager if I would have had the tools, mentoring, and discipline to undertake the Zoreas' methodology. With so many valuable techniques in the book, there is something every manager can implement to improve his or her organization. Thanks to the Zoreas for writing a comprehensive and thought-provoking guide to organizational analysis, improvement and self-growth.

Manage It Right! is a unique, easy-to-read guide to enhancing business performance through a rigorous process of analysis, system improvements, team building, monitoring and control. Written in narrative style, the book chronicles the journey of a midcareer manager, Dennis, facing the monumental challenge of turning around a failing division of a major company. Through extensive counseling with his seasoned mentor and consultant, Chuck, we learn the steps necessary to evaluate and transform organizational performance in a refreshingly new way.

Although this book is a quick read, it leaves the reader with a textbook's worth of tools to analyze a business's performance, identify and prioritize problems and solutions, and balance budgets to focus on critical needs. Its many tools are common-sense approaches to creating systems and procedures that help managers define progress and keep it on track. Advice for managing above to superiors and below to subordinates is beneficial for both new and experienced managers. Tools for self-evaluation and evaluation of subordinates are useful in performing a task that most managers dread. The techniques provided are ones that successful managers will return to often throughout their careers as they face the challenges of our fast-changing business environment.

Get this book and take a few hours to read it. You will undoubtedly find techniques and tools applicable to your own organization. You will probably identify with the challenges Dennis faces as he overcomes adversity and grows as a manager. Let this book be your mentor as you grow in your career. The tools and techniques that the Zoreas developed over fifty years of business experience have applicability to all organizations regardless of their current success. Take this book to heart and let it positively change your own managerial effectiveness. Return to it often and adapt the tools to your own organization and style. This is certainly a book that will benefit all managers and become a reference for years to come.

—Hunt Harris
Entrepreneur and philanthropist
CEO (retired), Star Forms

PREFACE

Manage It Right! is a legacy of its authors' years of business management experience. We have the opportunity to empower middle managers with better business management know-how, tools, and decision-making skills to effectively improve their individual organizations, and our economy as a whole.

This book provides a comprehensive method for improving the performance of business units. It translates experience and creativity into an education. It conveys the principle that anyone who is motivated to learn and take some risk can convert his or her thoughts into practical execution. It reveals the bridge between good ideas and success through detail-oriented execution.

Manage It Right! also emphasizes the extraordinary value that an outside consultant can provide to a client. The consultant brings unbiased and nonpolitical perspectives based on years of challenging experiences. Clients have the opportunity to sharpen their skills, to better understand and evaluate people, and to persevere in converting beliefs into action.

Stiffer competition, stricter regulations, and advancing technology continually challenge today's leadership with new demands and rapid change. *Manage it Right!* details practical guidance for private and public companies, as well as for not-for-profit, governmental, and educational organizations. It applies to CEOs, COOs, executives, managers, aspiring managers, manager mentors and coaches, management professors, teachers, students, trainers, external and

internal consultants, human resource specialists, and all those
wanting to better understand and implement critical enterprise
decisions and business operations.

Out of one hundred possible ways to respond to any given
business situation or challenge, ninety-eight will likely be incorrect
or very wrong. It is important to get to the one or two that will
work. This book covers the proper sequence of critical decision
making needed to substantially improve business performance. This
sequence was developed, field-tested, and refined over a period of
twenty-five years.

Readers will learn to select the best ways to respond to a variety
of challenges, improve employee motivation and pride, identify key
performance parameters, and increase profitability in the process.
They can customize the tools and methods presented here to fit
their specific needs, to lower costs and delivery times of products/
services, to save critical company time, and especially to enhance
performance.

The authors of *Manage It Right!* have worked with organizations
across the board: for-profit and not-for-profit, product and service,
public and private, small and large, R&D and manufacturing.
They have experience in a variety of industries, including defense
systems, semiconductors, fiber optics, software, automation, CAD/
CAM (computer-aided design and computer-aided manufacturing),
Internet retail, movies, utilities, services, manufacturing, medical
equipment, hospitals, and more. Ninety-five percent of these
clients' business challenges were related to internal management
issues. Each challenge revealed another lesson or led to another
management tool. *Manage It Right!* shares the field-tested, client-
approved, comprehensive method to increase organizational value.
Because these business management concepts are based on real-life
challenges, and because they have universal application, readers can
use them in their own organizations.

One of the factors in humanity's progress has been specialization.
With the advent of universities hundreds of years ago, societies

further formalized their focus on this concept. They realized that most individuals couldn't learn all the material available in all disciplines; therefore, knowledge slicing would facilitate its absorption. However, slicing life into small pieces is against what life entails. Life is integrating multiple disciplines. Leonardo da Vinci understood that over five centuries ago. He was a physician, a sculptor, a painter, a war engineer, an aeronautical engineer, and more.

Specialization has become the enemy of integration, and many individuals do not or cannot think in multidisciplinary ways. In an attempt to integrate business education, universities invented the MBA. The hope was that two years of multidisciplinary business theory would suffice to fill the voids surrounding specialization. In spite of this, business integrators are still few and far between.

Readers can look at their own organization, recognize the silos that have been created, and notice the barriers that separate employees from each other. Often, the lack of integration is the major impediment to a company's progress and underperformance. The problem can be further complicated by the lack of a common nomenclature, ineffective autopiloted processes, bureaucracy, and funding barriers.

Interdisciplinary integration, or the ability to simultaneously deal with various business disciplines to achieve results, has proven its benefits in some industries and has yet to be applied in others. The aero industry has enjoyed the fruits of interdisciplinary integration. It starts with the way this discipline is taught in the classroom. In contrast, the health-care industries suffer from limited diagnostics integration and collaboration. Consequently, service is inefficient and health-care costs have spiraled out of control.

Using the proven strategies in *Manage It Right!*, readers can improve their organizations' operations, growth, profitability, and value.

Acknowledgments

Thanks to our family, friends, neighbors, and clients who encouraged us over the years to write a book about business management as we see it.

Special thanks to Ed Henderson, whose thoughts, numerous discussions, and contributions were instrumental in helping us write this book.

We appreciate the efforts of Carole Lewis for her thorough review and comments on the first-draft manuscript.

We are grateful to Ed Waltz for his in-depth review and comments on the first-draft manuscript.

Thanks to Ray Wise for his review and comments on the final-draft manuscript.

Thanks to B. Beacon, whose deep knowledge of the English language found the right words to convey several concepts and ideas.

Thanks to Silvia Zorea, wife and mother, who offered invaluable comments, encouragement, and understanding during this journey.

Finally, thanks to the CreateSpace team, whose endless patience and untiring efforts helped convert our manuscript into this book, notably Erin Rocha, Chris Willemse, Virginia D. Kerr, and Carina Petrucci.

Thank you all for being persistent and tolerant. Here it is. Enjoy!

—*Carlos Zorea & Dee Zorea*

Introduction

Dennis is a manager who has been selected to revive BLM, a failing business unit. He realizes that managing this business unit would be an impossible undertaking if it were not for Chuck, an enigmatic and wise consultant, who tirelessly shares decades of proven management strategies. Dennis faces very serious challenges that affect both his career and his private life. During this engagement, neither Dennis nor Chuck enjoys much free time with their families or hobbies. Through it all, can Dennis save a business unit that no one else has been able to revive?

This book reveals lessons about intrapreneurial management concepts and sequential integration theory. These same lessons have helped managers apply implementable solutions to real-life business problems. These managers have been able to transform their businesses (be they failing, losing money, stagnant, or profitable), achieve and maintain excellence, secure growth and prosperity for their stakeholders, and increase the value of their businesses.

The book is divided into four sections.

Section 1 introduces the diagnostics process and methodology to identify organizational weaknesses. It continues with the change design process that converts these weaknesses into strategic issues, strategies, and changes in functional and transitional organizational structures.

Section 2 focuses on building a team. Because people manage processes, it is important for managers to leverage the power of the change design dashboard to recognize when weak teams can doom processes, build the right teams, and schedule and manage projects accordingly.

Section 3 deals with operational management. Managers learn the skills of blocking and tackling, including managing quality meetings, coaching, and training. This section deals with funding projects in spite of limited budgetary resources. In addition, readers will explore informal management styles.

Section 4 relates to the monitoring and control of the new organization. After identifying and eliminating weaknesses, it is important to foster growth. Once all the projects are launched and tracked, managers need to review the sustainable organization for the long term, to define the business metrics, to assess the quality of their people on an ongoing basis, and to align the business activity with the business unit's and corporate goals and objectives.

Appendix 1 includes a detailed version of the "Request for Materials" introduced and described in Section 1.

Appendix 2 presents "Chuck's Words of Wisdom" which is a collection of many unique and borrowed sayings that Chuck often shared with Dennis when imparting different business management lessons.

SECTION 1

DIAGNOSTICS AND CHANGE DESIGN

- 1 -

THE MANAGER

After a spirit-sapping day of negotiations in Pittsburgh, where the cold, wintry day penetrated all the way to the bones, I returned to the airport to catch my flight back home to Chicago. My flight from Pittsburgh was running late. Not only that, but while en route to Chicago, the plane kept bouncing off the airstreams like crazy. I couldn't remember the last time I suffered so much turbulence; it was almost like riding an old wooden rollercoaster. At least the landing at O'Hare was pretty smooth. It was nighttime already, and the skyline was pitch black.

As the pilot maneuvered the plane to our gate, I picked up my cell phone and called my wife.

"Cheryl, how are you?"

"I'm fine, Dennis. Where are you?"

"I just landed at O'Hare, but I can't predict when I'll get home. I hope I don't get delayed in baggage claim like last time. How are the girls?"

"They're fine; they went ice-skating this afternoon, and now they're working on their homework."

"Okay, sweetie, I'll call you when I get to my car, okay? I'm getting off the plane now."

"Okay. Talk to you soon," she said.

I picked up my suitcases and waited for the parking-lot shuttle bus to show up and take me to my car. I lived about an hour's drive from the airport. That gave me some time to think and introspect. You know, do a little soul-searching. There I was, about to turn thirty-five—a real wake-up call to reevaluate my life's purpose, values, and priorities. I was a middle manager with a wonderful wife and a proud father of two great daughters. I thought about how I had always been extremely responsible and reliable, but those qualities had never really gotten me as far as I thought they should have.

As I thought about my life, I realized that something was missing. It didn't have anything to do with my family—I had a great relationship with my wife, who was my high-school sweetheart, and I was a devoted father who was very involved in my two daughters' extracurricular activities. And although my parents and siblings were spread out across the country, we kept in touch regularly. Plus, I was a pretty decent fly fisherman and enjoyed working out at the gym and playing the guitar. No, this feeling had nothing to do with my personal life; it had everything to do with the fact that I was in a rut professionally.

In essence, that special spark of mine seemed to have gotten edged out over the years, though I desperately wished to find it again and reclaim it. In a futile attempt to fill in the void, I had secured a supplemental position teaching a marketing course for an evening program at a local university, which seemed fine. It offered a little extra income, which helped pay some of the bills, and I got to do something else I turned out to be pretty good at. And yes, that job was fine, but fine wasn't where I wanted to be.

This time, I let myself listen to the whispering cries of my soul for something new, something different, possibly even life-changing. I needed a new challenge; I needed more satisfaction from my day job. What I really needed, I thought, was actually a whole new day job, full of unexpected twists, like the kind you'd experience on an exciting adventure. I felt ready to take on new responsibilities, maybe even take on a new position at work.

As for the Pittsburgh negotiations—well, they had to do with my day job. They concluded my last formal assignment for the year, and I felt very proud of them; they turned out very well. After that, to finish off my duties for the year, all I had to do were the follow-up reports. I'd been working for the same company for twelve years. That's about a third of my life. That's real loyalty, real dedication. I had poured my heart, my soul, and my spirit into helping this company succeed and into raising my kids and supporting my family.

I called Cheryl and asked her not to wait up for me, reassuring her that she could go to sleep. Yes, it was very late, but an hour later I arrived home, barely able to keep my eyelids open. I was tired. I prepared myself a cup of tea, took a few sips, found my way to bed, and crashed on the mattress. I slept like a baby.

The next day, I woke up at 5:30 a.m. and, while they were still fresh in my mind, summarized the pros and cons of the Pittsburgh deal. I wanted to minimize the number of surprise questions that my new boss might pose. I finished the work and then joined Cheryl and the girls for breakfast. I decided to wear my lucky blue suit and my red tie. When I drove to work in my Ford Taurus, traffic wasn't bad. I was even early, but since the workplace had flex hours, many people came in earlier than usual so that they could leave early as well.

When I arrived, my assistant, Jennifer, was already there. "Good morning, Dennis; Peter's office called me a few minutes ago. He wants to talk to you as soon as you're available."

"Good morning, Jennifer. Okay, thank you," I replied. I grabbed a half cup of coffee and headed to the elevator.

This year my division had undergone some changes at the top. My new boss, Peter, had transferred over from a Fortune 100 company and had been given the title of senior VP. He was tall and in his midforties; he was also aggressive and demanding. His main pastime was hunting and "going for the kill." During the winter season, he could be atop a tree for hours, waiting with his rifle for a deer to appear within range. He had an innate patience to see the right opportunity at the right time. Peter's office was on the top floor of the adjacent building, next to the CEO, the president, and the other top executives' offices.

I went down to the first floor, crossed through the connecting hallway to the other tower, finished my coffee, and tossed the paper cup into the nearest trash bin on my way to the executive elevators. As soon as I got into one of them, I swiped my access card next to the control panel and pressed the button for the fifty-fifth floor.

In very short order, I reached the top. The elevator doors opened, and I stepped into the reception area, only to be greeted by a security officer who first had to clear my visit with Peter's creative assistant, Claudia, and to make sure that Peter was ready for my visit. I was let in and walked down the corridor, and there I saw Claudia with her usual friendly smile.

"Hi, Dennis," she said. "It's really good to see you again. By the way, Peter is on the phone right now, but he will be with you shortly; he really wants to talk to you. I wish I knew what about, but I bet you'll find out soon enough. Just give him a few minutes, okay?"

"Okay, Claudia. I'll just take a seat until he's ready."

While I was waiting, I overheard Peter saying, "Okay, Greg. I'll move in that direction right away."

Greg, the company president, was an engineer by training who exuded a charismatic aura that had earned him the love and respect of his employees and subordinates. He was intelligent, hardworking, devoted to making the company better, and he just loved coming in early and making every minute count. He knew that he needed greater discipline in the company and that Peter could make that happen, but Greg wasn't quite sure about how well Peter's aggressiveness would be received in the existing environment.

Peter hung up the phone, turned around in his comfortable chair, came to the door, and said, "Hi, buddy. Come in."

I entered his office and glanced around very quickly, just to refresh my memory on the kind of luxury afforded to the higher-ups. I knew that senior VPs enjoyed huge office spaces, and his was no exception. It just happened to be full of Red Sox memorabilia. He had come to Chicago all the way from Massachusetts. He had bought a huge house in the suburbs for a steal after the real-estate crash.

"Please sit down," he added. I sat on the left side of the T-table at the seat closest to the entrance.

"Dennis, based on the results of your meeting yesterday, your temporary assignment is nearly done. I felt very satisfied when you called yesterday from Pittsburgh with the negotiation results. I already updated Greg about it, and we got into a discussion about potential new assignments for you. I know you have a few reports to write before you'd be ready to take on a major new assignment. I know these reports will take some time to finish, but the sooner you get them done the better." These words caught my attention. I nodded to let him know I was really listening.

He continued: "Greg is worried about the BLM unit, which operates under Jack. It turns out that unit has been so underperforming lately that the local press has even written a number of unflattering articles about it. In fact, Jack doesn't want BLM anymore."

He paused for a few seconds and then resumed. "Greg told me that he'd like to put BLM under my command, but he made it very clear I'd first have to find the right person to lead it. He also mentioned that several months ago he engaged Chuck for consulting services. Greg believes Chuck to be a remarkably seasoned individual and has worked with him for over six years. He initially hired Chuck to make sure that everything in the organization was being done right both strategically and operationally—sort of like having a second opinion. The results have always proven fruitful, and that's how Chuck has come to be known as Greg's senior consultant. It's also why he trusts Chuck's originality even if his opinions occasionally clash with our other consultants from McCain Consulting. I'm sure you already know that Greg works very closely with McCain on all our major projects."

"Yes, Peter, I'm aware of McCain. One of their teams worked with me in my previous assignment, and I've also worked with Chuck before. I know he has a different way of getting things done, and I believe and respect Greg's position and approach. It sounds to me like he wants our division to take over BLM and improve its performance and reputation."

I recalled how about six months ago I worked on a project with a whole bunch of consultants from McCain. McCain had been working with the company for decades. They came well equipped with numerous MBAs. However, there had also been this independent consultant who had caught my attention—Chuck. His style was very reserved, though he kept coming up with effectively suitable answers to many of the challenges we were facing at that time.

"Dennis, I brought you here today because you've proven yourself to the company on multiple fronts, and you're a veteran employee with many years of dedicated performance. What Greg and I want to do is have you take over the helm at BLM. It won't be like anything else you've ever done. This won't be a walk in the park, let me tell you. But I know that when you set your mind to doing something, you come through for those who rely and depend on you. I don't think anyone can go at this alone, but Greg reassured me that we could bring in Chuck to coach whoever becomes the new BLM manager. With my support and Chuck's help, I believe you could make it happen. I think you should lead BLM." He paused for a bit and then said, "Will you do it?"

I could tell he was feeling pressed to select a new leader for BLM and to initiate the change process. I had the feeling that Peter didn't really have any other decent alternative assignments to offer me, and if I hesitated to accept his offer right on the spot, he would have offered the job to someone else, and I might have lost out on a pivotal career-making opportunity. Plus, I yearned to try something new. BLM was a larger unit, and a promotion would surely be granted upon my acceptance. I didn't know much about BLM, and I didn't have a clue about the sort of mess it was in, but my gut screamed out to me, "Opportunities such as this one rarely ever come up in this company, so don't you dare leave this room without accepting!"

First, though, I needed to know exactly what type of challenge I was facing. So I said, "Peter, can you tell me a little bit about the types of problems BLM is experiencing?"

"Sure," he said. "In a nutshell, our company has run BLM for several decades, and BLM started to deteriorate years ago. Knowledgeable employees have retired, new customer demands couldn't be satisfied, and the unit failed to modernize. Various personnel have been assigned to manage that unit. They knew it would be a complex but temporary career milestone to continue moving up the company ranks. They moved on as fast as they got there.

"The situation became so dire that customers have approached our COO, CEO, and even board members, asking them to resolve their 'burning issues.' It's been extremely embarrassing for our company's leadership when newspapers attack the unit and the company. Our company's reputation and leadership are suffering. The problems have also negatively impacted the sales and performance of our other units. As the number of complaints continued to mount, I and other top executives wanted a large consulting company to explore outsourcing the work. Although we'd miss out on additional revenue from the unit, it would hopefully stop the avalanche of bad publicity. But Greg still wants to save this darn thing. So here we are. Does this help?" Peter asked.

"Yes, thank you," I replied. "That gives me a general idea of the history."

Upon hearing how extensive and entrenched BLM's problems were, my gut wrenched with anxiety. How could I possibly turn around a unit with such monumental problems that dated back so far? I had to do it, though. If I didn't accept the job, the company might not offer me anything else. And if I did accept it and succeeded in turning BLM around, it would be a huge personal accomplishment worthy of great rewards. I had to make a decision quickly.

"It sounds like a challenge that I'm willing to take on. I'll be glad to do it," I said firmly. "Thank you for the opportunity."

Was I nuts? To run such a large unit, not knowing anything about it, except that it was in really bad shape? I had never done anything like this before. I might have made a mistake by rushing to accept this new destiny, but we're often fashioned by the defining moments of our lives, and this was mine. I committed to this newest and greatest professional challenge.

"Thank you for thinking of me. By the way, it'll take me several weeks to complete the final reports for my last assignment."

"No problem," Peter replied. "I'll let Greg know that you're on board with BLM's transition to our division. Also, just so you know, Chuck has already gotten the ball rolling with BLM, and he's doing some fantastic groundwork, figuring what's what and so on. He's been sending me reports, but I can't seem to wrap my head around them. Frankly, I've never seen this type of comprehensive work and reports before. After you return from vacation, I'll let you and Chuck sort out the details."

We stood up and shook hands. "Merry Christmas, Dennis. My regards to Cheryl and the girls. I'll be on vacation next week as well, so Happy New Year to you too!" he added.

"And happy holidays to you and your family, Peter," I replied.

When I arrived back home, I told Cheryl about my new job and the rumors I had heard about BLM.

"If the situation is so bad, do you think you'll be able to make it work?" she asked.

I didn't keep secrets from Cheryl. I looked her straight in the eyes and said, "I really don't know, sweetie. I really don't know enough about the job yet, but when the time comes, I'm sure I'll find out. Sometimes you just have to take a leap of faith, plunge into uncharted waters, take control of the situation, and leverage your resources as best as you can. And that's what I plan to do."

- 2 -

THE CONSULTANT

During those last cold days in December, I worked as fast as I could, but it seemed to me as if I didn't accomplish all that much. After all, year's end wasn't usually the best time to get a lot of work done. Our family reunion was coming up, and it has been our tradition to celebrate together in Florida, where my parents lived. That's how we spent our winter vacations.

I knew that new, "special" responsibilities were about to be sprung on me at work, and then it struck me—next year, I might not get to enjoy as much quality time with the family. Ten days later, we returned. The remaining weeks in January passed very quickly. I concentrated on finishing my outstanding reports so I that I could shift my focus to finding out more about BLM.

No matter who got appointed to direct BLM, no one was willing or had been able to effectively lead the unit. Five years ago, BLM's director was not sufficiently competent to handle the unit. That director's responsibilities turned out to be far too complex for him to manage, which also happened to be the case for others before him. In fact, before leaving his job, he had even suggested to "outsource the darn thing."

That same director thought he could save the cost of a salary by having one person managing another unit and BLM; he promoted Mary to manage BLM along with her lieutenant, Charlotte. However, managing this business unit on a half-time basis simply wouldn't work. When BLM transferred to Peter's division, Mary transferred to another unit.

Charlotte was very nice, very energetic, and technically knowledgeable, but she feared that the decision makers would outsource her work to a third party. As a single mother and the sole supporter for her family, she decided to leave the company to work for one of the company's vendors.

Both Mary and Charlotte had worked long hours, but it seemed that no matter how much dedicated effort they poured into their work, the number of critical problems kept piling up way faster than the needed solutions. I already knew that they had worked very diligently to provide Chuck the information he sought from BLM to assess whether the company could keep the unit in house, but their hopes seemed to have been dashed when they had learned that McCain Consulting favored outsourcing. McCain simply didn't see the situation as salvageable. Both of them had seen the message written on the wall and had gotten out.

Last summer, Greg had tasked Chuck with exploring the intricacies of the unit. The mandate was very specific: figure out how to turn this unit around so that it could be managed sensibly and effectively, and to the point that the rampant negative press coverage would dissipate and even vanish. The goal was simple: no more negative articles in the local newspaper. It was easier said than done.

January was coming to an end, and I let Peter know I was ready to take charge. I was introduced to the key employees, and I quickly found out who would be working for me directly. That same afternoon, I found a rather large package on my desk from Claudia, Peter's assistant. It included four white three-ring binders. I looked at the binders. These were the same ones that Chuck had prepared and delivered to Peter the previous quarter. I opened them one by one, scanned their tables of contents, and quickly flipped through a few pages here and there.

I wondered, "What are they doing on my desk?" Clearly, Peter must've had pretty good reasons to hand them over to me. They all covered different subjects. There were no graphs, no diagrams, and no visuals. How was I supposed to make heads or tails of them? He could have just as well dropped a ton of bricks on me. I could feel a migraine coming.

So there I was, feeling somewhat dumbfounded and quite overwhelmed. I knew I had to meet with Chuck right away for a meeting of the minds. I needed some clarity in the midst of it all. The sooner we could sit down together to discuss these materials, the sooner I could begin to crack the code on how to proceed. I had to know how these reports applied to my new role at BLM.

I don't recall who called whom, but in short order, Chuck and I met in the company's cafeteria.

"Dennis, I know how important this is for you, and I don't know what motivated you to take over this unit, but it's a tremendous undertaking and a formidable challenge," Chuck said. "I've completed the diagnostic assignment that Greg requested of me, and the details are in these binders. These materials are not just for you to read, but to actually absorb and make your own; you'll have to read these from cover to cover at least three times before they really start to sink in."

"Are you going to help me figure this out?" I asked. "Peter told me that BLM's situation is complicated, and given what you've just told me and the reports you've put together, I believe it."

"I did what Greg assigned me, the results of which are in the white binders you now have in your possession. I also believe you'll need to be properly coached to succeed in your task ahead. So I'll be blunt. Right now, the way it's running itself, it looks like BLM has a death wish, but because I believe we can save it, Greg would like me to coach and mentor you. If you want me to help you personally, you'll need to agree to certain rules. And if you'll accept these rules, I'll let Greg know that we'll start working together pretty soon."

Chuck's language was not fully clear to me. He talked about certain rules, and I didn't know what he meant. It was clear from the tone of his voice that I might have made a mistake when I agreed to take the job, and so I remained silent, just thinking about my new situation.

Chuck continued: "You and I worked together a couple of years ago, and that worked out very well for us both, but this situation is different. Right now, you are in the spotlight. I'm sixty-seven years old now, and I do consulting work because I love the game of business. I also like to teach all that I have learned over the course of nearly a half a century of genuinely interesting work. I'm sure you are well aware that as a consultant, I don't have operational authority. You are the one empowered to implement the decisions. If we work together, I'll assume you will implement whatever decisions we discuss and agree upon. Now, if I take on this responsibility to coach you, you must take on the role of a real partner in this mentorship relationship."

"When you say a 'real partner,' what exactly are you saying?" I asked.

"I know you're a very honest guy. I've noticed your dedication and earnest performance these past few years. I already know that you're very responsible, but…" Chuck trailed off.

"But what?" I replied.

Chuck answered, "I'm willing to guide you on how to reign in this monstrous BLM situation, but only if you promise to fully dedicate yourself by making sure you get your skills up to speed as required, even if it means immersing yourself in handling and supporting your job responsibilities up to seven days a week. And why is that, you might ask? Well, it's because you actually have two jobs to perform. You see, your first job is your operational job. It demands that you manage the daily business activities of the unit and handle or resolve the daily problems or issues that arise. And believe me, they've got more challenges than they can handle, and the number of outstanding problems steadily increases with each passing day.

"Your second job is your professional development. It involves the work you'll be doing during and in response to our coaching sessions, which will empower you to get this unit on the right track and come out successful. Now, I have to be very realistic with you. If you want to work with me, you'll have to sacrifice a lot of personal time for quite a while. But that, my friend, is only part of the price you'll have to pay to make BLM run smoothly before you can have your personal time back. I also have a set of iron-clad rules that I'll ask you to abide by. Please open your notebook and write the following."

I opened my notebook and said, "Okay, Chuck. Shoot!"

He looked me straight in the eyes and rattled off a quick, short list: "Long hours, no excuses, willingness to learn, doing homework on time, self-discipline and periodic self-evaluation, and the most important rule of all: trust that all I want for you is for you to be successful. In addition, we will meet periodically at my place over several months until you're able to command your troops." He waited for me to write down everything and then added: "Whatever choice you make in the end, call me and let me know your decision."

I didn't know how to react. My "interview" with Peter for my new job flashed through my mind. And this time I didn't want to rush my answer the way I did with Peter. Within a couple of seconds, I said, "Let me think about this, and I'll get back to you soon."

"Thank you, Dennis," Chuck replied.

By now, I had spent some time with the key personnel in BLM and looked over some of the numbers. The situation was bad. Before I accepted this opportunity, the unit had already been operating without a manager for several months. The phones rang constantly; customer complaints kept racking up; customers and media were barking up the chain of command and hounding company execs and board members. No one in the hierarchy knew what to do to solve the problem. The boat was sinking, and it seemed like it had too many holes to patch, not just one or two, like I had hoped. I recalled Peter's guidance when I came on board, "I don't want any more phone calls at the top; I don't want any more negative articles in the newspapers. Chuck will help you. Fix it fast."

So what could I do? I needed more people and a better operation to deal with so many hostile customers and all the negative press. But the financials were so confusing that I could barely make sense of them. I didn't have enough people to run the current operations. My budget was already so lean that I couldn't cut other expenses. I thought about upgrading our technology to be more competitive, but I had no budget to invest. We were underbudgeted and understaffed. I realized it called for better skills and experience than what I had, and I started to question whether this was in fact a real opportunity or if I had been deliberately set up to fail. It had been weeks since the Pittsburgh meeting, but now, for the first time since then, I started to feel the stress mounting. To say the least, the pressure on me was heavy.

I drove home and thought about Chuck's rules, the unit's situation, and how my next decision would affect my family. My first impression of Chuck was that he was tough, knowledgeable, experienced, demanding, and sort of scary. I had asked some other people in the company about him, because I needed to know more about this mysterious man who could have such a huge impact on my career. Those who had worked closely with him saw him as very human, friendly, sometimes funny, supportive, helpful, down to earth, and one hundred percent trustworthy.

Once you got to know him well, they said, Chuck had a rare ability to blend humanity and warmth with impeccable business discipline. For decades, he had helped numerous executives, entrepreneurs, and managers become highly successful. From various sources, I learned that he liked to play chess, collect stamps, go to the theater, and watch foreign movies. During this intense engagement, however, I sensed that he probably wouldn't have much time to enjoy any of those activities.

At dinner, I remained pretty quiet, and Cheryl took notice. Usually, I was rather conversational during our evening meals together, but that night things were different; she could tell something was bothering me, but she couldn't contain herself and had to break the silence. "Dennis, what's up?"

"Sweetie," I began, "I'm starting to get the feeling that I might have jumped the gun when I agreed to take this new job. There is someone there, however, who already knows how I should proceed. He's the best chance I've got for coming out of this quagmire alive, and I do want his help; don't get me wrong."

"Well, dear, so what is it? What's eating you up? I haven't seen you this nervous since you had to face some negotiators out in Pittsburgh, but that was months ago, and you came out of it just fine. In fact, I still remember how proud you felt after you finished that challenge. See, honey? It was just a challenge, and you came through with flying colors. The more impressively you perform, the greater the next challenge becomes. It's like you said yourself— we're here to explore and engage the world to find out who we are and what we're made of. This challenge is just your newest one. That's all."

"Thank you, sweetie. You're right," I said.

"You don't have to lose any sleep over this. Who knows? We can figure this out; we always have. I don't think this has to be any different. So tell me, who's this guy who can help you out?"

"Well, it's Chuck. You remember Chuck, right? Last year you met him and his wife at Peter's fancy celebration party at the Drake Hotel. Peter threw the party to celebrate our division's very successful business campaign."

"Yes, I remember now. He and his wife were very nice. Yes, I remember Chuck. He looked very experienced, both in business and as a family man too," Cheryl said.

"Well, sweetheart, the truth is, I'm at a crossroads. I finally had my first meeting with Chuck, thinking we'd get started on unraveling his diagnostics reports. I never expected, however, that he'd put up conditions before coaching me. When Peter spoke to me about this assignment, I thought it had already been agreed that Chuck would just do his part."

"What kind of conditions?" she asked.

"Just some rules to hold me firmly accountable to him. He won't take me under his wing unless I commit to sacrificing my personal time for some intense personal coaching and study time, which could last for many months. Who knows? Before I thought I'd only have Peter for a boss, but now it feels like I'm going to have two. I don't know, sweetie. Maybe it's just that I'd have to cut down a lot on my time with you and the girls. I already spoke with a bunch of the guys in the unit who carry a lot of weight there, and from what I've learned so far, this new job is way over my head. Chuck has Greg's blessing in this matter, so the way I see it, I'll have to do whatever Chuck says. I don't feel too comfortable with the prospects of hardly getting to spend any quality time with my family. Honey, what do you think? What do you think I should do? I either have to accept Chuck's rules, or I swim alone. I'll probably sink if I attempt to go at it alone. But if I agree to his conditions, to abide by his rules, at least I'll have a decent chance to find safe harbor."

"You know that I always want you to be happy. I don't know. Could you get back to Peter and ask him for another job?"

"Well, our corporate intranet says the job has already been filled, and I've already been congratulated by our president for taking the position. I've already been introduced to the unit and its personnel, and customers are calling me. It's really too late for me to backtrack now."

"So what can you do? You know that the girls and I will support you. I'll talk to the girls tomorrow."

"Thanks, dear."

Cheryl made my decision easier. I knew I needed some help to sort it all out, and I knew it wouldn't be easy. I e-mailed Chuck, requesting to meet him again. We volleyed a few more e-mails back and forth and finally settled on meeting at his home in Naperville, a western suburb of Chicago.

It snowed that day, but I arrived on time and parked in the circular driveway; the walkway was properly salted and clear. I rang the doorbell, and he welcomed me inside with a smile. "Hi, Dennis; I hope you had a good ride. Please come on in."

His home was a custom-built house originally intended to accommodate his whole family. But his kids, already grown, had moved out long ago and lived on their own. He handed me a pair of "booties" to cover my shoes. His house looked immaculate. As I passed through the two-story grand foyer, I glanced around and noticed several elegant modern sculptures along the walls. We entered his nicely furnished mahogany-style office. We sat facing each other across a large table. The walls proudly displayed his academic diplomas as well as laminated business articles about his entrepreneurial contributions to Chicago's business community and economy.

Fortunately, I came with a bag large enough to hold all the white binders that Chuck had originally prepared for Peter and Greg, the same ones Peter had sent to my office.

"Did you have a chance to read the materials?" Chuck asked.

"I glanced at them, but I haven't studied them yet. I've been putting out fires all day. Plus, the way things are going at the office, I find myself getting home very late, only to repeat the same cycle of activities the very next day," I said.

"Have you thought about the rules?"

"Yes."

"And what is your answer?" Chuck asked, already knowing full well what the answer would be. He knew I must've been there for a very good reason. He just wanted to hear it straight from the horse's mouth. Well, I knew I wouldn't be able to successfully turn around

BLM without his guidance and determination, so I surrendered to my new reality and submitted myself to his conditions for cooperation.

"I know now how difficult the situation really is, so I'm ready to play by your rules."

"Okay, Dennis. Very good! I'm glad to know that the litany of excuses you just mentioned were your last ones before we get started. Welcome, and congratulations on beginning your most fantastic journey in the world of business. Very few people know what you're about to learn."

"What do you suggest we do next?"

"There is one more rule for you. I want you to spend at least half a day, every week, either at home or at a library to do whatever we decide needs to be done. I want you to take time to think—undivided, uninterrupted time for yourself. You will not succeed by only calming your customers. Going to work and dealing with difficult fires every day will not solve the core challenges. It's important to know exactly what to do."

This felt like my last hope. I knew I couldn't expect guaranteed success, but I didn't want to fail either. I had a sense of relief. I knew that from now on, I would have an ally. I took the white binders out of the bag and placed them on the table.

"Chuck, you've been working with the BLM group for several months. Could you please tell me how you collected all of this information and how you derived your conclusions?"

"I'll be more than happy to do so."

- 3 -

Intrapreneurship Technology

Since I didn't know how long Chuck would spend with me, I had budgeted my entire afternoon for our meeting. I quickly learned that with Chuck you don't schedule meetings for merely an hour. After two hours we took a short break; he invited me to have a granola bar and some mineral water. Chuck was a heart patient and was very cautious about eating and drinking. Through our meetings he made me more conscious about my health.

Chuck said, "I'll walk you through the methodologies I developed over nearly five decades of business experience, because, on top of solving problems, you need to know how to do these types of analyses by yourself. Although I'll 'monologue' a lot, I expect you to capture the principles in your notebook and study them at home every night. Practically speaking, this is a process of intrapreneurship technology transfer."

"But why do you call this intrapreneurship technology?" I asked. He handed me a card that read:

Definition

Technology makes, modifies, or uses tools, techniques, and systems to solve a problem or improve an already existing solution to a problem, so as to achieve a goal or purpose.

"Based on this definition of technology," Chuck said, "it seems we have developed an *intrapreneurship* technology. You see, many business problems are all too often wrongly attributed to an external reality. Customers get blamed for loss of market share, for reductions in periodic sales, and for declines in overall periodic profitability. Those are all excuses, and I don't like excuses. The truth is, in ninety percent of the cases, the problems of any unit are not related to externalities but rather are inherent to its own organization. In this and future sessions, we'll make sure to discuss and concentrate on the *what* of business management."

"Like what to do next?" I asked.

Chuck looked at me with his deep gaze, exploring to see whether I was properly tuning in and understanding what he was going to say next, and then he added: "This is the number-one challenge you are facing. The *what* comes first. Errors in deciding the right *what* all too often produce irreparable consequences."

I interjected, "But I have to show quickly that I'm doing something, to show Peter and Greg and the employees that I am in command of the situation."

"Listen, Dennis, I'm about to share with you my many experiences learned over forty-five years in business. Remember the old board games we used to play in our childhood, where we used to roll the dice to advance our token, and if we landed in the wrong square, we had to return back to the starting position, back to square one? Well, in business, going back to square one is painful. It means loss of credibility, time wasted, and many resources lost, to name a few."

"But what should I do in the meanwhile?".

"To know the right *what*, you have to invest part of your life to long hours, to acquire new skills, to think without sitting in front of a computer…long weeks, long days, long hours. Did I mention long hours before?"

"Okay, you have my commitment, but what do I do now?"

"When you go back to work, you'll keep doing the best you can, and it probably won't be good enough. But that's understandable; the skills you need take time to develop, and as we all know, there's no such a thing as fine wine before its time. In the next few sessions, I'll try to explain to you the logic we used in deriving the *what*. I know that BLM needs change to make it different from what it already is. Change requires the direct and indirect collaboration of three different types of individuals: stakeholders, transformation agents, and adaptation agents.

"Greg and Peter are the major stakeholders. Their expectations drive change in the organization. They know that they don't want noise coming from BLM, but they don't know the *what*. That's why they hired me and you; they hired us to figure this out. The *what* requires a lot of detail, and they don't have the time for it. Sometimes change is needed after extreme aversions to risk. Other times change is needed to offset precedents of retaliation against failure.

"A do-nothing policy fosters an environment that lacks risk taking, creativity, and innovation. Doing nothing and being forced into a routine yields failure. The only variable left to know is *when* this will happen. In the modern world, taking some level of prudent risk is necessary to maintain leadership. A culture needs to welcome novel ideas and make an effort to make these ideas work."

"I have been in this company for twelve years," I said, "and I know all too well what you're saying. BLM is where it is because of everything you just mentioned—and the way things stand now, we're already operating in a failure-oriented mode."

Chuck looked at some notes and said, "Change is in the air. You need to look around and notice the changes in people, markets, technology, competition, customers, performance, expectations, and regulations. Company leadership sometimes reveals its confusion over the meaning of change by blindly changing practices while ignoring the company's principles. More often than not, the principles are the source of the company's problems, and these are the ones that need to be changed first.

"The principles and methods I teach come from almost five decades of observing, managing, and learning how companies operate. These methods and tools have been implemented in small and large companies, private and public, across many different and unrelated industries."

"How come the same methodology works for all? Aren't methods different when you deal with different size companies?" I asked.

"Molecular biology deals with the structure and function of molecules essential to life, especially with their role in cell replication and the transmission of genetic information. Similarly, in what I call *business molecular biology*, corporations are based on their business cell health, structure, and function. Independent of their size, or whether they are public or private, or in a certain industry, all companies have business cells that are managed by a leader.

"Generally, business units have several business cells. A business cell is the smallest unit that can generate a P&L statement. In some cases, business cells may not have a separate balance sheet—but they should, even if it's only approximate. Having an imperfect balance sheet is oftentimes much better than not having one. Not all cells in a given business require the same type of attention. The business unit manager can use basic P&Ls and balance sheets to identify which cells are a problem and which are fine.

"The business unit leaders should be *intrapreneurs*, having an entrepreneurial spirit but functioning within a corporate structure. They should feel a degree of independence with the rights and the obligations that come from balancing freedom and discipline. Business unit leaders should leverage the company's resources to the fullest extent and shouldn't be held hostage to centrally provided services. Whatever is required from the business unit leader is also applicable to every business cell leader.

"In my consulting practice, we mostly face business cells that were deficient and produced pain to their hierarchy, independent of size and type of ownership. Proper management leads to business health. Many healthy business cells will integrate into healthy business units, product lines, and companies. This is the main reason why the methods and processes you're going to learn work for companies that are small, medium, or large; product-producing or service based; public or private; across different business segments."

"But in my company, a business cell doesn't operate in a vacuum," I said.

"Correct," Chuck replied. "They are part of a business nervous system that is linked to other cells in their own business unit and to business cells in other groups. It's the cells' successful coordination that results in the success of units and companies. While the executives, leaders, managers, and supervisors work to connect cells and units vertically, it's the employees who mostly connect the cells and the business units horizontally. Their responsibilities and rights have to be taught and clarified to allow them to become major contributors within their unit and their company."

We continued to exchange questions and answers until he said, "Wow, it's starting to get pretty late."

"This is fascinating for me. I get the feeling that whatever I learn while working with you will stay with me for the rest of my career."

"You're right. You are right."

After another three hours, I felt like my brain was about to explode. We called it a day, and I headed to my car. It had been snowing this whole time. I opened my driver's door, got the scraper, and cleared the white sheet of snow from the windshield and windows.

To date, my standard modus operandi had been so different from Chuck's conceptual thinking. I started feeling a new spirit of hope growing inside me, and I kept wondering, "Is this really happening?"

I headed home, arrived just in time for dinner, watched the news, kissed the girls good night, and fell into bed, completely exhausted.

- 4 -

SELF-EVALUATION #1

I already knew that Greg's exacting nature demanded the best in people and that he relied on Chuck. And mentally I knew that Greg and Peter's choice to pair me with Chuck was the right one. I was fine with that, but I still felt I had to do my own due diligence. I had to find out if Chuck was for real.

The next day, I arrived at work early, looked online, and found many articles about and by Chuck related to business management. Reading these gave me added relief that he had agreed to work with me. The problems at BLM kept mounting, conditions kept getting worse and worse by the day, and sometimes I even felt sorry for myself for having bitten off more than I could chew. The gap between the manager I was and the manager I had to become seemed unbridgeable.

That night I was talking to Cheryl, and she said, "You should reach out to Chuck. I think he could shed some light on what you're going through and possibly even give you the kind of emotional support you seem to need right now. Greg trusts Chuck's experience. I think you should too." Luckily I had Chuck's cell phone number.

The next day I took Cheryl's advice and called Chuck.

"Hello, Chuck speaking."

"Hi, Chuck. This is Dennis. Sorry to bother you, but I felt that I needed to call you. I have some things on my mind I need to figure out and a few things I need to get off my chest."

"What is it? What's up?"

I leveled with him and told him what I was going through emotionally. He listened and then said, "I'm in Grand Rapids, Michigan, right now, on my way to see a client. I have something in my briefcase that I always carry with me. I'll send you a PDF copy. I believe it'll help clear things up for you." A few minutes later, I got an e-mail from him.

From: Chuck

To: Dennis

Subject: From Shock to Action

When a manager is shocked with criticism about his unit's performance or with the task of turning around a business unit, that manager goes through seven phases of emotion before phasing into action. The length of each phase is a function of the manager's character and support systems.

Phase 1: Shock, disbelief, and denial.

Phase 2: Guilt—"If only I had done something different..."

Phase 3: Anger—brought on by frustration.

Phase 4: Depression—this feeling comes and goes, and you may sense despair.

Phase 5: Acceptance—finally, the leader accepts the truth.

Phase 6: Transcendence—realizing that there is a whole new way to engage the opportunity to achieve better results.

Phase 7: Hope—understanding that the opportunity to perform better exists.

Phase 8: Action—working the new plan.

Please contact me tomorrow at my office and let me know which phase
or phases you think you were in this morning before you called me, and
now, after you've read this e-mail. I've been there before.

I reread the e-mail several times, and then it dawned on me
that since the day before, I had experienced the first four phases.
I also understood that there were surely others out there who had
felt similarly distressed, having been thrust into extraordinarily
challenging predicaments before, like Chuck. The epiphany was
strikingly clear, and in Chuck I now saw a veteran business mentor
and ally.

It felt refreshing; I had just entered phase five. I accepted the truth
and decided to work as hard as possible to quickly reach phase eight.

I had a new session with Chuck scheduled for the next day; this
time, I was actually looking forward to it.

- 5 -

TURNAROUNDS

It was another wintery day. Chuck and I had agreed to meet every Wednesday from 2:00 to 5:00 p.m. The rest of the week, I'd be dealing with BLM and Chuck's homework, and he'd continue to prepare more reports and new homework assignments for me. As for me, I found his reports to be groundbreaking. With each new report he'd share with me, I'd gain a new business perspective. And with each new perspective, I'd see how I could better prepare for what I had to do, and then just do it.

Chuck was very devoted to his work. I occasionally even thought of him as an overachieving workaholic who expected anyone and everyone he did business with to perform at his same caliber and level of intensity. Frankly, I sometimes felt it to be too much. But to his credit, he happened to be a man of integrity; his work ethic was above reproach, and his unflinching honesty vacillated between pleasant and brutal.

"Today we are going to add one more rule to the list," he said.

"Another one?" I replied without thinking. I was concerned that any additional rules would only further strain my already fragile schedule.

"Yes, one more rule. That's right. From now on, everything that we discuss in this office will stay here. Neither one of us is going to share what we discuss here with anyone else. It's a gentlemen's agreement. Agreed?"

"Yes," I answered. I wanted that. I trusted Chuck, and this was taking our professional relationship to a whole new level, to a much higher plateau.

"Okay, today we'll begin our session with a discussion about the concept called 'turnaround.' Your unit is in need of a turnaround."

"I thought that turnarounds were for units that operate in the red, and we're not losing money."

Chuck quickly cut me off. "True, BLM is not losing money. Nor is it making any money. Moreover, its dysfunctional behavior is needlessly robbing top management of its peace of mind with all of that bad press that's been hounding you recently. The company would be much better served if its executives didn't have to get sidetracked by all the bad news that's being written up out there.

"BLM is forcing top management to underperform, thereby making the whole company underperform. The company's other units shouldn't have to suffer due to inadequate attention from top management. Right now, the way things stand, BLM is a big liability to the company. It desperately needs a turnaround."

"I see. Well, that puts things in a whole new perspective," I remarked. There was always something new to learn.

"First, let's review the different kinds of turnarounds that exist," he began.

I figured I'd start taking some notes, but as I began to reach for my notebook, Chuck interjected. "I've prepared a one-page summary to save us some time. Let's review it," he said, and handed me the following copy:

Exhibit 1:

The Best-Known Types of Turnarounds

Financial Turnaround

Best known to the public; it is intended to make the bottom line go from red to black. The theory is simple: increase revenue and reduce costs.

Behavioral Turnaround

It is critical to change the organization's behavior before other changes take place. Our experience shows that as soon as the need for change is recognized, legitimized, and authorized, all types of turnarounds have to be considered almost simultaneously. Without a behavioral turnaround, the rest is difficult to achieve.

Strategic Turnaround

The unit/company is following the wrong business path and needs a new strategy while there's still a chance to correct course (e.g., many years ago, K-Mart's profitability lagged behind Walmart's; consequently, in spite of its profitability, K-Mart replaced its CEO).

Organizational Turnaround

The company, group, division, line of business, or business cell needs a realignment of organizational reporting structures, according to which certain personnel may have to be reshuffled into other groups or new groups, thereby fashioning new teams.

"In a nutshell, a turnaround is a transformative process that changes a condition from being dysfunctional to being effectively functional. This means that first of all, before attempting to implement any changes, you must first get a handle on what it is you're trying to change and why. In other words, before leaping to prescribe a treatment, you'd be wise to first conduct a meaningful diagnosis of the condition. This may sound a bit like I'm using medical jargon here, and that's okay. In a very real sense, the analogy between a medical patient and an ailing business is quite valid. The goal is to stay healthy. Always remember that. A turnaround process aims to heal a major business condition. So, before you try to fix the condition, what must you do first?"

He paused to hear my answer.

"What should I do first?" I repeated the question back.

"Yes, Dennis. What should you do first?" he repeated again.

"Diagnose it!" I finally answered.

"Exactly. I know you had many questions about the diagnostic process that led to the white binders. Diagnosing a business problem is similar to the challenge of diagnosing a medical condition. If the diagnosis is off-track, the treatment can be ineffective or possibly even make things worse."

"Okay," I said, inviting Chuck to continue. "Just please go slowly—I want to take notes," I added.

"Your first step is to find meaningful clues. Then it's up to you to piece the clues together and figure out what kind of a challenge you're up against. In the medical arena, you'd first run a panel of basic tests to get your initial set of clues. In our case you get your initial set of clues by establishing meetings and dialogues with the key decision makers—the president, VPs, directors—and any other relevant stakeholders who must be selectively chosen to participate according to how relevant their likely contributions may turn out to be. They are there to reveal what they believe to be the issues related to the unit's underperformance." After a short pause, Chuck continued. "When meeting with the principal stakeholders, I channel the contents of my discussions into four general categories: the *field*, the *jockey*, the *horse*, and the *care*." Mentioning each of these four terms made him smile.

"You're starting to sound like a race-track commentator trying to predict the results of the Kentucky Derby," I said.

"No, no. Forget the Derby. This has nothing to do with the Derby. These four category words simply help you remember the most important elements that you must focus your attention on during your preliminary investigation. They help guide you as you're forming your first impressions of what needs to be reviewed. This is especially crucial if you don't know anything about a business unit that you're trying to study and better understand."

"Okay. So what does each of these mean? Please elaborate."

"Absolutely! With pleasure!" he said with a grin as if he was about to award me the state lottery. "Let's start with the *field*. The *field* represents the business opportunity, or the value proposition. I jump-start my assessment by asking myself these cardinal questions:

- How important is this business to the company?
- Is this business sound?
- What is its potential?
- What are the dangers of failure?
- Why should this business be pursued?
- How large can this business grow?"

"Okay, I think I'm pretty familiar with these *field* matters. Now, what about the *jockey*?" I asked.

"Yes, the *jockey*. The *jockey*, as you can pretty well guess by now, represents the leader of the business operation. It's important for all parties involved—the hierarchy, the consultant, and the leader—to understand how well suited the leader may be to the demands of the business in the current environment. The challenge is to determine whether he or she could steadily evolve to fully handle the demands, either by him or herself, or with the help of a consultant."

"So did you ask Mary this question?" I asked out of curiosity.

Chuck replied, "First, I interviewed all the stakeholders. They provided their own opinions on what they deemed to be the unit's strengths and weaknesses, and I carefully dissected their answers. You want to be very cautious, because people's careers are at stake; this is a very delicate matter.

"When I met with Mary, it was obvious to both of us that she couldn't manage it all. She had the right kind of gung-ho energy and an impeccable work ethic, yet she lacked specific essential knowledge and leadership talent to properly steer the business onto the right path. Plus, she wasn't prepared to make the necessary personal sacrifices if she were to evolve into the kind of person that this job truly demands."

"So what do you do under those circumstances?"

"Well…" Chuck paused to clean his bifocal glasses. I sat there, completely tuned in, yet I never expected to sit in complete silence for a full five seconds. It was as though Chuck had decided to weigh his words before saying anything, as if he was trying to protect my sensibilities.

"Listen, Dennis, you have to take a step back and ask yourself these same tough questions. If you conclude that your situation is untenable, then in the interest of everyone's well-being, it would behoove you to find a more suitable, or shall we say more *compatible*, position.

"Languishing in a job is bad practice. It doesn't nourish the soul. Beyond that, the effects it may have on your soul may ripple through and affect your lieutenants, employees, the business itself, and ultimately your family. It's a phenomenal responsibility."

"Although I know I'm not yet prepared to be your ideal *jockey*, I do trust that you know what to do, and I'm willing and ready to internalize and apply whatever you intend to teach me."

"Okay, so let's end our session today with two more concepts for you to investigate. I call these the *horse* and the *care*."

"I'm all ears."

"Understanding the *horse* means fully comprehending the culture of the unit, the existing business architecture, the way the business is organized, the hierarchical decision-making process, the current managerial rights in place versus those that may be required to meet the expectations and obligations by the same management, and the clear rules by which current accountability is measured—in other words, metrics.

"Understanding the *care* relates to both the manager's leadership actions toward his or her subordinates—training, budgets, tools availability, demands, help, et cetera—and most importantly, the attitude and behavior of the hierarchical leadership toward the unit and the leader. Decision making and resource availability require special attention."

As Chuck started to flesh out each conceptual category mnemonic, I took notes, trying to physically record and mentally grasp as much as I could. Many of these ideas and concepts were foreign to me, and too many of them were floating in my mind. In fact, although I didn't totally get all the details during our session, I was determined to learn them all. And not only learn them, but to master them as well and be able to apply them.

"Do you have any questions before we adjourn?" Chuck asked.

"Well, I may actually have too many," I answered. "But instead of asking them all now, I want to study what I wrote down. I'll take a rain check for now, and we'll discuss this further at our next meeting."

I left with mixed feelings. On the one hand, I was saddened by the thought that the next day I would have to personally face unpleasant customers, and my mind would have neither the time nor the serenity to focus on Chuck's materials. I was also worried about my lack of preparation and training to be able to succeed in such a demanding environment. At the same time, however, I also felt encouraged. My personal coach was completely on top of his game, and he believed in me. He totally believed that, as long as I fully committed myself to his prescribed course of study and action, I would pull through and make it all work.

I drove home cautiously through the icy roads; it was a tough winter. I had to focus on my driving, but my mind kept playing back my last discussion with Chuck. "The *field*, the *jockey*, the *horse*, and the *care*…the *field*, the *jockey*, the *horse*, and the *care*…" I repeated his four mnemonics until I finally got them committed to memory.

I arrived home just in time to have dinner with Cheryl and the girls and catch up on ESPN highlights. I grabbed a cup of tea and went back to my notes. According to Chuck, all of the information that he had gathered from the executives and the other key stakeholders helped to get a proper pulse on the current health of the business. It all served to fill in the jigsaw puzzle pieces on the four perspectives— the *field*, the *jockey*, the *horse*, and the *care*. "But what do I do with all these concepts? How do I translate them into relevant action?" I wondered.

So far, I wasn't fully clear on what he had done with all that information. At night, I would review my materials from our previous sessions and drill any new nomenclature into my head until it became part of my active vocabulary. I even started to put together a little dictionary to help me remember the meanings of these new concepts and metaphors.

Peter had scheduled a staff meeting that happened to overlap with my regular afternoon time with Chuck. I was so eager to meet Chuck that I e-mailed him to reschedule our coaching session to the morning. He responded, "Dennis, looks like we have a pretty tight schedule tomorrow. I already have a high-level morning meeting with Greg and Peter on another project, and it runs until noon, and you have your staff meeting at 1:00 p.m. How about we take forty minutes over lunch?"

"Absolutely!" I confirmed.

By 12:20 p.m. we were sitting under the glass-paneled cafeteria ceiling, each with our own food tray, enjoying the sunny blue skies.

"Chuck, tell me something. After you got the initial perspectives from your contacts at BLM, how did you take advantage of the material you collected?" I asked.

"I'm glad you're taking the initiative to probe deeper. This is a crucial habit that you must hone at this stage of the game. Thinking before acting will prove essential to your success. By the way, do you have your notebook with you?"

"Yes, I've already learned to bring my notebook whenever I come to see you. Ah, yes. Here it is." I opened the notebook to a fresh new page.

"The key, you see, is to catalogue the information received from every interviewee into a table of alleged weaknesses. Out of each and every interview that I conducted, I made sure to unravel as many weakness-insight nuggets as I possibly could. Everything that sounded like a weakness got recorded, numbered, and classified according to whichever of our four perspectives they best fit into: the *field*, the *jockey*, the *horse*, and the *care*. Do you see where this is going?"

"But those you interviewed may not know the whole truth. Do you believe you can really discover the whole truth with this process?" I wondered.

"Not at all."

"So then why do you do it?" I asked, and just as soon the question escaped my mouth, I realized I had made a mistake. Chuck was famous for his problem-solving logic. I knew that he also happened to be a chess player who played online tournaments and often won against high-ranked players. I knew there had to be sound logic backing his approach. I just had to find out what it was.

"The interviewing part of my process gives you a lot of info, but it's not the whole enchilada. It gives you a preliminary set of perceived weaknesses. But there's more to it, you see, because after I capture the overall feel of how the key stakeholders see the situation, I imagine how other groups view these same perceived weaknesses. Sorting through the perceived weaknesses is instrumental in tackling the next phase. Are you clear now?"

He looked at his watch, and said, "Sorry, Dennis. I'm late for my next meeting. Please be in touch."

I remained seated for a few more minutes, thinking about our conversation and feeling pretty content. For the first time since I took this job, I actually felt like things were beginning to make sense, like I was being clued in on how to learn to read the code underlying my daily chaos. I mean, here was Chuck, teaching me how to properly map out my business terrain and how to fashion and use the right keys to each new situation as circumstances would prescribe. I was really starting to like this guy. This was pretty exciting for me. I knew that in our next session, I would begin to learn how to apply Chuck's intrapreneurship technology to the contents of the white binders. I found myself very much looking forward to our next lesson.

Suddenly, remembering that I had Chuck's e-mail printout on the eight phases of recovery in my coat pocket, I found it, unfolded it, and looked at it again. As I read it, I felt I had once again shifted phases, going from number five, acceptance, to number six, transcendence. I was elated.

- 6 -

Diagnostics

I was starting to be a real fan of Wednesdays, and today was Wednesday again—the only day of the week when I could escape the explosive hellish situations from work and reach an oasis of calm. I started to think about identifying weaknesses, and now that I was clear about how Chuck had gotten started, I felt more interested in learning the contents of the four white binders.

It was a cold day, but the sun could still be seen at times as the clouds passed on by. As usual, I arrived on time, parked in the circular driveway, and followed the walking path to the house. I rang the bell, and Chuck opened the door. With a smile he said, "What a beautiful day. Please, come in."

I knew the routine. Put the booties on, go through the foyer, admire the sculptures and the gorgeous floor with Spanish ceramic designs, and enter the office. It was the first time I noticed a lot of natural light through the grand office window, behind where Chuck sat at his desk.

I took out one of the white binders titled "Request for Materials (RFM)." It had a long table of contents, and it was full of the questions that had been directed at the business unit team.

"Well, do you have any questions for me?" Chuck asked.

"Yes," I answered. "Could you walk me through the same process that you went through to produce this document?"

"Sure. Let's just go through this one step at a time. And by the way, although what I'm about to tell you may sound a bit like a lecture, just jump in with any related questions or concerns, okay?"

I nodded in agreement. The rules were clear.

Chuck continued: "I have the advantage of having worked for years in venture capital. I had to evaluate business plans within severe time constraints and under a great deal of pressure. And because of that, I learned how to ask all the right questions very, very quickly. In other words, I managed information and people very effectively under conditions of uncertainty. That came in very handy when I realized that the quickest way I could determine the absence or presence of essential operational details was by asking the right people certain specific, probing questions.

"Gradually, over the years, I fine-tuned the questions and compiled them into a coherent questionnaire. It's a powerful tool I call the 'request for materials,' or RFM. It's powerful because, by the time I'd get the RFM answers back, all of the information from those answers would give me roughly ninety to ninety-five percent of what I needed to know in order to design necessary change.

"I customized this tool for BLM into seventeen major subject categories, or themes. Now, depending on the business you're looking at, categories may be added, slightly adjusted or modified to better reflect the nature of the business, or even get completely dropped from the list if they don't apply. As for BLM, my preliminary meetings with the executives and business managers gave me a good macro-level feel for the unit's business environment. To really crack the code on this unit and find out what its real issues were, I had to dig deeper to get at the micro-level operational details.

"Remember, before you try to change anything, first perform a high-resolution reality check and gain a detailed understanding of what you're trying to change. Figure out your current starting point and conditions before you lay in a new navigation plan."

"I don't have your kind of background. How am I supposed to handle all this?" I asked.

"Look, your current objective is to study the binder materials; they map out your unit's present condition pretty clearly. Also, Mary, your predecessor, was the first person from BLM to give me information about the unit, and that gave me a pretty good sense of what was going on over there. Later on, I did the same with the executives, and they offered their own perspectives and supplemental points of view. All of that information was catalogued into the subject-specific categories that make up the table of contents of those binders. Okay, please take a look."

I opened the binder and read through the list once more:

EXHIBIT 2:

REQUEST FOR MATERIALS (RFM)[1]

Section 1: Business Fundamentals

Section 2: Business Analysis

Section 3: Market Analysis

Section 4: Marketing Activities

Section 5: Sales Force and Sales Activities

Section 6: Financials, Billing, and Forecasting

Section 7: Expenses Analysis and Capital Equipment

Section 8: Organizational Structure and Personnel

Section 9: Technical Support

Section 10: Customer Support

Section 11: Additional Business Information

Section 12: Partnerships and Joint Ventures

Section 13: Union Relationships

Section 14: General Management

Section 15: Executive Time Management

Section 16: Miscellaneous

Section 17: Major Challenges

---

1 *See Appendix 1: RFM—The Detailed Questionnaire.*

"Chuck, I have some questions."

"Shoot."

"You have tremendous experience, but this is my first time attempting to manage a business from A to Z. How can I possibly come up with the right list?"

"This RFM is your working list for now; the experience you'll gain during this assignment will help you develop your own list with a high degree of confidence. You can use this list as a reference in your future work. Please, take the time right now to read the subject headings for each of the seventeen sections, and let me know if you have any questions."

While I was reading the document, Chuck decided to proofread one of his reports. I read all the pages, asking for clarification when needed, and got all my questions answered. My first impression of it all: overwhelming. There were topics on that list that I was sure had never been discussed before by anybody in the company. Plus, I honestly didn't know how to effectively juggle all of these responsibilities simultaneously. In fact, had it been up to me—based on what I did know—I would have never been able to come up with the kinds of questions that appeared in that binder.

On the one hand, I felt badly about how poorly the hierarchy had prepared me for my assignment. On the other hand, I felt uplifted because of Greg's and Peter's foresight to partner me with Chuck; the direct support he kept giving me was proving to be invaluable. With his guidance, I knew I could chip away at my deficiencies and gradually bridge the gap between the skills I had and the skills I needed to acquire.

Chuck said, "Complacency erodes the future, especially in units that underperform. The hierarchy used to think of BLM and its performance as satisfactory. The questionnaire answers and their quality, or lack thereof, all tell a more complete and compelling story of the unit's actual reality. In business units that require turnarounds of any kind, you may find people assigned to tasks and processes that are sometimes obsolete, weak, or downright broken. Some employees perform their jobs 'by the book' and isolate themselves from the environment. They know that some things are wrong, but they either don't know how to fix them or don't have the power to do that. Are you with me so far?"

"Yes."

"Good. The questionnaire is comprehensive. Its answers mainly reveal:

- The requirements mandated by the business leader;
- The missing or deficient functionality;
- How relevant each work activity or project really is;
- The unit leadership's relevant organizational knowledge base, expertise, skills, and talents; and
- The extent of the unit's ability to analyze its own issues and challenges posed by its processes and personnel.

"Although they're rarely scrutinized, very successful business units have answers to *all* of these questions. In weak business units, however, few if any employees know the unit's mission or *business definition*, which answers the question 'What is your business?' or 'What is the nature of your business?' or 'What is the essence, function, and purpose of your business?' The *essence* is what it's made of, the *function* is what it does, and its *purpose* governs its sense of direction.

"All too often, the success criteria, in the form of goals and objectives, happen to be ill-defined or unknown. This restricts the flow of quality communication. The condition of these business units may indicate neglect because the current leader is too weak and needs additional training, or the hierarchical chain of command has a weak link, or other business units draw greater attention from management because they are more important or more troublesome to the company, et cetera.

"Answers to the RFM tell the full story, and it's a pretty safe bet that the larger the gap is between the total number of questions asked and the number of satisfactory answers provided, the more dire the predicament of the unit. If the leader wants to improve performance, he or she will have a unique opportunity to do things right by extending his or her horizons to allow for further personal evolution to quickly acquire new essential skills and tools. For some, this type of experience may feel quite intense, while for others it may even feel like a radical but necessary change.

"By September of last year, Mary was facing the challenge of dividing the unit's questionnaire assignment among her unit's key contributors. Since I had insisted that the RFM responses be returned to me within a brief time frame of just a couple of weeks, practically speaking, no new information could be generated besides what was already available; only the information that was actually available could be presented."

"What happened after you prepared the RFM?"

"When I met with Mary and Charlotte, I explained to them all the details. I also explained that intense concentrated effort and timely responsiveness were crucial to the success of this diagnostic phase, that I knew they might not have all the answers, and that a lack of answers was okay."

"What do you mean? How can that be okay?"

"To discover the cracks in the business management structure, whether minor or severe, you follow the path of the missing answers. Remember, what we want to do is quickly discover what exists and what is missing, what's working and what's broken, what's being done right and what's being done wrong. I told Mary to write 'not available'—N/A—for any item that lacked backup."

"Did you establish any special guidelines for how the response materials were to be prepared?"

"Absolutely," Chuck said. "It's important to specify the rules of the game for how the information should be organized and presented to the requester. These should include your preferred media format, such as hard copy, electronic, et cetera, the time allotted to complete the assignments, and the format, style, and manner for how the answers should be prepared and presented.

"I'm old school, so I asked for hard copies. The answers were to be delivered within two weeks, and it was up to the business leader to determine who would prepare the different sections. Mary took on that responsibility and distributed the questions to the different groups."

I looked at my watch. "Chuck, excuse me for interrupting. I forgot to tell you. Tonight, Cheryl and I are celebrating our wedding anniversary, and I have to leave a bit earlier than usual. I promise I'll read up on the subject so we can talk about the answers next time."

"I know that your situation at work is complex and in a way unpleasant, but things are going to improve. Knowing what to do and hard work are good healers."

We both stood up, and I put my binders back in my bag. I knew we were starting to see eye to eye, and though I was starting to gain an initial understanding of Chuck's intrapreneurship technology, I knew that we were still in the very early stages of turning BLM around.

I walked to the door, took my booties off, and said good night.

"Happy anniversary, and congratulations to you and Cheryl and the girls," Chuck said.

Two days later, upon returning from a departmental meeting, Jennifer, my assistant, said to me, "Dennis, about an hour ago, I got a phone call from Chuck. He is visiting another division in the company, but because of some changes to his schedule for the day, he's got an open block of about two hours starting around noon. He'd like to meet with you and wanted to know if you'd be available."

I had to prepare some material for a meeting next week, but I couldn't pass up on the opportunity to meet him. "Jennifer, please call Lulu's to reserve a table. Please call Chuck back and ask him to meet me at my office. Let him know that I'll drive us to Lulu's for lunch."

A few minutes later, the meeting was arranged, and around 11:30 a.m. Chuck showed up in a nice blue suit and a red tie. We headed to Lulu's, and I ordered my favorite, chicken salad. Chuck ordered salmon, well done, along with a side order of asparagus.

"Chuck, I'm interested in the content as much as I am in the format. These past couple of days I've been thinking about our last conversation, and I'm eager to find out what happened after you gave Mary the RFM assignment."

"Well, Mary and Charlotte were very appreciative of my efforts to help them make better sense of it all. Accordingly, they made this project their top priority; they proved to be very responsive and diligent. I'm really pleased with the quality of the professional relationships we formed.

"A couple of weeks after we issued the RFM, large quantities of documents came back. This was a very intense period. Every document received was carefully categorized, read, and reviewed. During this period, I started to record as many questions as would come to mind while I was reading. In parallel, I also identified and recorded as many weaknesses as possible. The answers to the questions were tabulated in four categories as satisfactory, unsatisfactory, partially answered, or missing."

"And how satisfied were you with the answers you deemed satisfactory?" I asked.

"The satisfactory answers are not what we need to focus on. Actually, when you look at the big picture, you'll begin to notice that the other three categories are where we should place our attention— questions that were answered unsatisfactorily, partially, or not at all. These are the areas where we have opportunities to correct various deficiencies."

"Well, some of my people told me that sometime after they sent you their answers, they met with you. So, what happened then?"

"I see that you're done with the meal. Do you have your notebook?"

"Of course." I pulled out my notebook and my pen. "Is the main purpose of the preliminary analysis to find more weaknesses?"

"Yes, but there's more to it. You see, the work we did after receiving the materials served three main purposes:

a) to prepare questions for further clarification from those employees who had responded with answers;
b) to identify and list as many previously unrecognized weaknesses as possible; and
c) to merge the list of newly recognized weaknesses with the list of weaknesses that became apparent in the diagnostics preparation phase.

"Later, we worked for weeks rechecking and making sure that the weaknesses listed on the merged list were in fact real and legitimate."

The waiter came by and left us the check. Without skipping a beat, Chuck took out his credit card and paid the bill. He didn't even give me a chance to cover my share of the meal. Our lunch break had lasted a little longer than planned, but it was worth it; I was learning how to initiate a turnaround project, what kind of information to ask for, and with a counterintuitive approach, to zoom in on operational areas whose information responses revealed deficiencies or dysfunction.

We drove back and talked about the weather. I went back to the office. Jennifer handed me some paperwork and patiently waited until I finished signing it all. I asked her if she knew who in the unit had met with Chuck one-on-one during the diagnostic period. She answered that he mostly met with Mary and Charlotte, but I had a hunch that he had also met with Dustin, especially after McCain Consulting had concluded their assessment work. Dustin had nearly a decade of work experience in the unit and was now working there as a supervisor. He was like a treasure trove, chock-full of useful information. All of a sudden I had an epiphany. I quickly asked Jennifer to get in touch with Dustin to see if he could meet with me in the afternoon. I figured I could seize an opportunity to glean relevant insights from him. And it was about time he got better acquainted with his new boss.

Jennifer came back and confirmed my meeting with Dustin for 2:00 p.m. He was a little late. I invited him to take a seat.

"Dustin, thank you for coming. I'd like to ask you a few questions."

"Sure. What do you want to know?"

"Did you previously meet with Chuck, the senior consultant?"

"Yes."

"When was the first time you met with him?"

"Well, it was a few months ago. It was after we prepared the answers to his questionnaire. He called it a 'request for materials.' It was no easy assignment, let me tell you, but it made sense. He really hit us hard with his RFM. We all felt we were in for a rude awakening.

"One of my friends in the sales division across the street told me about the work Chuck did for them a couple of years ago. He told me that underneath Chuck's tough exterior and directness is someone who truly cares about the company and its people and that he's repeatedly developed win-win situations for both sides.

"And, frankly, during all our years with the company, none of us had ever seen a more thorough information request than Chuck's RFM. After we sent him our response materials, we learned that we would be scheduled to meet with him to clarify anything that was vague, along with everyone else who completed an RFM assignment."

"So who called the meeting?"

"Mary and Charlotte called the meeting, and it took place in the large conference room. All of the business unit lieutenants and supervisors showed up, including certain process owners who worked in other units. We all felt our jobs and even pensions were now on the line. Based on the RFM we had to complete, we were convinced that this senior consultant would show up and grill us mercilessly.

"Chuck threw his questions at us like daggers. Of course they were all relevant. We couldn't answer most of them. One of the external process owners even broke down and unexpectedly announced that there was nothing he could do different because he hadn't been granted that kind of authority. Meanwhile, Chuck kept taking notes as the answers came shooting back, and there were no breaks until he finished asking his final questions. We told him who had left the company or retired, and who had transferred to other units who could possibly answer the remaining outstanding questions."

"Have you seen him since then?"

"Yep, a few weeks later, he met with me again. Yolanda, who was Charlotte's assistant back then, served as the liaison between Chuck and the business unit; she scheduled all of his meetings with unit personnel according to his request list. I'm sure it must have been pretty intense for him, but he took it in stride and made it seem pretty straightforward. From my own experience and that of my colleagues, he always showed up extremely well prepared. By the way, when he found out that I was the unit's liaison to McCain, he made sure to talk to me in particular. He knew that I had helped them understand our business and that I even helped them explore outsourcing as a possible solution."

"How did the meeting go?"

"The meeting went well, but I sensed he was dissatisfied with the results of our work with McCain. By then, McCain and Jack wanted to close shop and outsource the business liabilities. Did that bother us? Well, of course it did. And that was back then. Even now, BLM employees still believe that the outsourcing possibility still exists. It bothers us. We don't want that sort of threat around anymore."

- 7 -

From Weaknesses to Strategic Issues

I kept learning more and more about the conditions that had helped create the mess at BLM, and I was starting to grasp Chuck's massive undertaking with BLM's diagnostics process. Chuck told me that by the previous December, the diagnostics process had been nearly complete. It would determine if the company should keep BLM or not. It was a tough call to make; so many jobs were going to be affected by this one single decision. What a truly huge responsibility. But Chuck told me he could see how the unit could be saved, that he had shared his insights with Greg and Peter, and that's where I fit in. I was to become BLM's new fully dedicated manager.

I had to effectively juggle the needs of the business and the well-being of my personnel, as well as keep a clear head on my shoulders. Chuck never asked me how things were going for me. Instead, he mostly focused on sharing his strategic vision for my unit to better prepare me for the tactical decisions that lay ahead. Gradually, as I learned to adapt to this executive-style mentoring, I also learned to adopt a whole new decision-making methodology that would carry me through these turbulent times.

I knew I had to put in more effort and learn faster, but it was difficult for me to balance my work, Chuck, and my home life. Despite these challenges, I made sure to get better acquainted with my people. Their efforts, after all, would end up justifying our choices one way or another.

On the morning of our follow-up session, I had to drop off my car at the shop for some service. Fortunately for me, Cheryl graciously lent me her gray Chrysler.

I got to Chuck's, and he greeted me as usual. Chuck was so disciplined that for every meeting that he scheduled, and I mean *every* meeting, he would always prepare an agenda. He usually e-mailed the agenda, outlining the subject and issues he wanted to discuss. I always had issues I wanted to raise as well, and after giving him my input, we'd come up with a sensible joint agenda for our session. Both of us always made sure to prepare new materials ahead of time. By now, we were working with a current and complete list of BLM's confirmed organizational weaknesses. Accordingly, today's agenda emphasized understanding weaknesses, and I started wondering what the next step would be.

"Dennis, today we are going to make some changes to the way we work."

"Okay. What do you have in mind?"

"Well, so far I've been the one doing most of the talking, and you've been the one doing most of the listening, writing, and reading. Starting today, you will be given homework assignments that will help you to better understand the ins and outs of your business unit. I'll be sharing specific techniques with you that you'll be able to apply. You'll come up with your own answers, and I'll have my own. This way, we'll compare notes and have meaningful discussions. I'm sure that you'll quickly acquire the knowledge needed to face the challenges you're up against. What's the last thing we were discussing?"

"Well, I was starting to understand that by checking the validity of the unit's *alleged* weaknesses, we come up with a narrower list of *confirmed*, or real, weaknesses."

"That's exactly right. As you recall, inputs from the hierarchy, manager, employees, as well as my own analysis contributed to our list of weaknesses. It's quite normal to end up with hundreds of weaknesses. Getting to a complete list of real weaknesses marks a major milestone.

"In the second white binder, you'll find the list of confirmed weaknesses that we had pinpointed in our initial exploratory steps. These are the challenges you have to contend with. From this point on, we'll refer to these as simply *weaknesses*."

"Well, now that we have this staggering list of issues, what should we do with it?"

"Please open your notebook," Chuck said. Then he paused. I knew he was about to say something important; he was waiting for me to fully tune in to what he was about to say next before I'd start jotting down any fresh new notes.

"I'm ready."

He proceeded: "All of the weaknesses will be grouped by themes that, when possible, will correspond to strategic issues. These strategic issues will serve as building blocks for defining each business cell's strategy and ultimately goals and objectives for the business unit."

As I took notes, I remembered Chuck telling me that this managerial approach builds upon itself from one step to the next. I paused for a moment to reread his statement a couple more times, and I was intrigued. I felt like I was being introduced to a whole new paradigm shift that would gradually draw me in, bit by bit.

Could this way of thinking really pave the way to the kind of concrete results that Greg and Peter were seeking? I mean, I saw how my unit was doing business. And the way it was running, I used to feel terribly hopeless about it pulling through. In fact, I felt very skeptical about the prospects of any new approach. But now I was starting to view my unit from a whole new perspective. The real adventure had only just begun.

"Your assignment is as follows," Chuck said. "Number and catalogue every single one of the weaknesses listed in the white binders. But before we move on to the second step, I want to ask you a question."

"Go ahead."

"Okay, all weaknesses are not equal. They differ in importance, in nature—whether they are strategic or tactical—in the amount of time it takes to resolve them, in the amount of resources required, in the quality of leadership required to effectively deal with them, and in other ways too. Knowing that, how should we interpret this data, and how should we proceed?"

I figured this must be a rhetorical question, mostly because I didn't know how to answer it. Over time, I had realized that such questions were just part of his style. Whenever he asked me a question about which I felt pretty clueless, I had learned to see it for what it truly was—a light intro to his predetermined answer.

"To get a better handle on the data, what you'll initially do is put together a three-by-three matrix," he said. He quickly drew a diagram to show me what he had in mind:

EXHIBIT 3:

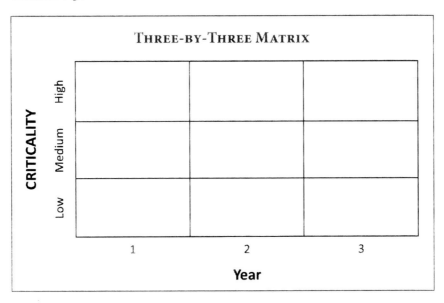

"Segment the vertical axis into three criticality levels: low, medium, and high. These represent the relative impact that a weakness has on the business unit. Similarly, segment the horizontal axis into three year times: one, two, and three. This represents the estimated lengths of time to resolve each weakness. Are you okay with this? Can you see yourself populating such a three-by-three matrix?"

I felt pretty comfortable with this fairly simple set of guidelines and replied, "Sure." Little did I know that, by the time I completed this exercise, it wouldn't be all that straightforward.

"As soon as you finish this exercise, call me and we'll schedule our next meeting."

I packed my papers and binders, headed to the front door, paused for a moment, and said, "Thank you for your help. I'm pretty excited to be working with you. I know I'm just starting on the journey ahead, but I'm glad you're on my side."

"Enjoy the weekend."

"You too," I said and left.

By the end of the weekend, I had become intimately acquainted with the unit's full list of real weaknesses. The next Wednesday we met again, and Chuck asked, "How was the homework?"

"I think it went well. I prepared the three-by-three weaknesses matrix, and here's how it looks." I presented my matrix:

EXHIBIT 4:

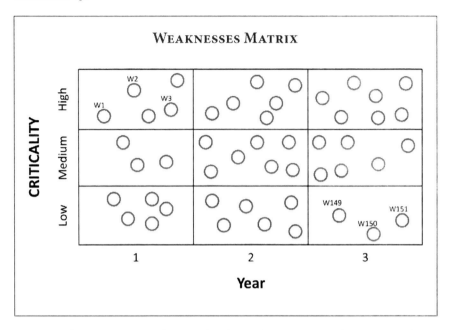

The facts were the facts. I had weaknesses listed in each of the nine matrix sectors, all numbered and catalogued.

"Very nice," Chuck remarked. "It looks like you did a pretty good job filling in the weaknesses matrix. Okay, what we'll have to do next—or rather what *you* will have to do next—is to translate the matrix of catalogued weaknesses into a corresponding matrix of strategic issues."

"Hold on. Wait a minute. You're jumping ahead a little too quickly for me. Before you continue, would you tell me how you define the term *strategic issue*?"

"Of course. A strategic issue is any unresolved challenge that affects the ongoing well-being of an organization."

"Okay. That makes sense. Then what?"

"Then you group the weaknesses by some common thread, denominator, or theme. Each of these themes is a strategic issue. For example, using your matrix, group weaknesses *W1*, *W2*, and *W3* into *Strategic Issue #1 (SI 1)*." He showed me the following:

EXHIBIT 5:

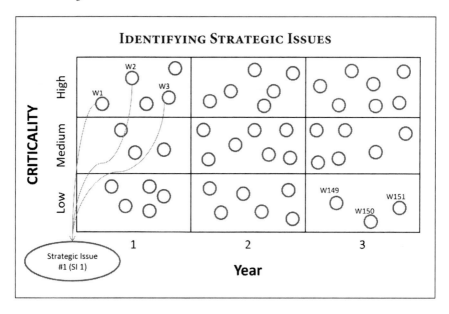

"You'll do that for all one hundred and fifty-one weaknesses. Then, similar to the way you mapped out the weaknesses, draft another three-by-three matrix and map out the strategic issues." He showed me the next example:

EXHIBIT 6:

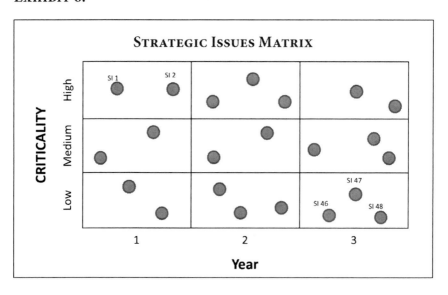

"We've just consolidated one hundred and fifty-one weaknesses to forty-eight strategic issues. The newly derived strategic issues now serve as building blocks for your business cells' strategies," Chuck added. Then he showed me the next example:

EXHIBIT 7:

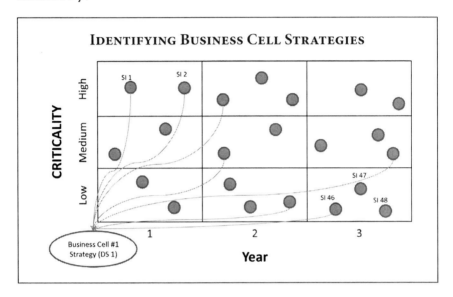

"You'll allocate the forty-eight strategic issues across the business unit's three business cells. In this example, we're grouping seven strategic issues into *Business Cell #1*. The different business cell strategies make up the short-term and long-term strategies for your business unit as a whole. In a future session, we'll discuss what we actually do with all these strategies."

Chuck stacked the papers together, handed them to me, and added, "On a different note, I'll be away for the next ten days. It's a brief new consulting assignment with a Spanish company. They read one of the articles that I was featured in and contacted me, so here I am, traveling again. I won't be here to meet you next Wednesday. Since we're skipping one meeting, I'm going to give you a little more homework this time. I'll still have access to e-mail. If you come up with any related questions or need clarification while preparing the work, please contact me, and I'll help you."

I had two weeks until our next scheduled session. The days went by quickly. I used the break to spend some much-needed quality time with Cheryl and the girls. The following weekend turned out to be very nice; temperatures were above average, and spring was just around the corner. I did what I believed any self-respecting family man would do to help strengthen his family bond at a time like this: I took Cheryl and the girls out on a trip up north to our cabin. We had a great time. It was my first weekend with the family in a very long time.

The two weeks had come and gone, and it was time to resume our meetings. While I did work on my assignment, I knew my work was incomplete. I got to Chuck's office; we greeted each other and sat down in our usual spots. He quickly summarized his trip for me and then asked about my homework assignment. I mumbled, as I began to open my bag, that it wasn't totally complete. I looked up, and his face showed a mixed look of disappointment, pain, and a hint of anger.

Chuck touched his chin with two fingers and said, "Dennis, you know that I support you and that I'm working hard to make you successful. But I also told you when we started that there were rules to our relationship. One of them was no excuses. I made this abundantly clear as a principal precondition to our coaching relationship, before we started to work together, and I still feel the same way about it today as I did back then; I have not changed my mind.

"To date, many of your predecessors have failed to effectively lead and manage the unit you have inherited. We both know that this isn't a quick-fix kind of deal, but I will guarantee you that you will not succeed if you don't fully commit yourself to the task at hand. You must realize that this is more like preparing to run a marathon all the way to the finish line. And right now it feels like you're struggling to barely finish a single mile, let alone a full marathon.

"It's doable, though. With the right kind of coaching and the right kind of commitment, it can be done. The challenges facing us both are nothing short of serious. In a few weeks, I'll have to face your bosses and update them on our progress. Presently, we are nowhere near being prepared for that. I suggest we skip this meeting and reconvene as soon as you get your act together and make sure you're ready."

I felt surprised and confused. I simply didn't know what to say. Was he being too tough on me? Or did I get too complacent? He sat there silently, and so did I. The mutual silence was deafening, and it started to feel too painful to bear. I bagged up my papers, stood up, and started heading toward the door. As I was about to leave the room, Chuck said, "Dennis, I'm your coach. Do you know what a coach is?"

Having just been cut down to size but a minute ago, I remained silent, still feeling a little too embarrassed to respond.

He continued: "Hall of Fame Texas football coach Tom Landry said, 'A coach is someone who tells you what you don't want to hear, who has you see what you don't want to see, so you can be who you have always known you could be.'"

These were some pretty strong words, but in the final analysis, I knew coaches got judged by how well their players performed. We had plenty of work to do, and I knew he really wanted me to succeed. I had to place as much trust in myself as he did. It sure was a lot to live up to, but sometimes you just have to grow up and evolve.

I looked up at Chuck. He cracked a reconciliatory smile. I smiled back. I had learned another lesson—be well prepared when I meet with Chuck.

- 8 -

UNIT DEPENDENCIES

"Dennis, remember, if you aren't prepared to tackle a specific task, then tackle an alternate task—one for which you are ready. Always do something productive. This way at least you're always accomplishing something and making headway on at least one of your projects. The same applies to everything you're learning with me," Chuck said. "Since you're already here, why don't we work on the issues of the next white binder, *Hierarchy-Dependent Issues and Intra-Unit Issues*?"

As surprised as I was by his refusal to review my incomplete work, I felt even more taken aback by his alternate offer. I let his words really sink in, shook his hand, and said, "Thanks, Chuck. Yes, let's work on hierarchy-dependent issues and intra-unit issues. I promise to catch up on my homework. I know you're trying to help me." I took my seat again, nodded, and waited for him to resume.

"First, I'd like to remind you of a number of ideas that we discussed in previous sessions."

"Yes, I'm listening."

"Good. This is key. We've already touched on the subject of turnarounds, of which there are several different kinds; the diagnostic phase, which includes the RFM, analysis of weaknesses, and strategic issues determinations. All of this preparation work brings you to a possible crossroads. What I mean by this is that you get to a point where you can begin to contemplate new possibilities for how to change some of the hierarchy-dictated conditions that regulate your unit from above, as well as how you could recondition your unit's behavior in order to change its nature."

"I could really use at least a couple of examples to help bring this home."

"Sure. Take, for instance, the possibility of spinning off this business unit as a fully independent unit. In order for such a possibility to exist, you'd have to figure out what kinds of degrees of freedom it should have, so that in the event that everything else goes well, it actually could be spun off and do well on its own. Accordingly, you'd also have to figure out how it should functionally interface with the rest of the company and the hierarchy.

"For example, if the accounting function is currently being handled by the company's accounting department, then to help your unit become more independent, you'll have to set up your own independent internal accounting system. Likewise, if the hiring function is currently subject to the administrative dictates of the corporate human resources department, then to help your unit become more independent, you'll have to set up your own internal HR capability. These kinds of changes, for example, would help morph your unit into a more self-sufficient, more independent, more autonomous form.

"Furthermore, these kinds of changes are pretty fundamental, certainly from the point of view of the hierarchy, and therefore they require approval from your higher-ups. Then, let's say that you get that kind of approval. Well, you'll have to make your own decisions about how to implement the new functionality within your unit. Does this make sense?"

"Yes, I think so," I said. "After you find out what the weaknesses and strategic issues are, you're able to consider how to refashion the unit so it can function on its own in the marketplace."

"Very good. I see you're catching on pretty quickly. However, the change needed to morph your unit into a spin-off candidate assumes full business success. Can we deliver? Can you imagine the disastrous cost to the company if the top executives were to spin off the unit only to have it fail later? Imagine how the press would react to a negative event like that! A spin-off failure scenario would get hammered by both the press and the shareholders and might even end up jeopardizing the CEO's position!"

I remained silent.

"So let's continue. Imagine now that you've already got all the weaknesses mapped out and all of the strategic issues as well, along with your strategic issues analysis. Notice how the strategic issues analysis prompts us to compile two documents. The first one would be derived from what I call hierarchy-dependent issues; the second would be drawn from what I call intra-unit issues. Now let's define these two terms first to help you get a better grasp of what these concepts are all about.

"*Hierarchy-dependent issues* are strategic issues that are dependent on the higher-ups. Said differently, these are strategic issues that demand operational changes that would help the business run more smoothly, and they depend on approval and decisions made from your higher-ups in the hierarchy.

"Just so you know, I did have a number of preliminary discussions with your boss before you came on board. The first time I raised this subject, he felt reluctant to discuss any of the details I was prepared to propose. When I brought up this subject again in a follow-up discussion, I actually won him over on some of the issues. What I'm trying to tell you, Dennis, is to do your homework from A to Z, know what the right moves are supposed to be, and your boss will come around to see the reality of the situation the way you do.

"Winston Churchill, England's prime minister during WWII, used to say that 'the nose of the bulldog has been slanted backwards so that he can breathe without letting go.' Be a bulldog. When all of your analysis tells you that your perspective is more complete, and therefore more valid than that of your boss, you need to persevere to the max to realize your vision. In the end, it's up to you to turn your unit into what you envision it should be.

"All right. Let's switch gears and explore the subject I call intra-unit issues."

"Okay," I said.

"*Intra-unit issues* represent desirable major changes that you can push through your business unit, independent of any higher-ups in the hierarchy. You initiate and approve the go-ahead on these changes. In my experience, many business unit managers hesitate to make certain decisions, usually because they are not clear on whether any higher-up approval is needed or not. But usually, upon further review, these managers realize the reach of their decision-making jurisdiction. With full authority over intra-unit issues, you're able to act more quickly on them than on hierarchy-dependent issues that do require approval from higher-ups.

"Your takeaway lesson here is the practical rule of execution speed. Remember it, memorize it, and etch it in your mind. Fewer hierarchy-dependent issues inevitably produce fewer delays. Misperceiving a legitimate intra-unit issue for a hierarchy-dependent issue will only cost your unit in speed of execution and needlessly slow you down. Don't fall into that all-too-common trap of misperception.

"Instead, learn to properly identify which issues really do depend on higher-up approval or decision making. You're taking a risk when you reclassify what you at first thought of as a hierarchy-dependent issue as an intra-unit issue. But when you think through your issues prudently and thoroughly, you'll find the risk is fairly manageable. Migrating strategic issues from the hierarchy-dependent level to the intra-unit level is more than just an interesting intellectual exercise; it has to be a key part of your managerial toolbox. It's a must."

Chuck walked me through both of these documents, which he had already prepared prior to my taking the helm at BLM. As soon as we finished reviewing both documents, he said, "Okay, Dennis, for our next meeting, make sure to bring your completed assignment on strategic issues that was due today, and we'll also add a few

more things. Once you have completed the diagnostics phase and
determined the weaknesses and strategic issues, it's time to define
the mission statement, to clarify the business definition, and then to
clearly determine your unit's list of transitional goals and objectives.
By the way, they're called transitional because they help stabilize the
organization temporarily and may change after that.

"So, your new assignment is to:

a) develop a mission statement;
b) develop a business definition as you see fit; and
c) determine transitional goals and objectives for your unit."

"Chuck, I have a few questions," I said.

"Okay. Go on."

"Well, it's about the mission statement. What exactly do you
mean by that?" I asked.

"That's a very good question. For me, a mission statement is
a statement declaring the purpose of an organization; it serves to
guide your decision making."

"Okay, I'll have to think about it. By the way, how should I
differentiate between the mission statement and the business
definition?"

"Your business definition expresses how you're supposed to
translate your mission statement into action. You can start with
a sentence like: 'We are in the business of...' and then fill in the
blank."

"Well, this'll be interesting. I come from the doing side more
than from the thinking side. Having to think this much is going to
be a bit difficult for me, maybe even a little nerve-racking," I said.

"Hard thinking is a very necessary part of your job, and you'll
quickly come to realize that your thinking efforts will take on more
of your daily activities. You've got a really big responsibility on your
hands; hundreds of individuals depend on your decisions. And like
any other skill you've developed, you'll need to train yourself in this

new style of thinking as well, gradually cultivating more and more of your thinking side."

"I have to admit that this is a whole new approach for me," I said, "That being said, I still have one more question: How do you differentiate between goals and objectives? In our company we've always used them interchangeably, and I've always thought of them as synonyms. Aren't they the same?"

"The methodology framework that I've developed uses the terms *objectives* and *goals* much like you do in the game of soccer. In soccer the objective is to win the game by scoring more goals than the other side. And so, each time you score a goal, you increase the chances of achieving your objective. In other words, your goals support your achievement of objectives. Objectives are qualitative in nature. They express broad general intentions of what an organization wishes to achieve—for example, 'Our company seeks to increase its market share in the New England region.' Goals, on the other hand, are quantitative in nature; they are very precisely defined and are usually expressed numerically—such as, 'We are determined to increase our sales in Europe by seventeen and a half percent,'" Chuck said.

"Thanks. I get it now. It sounds pretty clear."

"The work you'll put into articulating the three parts of this assignment will provide you a unique opportunity to really understand the nature of the business in depth and to later communicate your findings three hundred and sixty degrees. By the time we have our first meeting with upper management, you'll have already done a lot of homework, compiled your list of hierarchy-dependent strategic issues, practiced your justifications for their approval, come up with all of the possible reasons you could think of to support your persuasive presentation, and reflect a bull-dogged determination of success. However you cut it, it'll be a lot of work, but know that it's a journey of successive approximations.

"This will be a major test for you as the new business unit leader; it will test your ability to sell ideas that will shape your career and the organization. You'll also have to make sure to present the logic supporting each request, emphasizing the painful ramifications that not supporting each request would imply. Sometimes top executives don't want to allow for change. Sometimes they can't foresee how introducing a minor yet meaningful change to the unit's organizational infrastructure should improve the unit's prospects and yield greater value down the road. I believe this will prove to be the greatest challenge you'll face as the business unit leader."

We further chatted about some of the work I had prepared, and I even got some fresh clarity on how to continue my overdue assignment, and then I left, promising myself to absolutely go the extra mile and make sure that I completed each and every homework assignment that Chuck assigned me well before it was due.

"By the way," Chuck added, "the work you are going to complete, meaning the last assignment I gave you on strategic issues and the one I gave you today on mission, business definition, and goals and objectives, will become your foundation for how to translate your business cell strategies into well-defined projects."

- 9 -

CHANGE DESIGN

The weekend had come and gone, and it was Monday again. As usual I sat down to check my e-mail. This time, however, what appeared in my inbox put a smile on my face: my reservation for a spot at an upcoming symposium was finally confirmed. I had been looking forward to this formal event since Chuck invited me to attend.

The symposium was being organized by the Society of Practical Business Management. I learned that their last large conference had taken place about six months ago. Chuck had been granted a speaking engagement then, and apparently he must've really impressed quite a number of people, because he got invited to present again at this conference on modern management ideas.

People's interest in improving their managerial skills in their own specific business environments was on the rise, and the society took full advantage of the opportunity to reach out to more people and to grow its membership. The nonprofit organization's goal was to offer a forum for some of the sharpest university professors and consulting firm experts to share their most timely and relevant insights and perspectives with its members.

The format for the information sessions would be pretty straightforward—a formal presentation followed by Q&A exchanges between the speaker and members of the audience.

Well, I heard that Chuck gave the society its money's worth the last time he spoke about his diagnostics phase, and I'm sure he made a number of heads spin with his controversial lecture. I'd bet that's why he was invited to speak again. This time, however, given that the attached e-brochure said that the main theme for the upcoming conference was "The Role of Strategic Planning in Business Development," I knew I'd be in for a pleasant surprise. I wanted to see just how ready I really was for Chuck's upcoming speaking engagement.

Sure, we had completed a number of coaching sessions, and I'd been picking up quite a number of useful pointers on how to decipher this mysterious subject of strategic planning. But maybe it wasn't actually a mystery—well, especially to those in the know, of course. And that's a part of what I grew to love about Chuck; he was in the business of demystifying what at first seemed to be overly nebulous and beyond my grasp. In fact, it really was within my grasp to fully understand it all. It just took me a while.

I gradually realized, thankfully, that Chuck had tamed this conceptual beast over a lifetime of business battles and wars. He was a true business veteran who had distilled business complexities into level-headed, matter-of-fact processes that, when applied faithfully, would yield phenomenal results. What can I say? He made a believer out of me.

I called Chuck and let him know how thrilled I was to get his invitation. In his reassuring tone, he replied, "I'm glad to hear that you'll be attending. By the way, what I'll be presenting at the symposium reinforces and complements everything that we've discussed so far. I'm sure you'll find it to be right up your alley."

I thanked him and confirmed that I would be at his presentation. By now I was familiar with Chuck's diagnostics approach, and I was looking forward to hearing both Chuck's presentation and the audience's questions.

Finally, the day of the symposium arrived. Although I couldn't participate in the morning sessions (I had to be at a luncheon meeting that I couldn't miss), I arrived just in time for the early afternoon session and Chuck's presentation. I entered the large room and took a seat.

The symposium chairman walked up to the podium, waited for the audience to quiet down, and said, "I am honored to introduce the next lecturer. Those who follow our presentation series are familiar with Chuck. For those new to these events, Chuck has developed a unique approach to business management that has worked for his consulting clients in private and public enterprises, from small to Fortune 500 companies, and across a variety of industries. At the end of the presentation, please line up at the two microphones in the aisles and ask your questions. Without further ado, I am honored and pleased to introduce our next lecturer." Applause followed.

Chuck, stood up, approached the podium, and addressed the chairman, who took his seat. "John, thank you very much for your kind introduction, and thank you to the society for this wonderful opportunity."

Although I didn't have my notebook with me, I recorded Chuck's presentation with my smartphone. He began: "Ladies and gentlemen, it's a great pleasure and honor to communicate with you on topics that are very important to us. At the last society meeting, I presented in detail the diagnostics process.

"Independent of the size of a business operation, once we have completed the diagnostics phase, defined the weaknesses and strategic issues, stated the mission statement, and redefined the business definition, it's important for us to determine, with complete clarity, the transitional list of goals and objectives for the enterprise. The reason we call them *transitional* is because as the process progresses, goals and objectives may and do change. Meanwhile, these transitional goals and objectives help the organization navigate during a transition period.

"Our methodology applies the following definitions. Objectives are qualitative in nature. They express broad general intentions of what an organization wishes to achieve. For example, 'Our company seeks to increase its market share in France.' On the other hand, goals are quantitative in nature; they are defined precisely and are usually expressed numerically. For example, 'We are determined to increase our sales in Europe by fifteen and a half percent.' Goals are the contributing elements necessary to achieve the objectives."

While I already knew some of this material from my work with Chuck, it was great to hear it again, particularly because I was working on implementing some of these concepts. I knew that the material Chuck was about to present would be the next stage of my learning curve.

Chuck continued: "All the elements previously described—strategic issues and business-cell strategies, both short- and long-term—are great for convincing presentations, but execution may be difficult or even impossible without *change design*. To understand change design, we need to focus on four areas that will help beyond the leader's decision making as a great way to communicate up in the hierarchy and down to the troops." Here, Chuck referred to a slide behind him, which read:

CHANGE DESIGN: 4 IMPORTANT AREAS

1. Business architecture
2. Organizational structure—functional and transitional
3. Investment portfolio
4. Road map

Chuck said, "Let's start with *business architecture*. Business architecture usually requires drawing block diagrams that connect the major components of business functionality. Most of the business units we review in our consulting practice have several business cells, or lines of business. It's important to review how each business cell is performing and how it will contribute to revenues and earnings. Occasionally we find business cells that sell dollars for fifty cents. Sometimes these business cells operate within other business cells, and their performance isn't easy to follow. To clarify these types of situations may require understanding which market segments the business cell more accurately serves. Once this is completed, it calls for restructuring to determine how the business unit should operate, if at all."

Chuck took a sip of water and continued. "Some business units are serviced by other internal company service units. Sometimes this can result in an economic benefit because it's less expensive than hiring an outside vendor. However, many times these internal services are actually more expensive and/or deliver subpar-quality services. If the leader has no control over these service units, their subpar services will negatively affect the leader's business unit.

"All business cells are not created equal. Sometimes, management focuses on the weakest cells and forgets that the main cells require most of the resources—both managerial and financial—to grow revenues and earnings. Like a magnet, weak and troublesome business cells draw excessive management attention. Therefore, it's important to organize the business building blocks from the point of view of optimizing the value proposition. Later, we'll see that reviewing and changing the nature of the business will have a tremendous impact on how the organization is restructured.

"Please note that while there are many demands, some are more important than others. If the analysis is thorough and the leader is absolutely convinced that the change is doable and beneficial, it's critical to follow the sequence presented here as quickly as possible. To design the optimal new business architecture, it's important to first understand the 'as is' business definition and then to clearly identify the following items." He read through the following slide:

Understanding the Current
Business Architecture

- Business cells
- Transaction volumes for each business cell
- Necessary functions to operate the business
- Information requirements
- Hierarchy and intra-unit dependencies

"Good leadership recognizes that every business can be structured differently and explores different alternatives. The key is to integrate all of the business architectures developed for each business cell into one business architecture for the business unit as a whole. Without exception, after completing the diagnostics process, we can always improve on the existing business architecture."

Chuck continued: "After the business architecture is completed and we know how the pieces work, it's time to deal with the next topic: *organizational structure*. It starts from the design of the functional organization, which incorporates the functions needed to make the business perform better. It is reached after considering several possible functional alternatives. The outcome of this effort looks like an organizational chart, but the emphasis is only on the detailed functions required to run the business, not the individuals. Redesigning any organization is a very healthy exercise and contributes to better and sounder decision making.

"Once the functional organization is clear, it's important to remember that the business unit is still operating daily according to the existing organizational structure. The business unit leader, knowing now where he or she is going, can start immediately to make organizational changes to get closer to the optimal organization designed. These changes end up in what we define as the detailed *transitional organization*. Then the business unit leader needs to evaluate the true capabilities of existing or new lieutenants and determine if there is a solid match between their skills and the new needs of the unit.

"This transitional organization will operate the unit and will constantly evolve until all the pieces and the right skills are available and ready to convert it into an optimal organization. We call this optimal organization the *sustainable organization*. We aim to reach this ASAP. However, the most common limiting factor of this phase is skills availability. It takes time to find, recruit, and train the right talent.

"In order to satisfy the road map requirements—the fourth element in the change design process—the organizational structure of the business unit may change. The leader will proceed to conduct a review of the detailed organization and explore the kinds of changes that improve performance and achieve efficiencies.

"The business unit will progress across its different cells, although not simultaneously. While one cell is completing its business architecture, another cell may already be implementing its transitional organization. This process of change design is *iterative*. It requires iterative management of all the elements embedded in it. Iterations are needed because actions are followed by reactions, and in some cases you need to tune and modify ongoing lines of thought in accordance with the new reality.

"It's also important to consider that the business is an ongoing concern, and inputs from the outside—invited or not—show up every day and have an impact on this iterative process."

Chuck continued: "The third element included in the change design process is the *investment portfolio*. It's the complete list of projects that were derived from having identified the strategic issues, short- and long-term strategies, business definition, mission statement, goals and objectives, business architecture and organizational structure.

"The investment portfolio is the real link between the *what* and the *how*—between the big picture and the tactics. Creating the investment portfolio is the *bridge to execution*. Usually the size of this portfolio is large in comparison with the resources available to the unit. Successful completion of these projects will bring the unit to a new and better performance plateau.

"Each one of the projects identified during these several months of hard work gets listed, properly identified, and named. Managing the investment portfolio is like managing a stock portfolio. Some projects will perform better than expected, and some will end below expectations. Monitoring the portfolio is important, and continuous corrective action is intrinsic to the process. Each project will be assigned to a specific member of the business unit. This means that every project launched, large or small, will have somebody responsible for it. Responsibility includes obligations and rights for those in charge. The leader will make every effort possible to help the project managers succeed.

"Surprisingly, experience shows that many projects can be completed within the business unit's *existing budgets*. This is possible by redeploying existing resources. Others may require additional personnel, funds, or special resources. In many cases, the unit doesn't have the quality of personnel required to run all the projects identified to improve performance. In such cases, the hierarchy is asked to help the business unit with *temporary* personnel who have the right attributes to accomplish some of the identified projects. Requests for the needed resources usually take place during the leader's presentation meetings to the hierarchy.

"The unit leader can enable certain projects once he borrows qualified personnel who are currently outside the business unit. Typically, these assignments extend for periods of a few months to one year. Upon specific project completion, the business unit can return the loaned personnel to their original unit. It's a win-win experience. The business unit is able to absorb a substantial peak of activity that would be otherwise impossible to perform, and the visiting employees or managers get the opportunity to enhance their visibility and personal résumés.

"In other cases, needed skills are recruited from outside the company. The business unit leader has to deal with the trade-off between available personnel within the company versus more suitable but more difficult to get personnel from the outside. This difficulty becomes extreme if the company's HR regulations favor internal recruiting. Contrary to popular belief, situations in which business units need to change require a substantial temporary investment. But these investments, if well managed, ultimately provide very large returns." Chuck clicked to a new slide, which showed the following graph:

EXHIBIT 8:

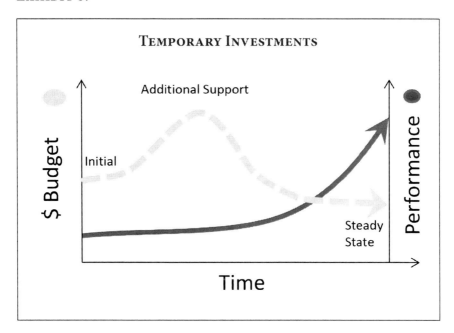

"What this shows is that improving your business unit's operations requires you to increase your initial budget with additional investment resources. As performance improves, the subsequent payoff to your unit is the ability to operate at a lower budget.

"At this time, let's take a brief five-minute break. When we return, we'll move on to the final element of change design called the Road Map".

- 10 -

Road Map

Everyone returned from the break. Up at the podium, Chuck looked around at the symposium audience. He continued: "While the business world often considers the notion of strategic planning as the game plan for a company's goals and objectives, establishing a strategic planning office to handle such functions has not always proven fruitful. In many cases, the strategic planning process has failed and a better tool is needed to improve operations.

"Supporters of strategic processes—not strategic planning—advocate using simpler and more effective tools. We use a tool called the *road map*, or RM, as a practical, down-to-earth replacement for strategic planning. RM leverages the effort invested during the diagnostics process and the change design.

"RM also replaces the classical strategic planning concept of simultaneously dealing with strengths, weaknesses, opportunities, and threats—also called SWOTs—and simplifying it into a simpler concept that deals *first* with weaknesses and threats. Only when these challenges are overcome and mostly eliminated do we deal with strengths and opportunities, that is, growth. The RM is built on a strong foundation. In other words, you don't build a second floor when the first floor is burning.

"A few months ago at this same forum, I did a presentation about strategic issues." Chuck showed the following slide:

EXHIBIT 9:

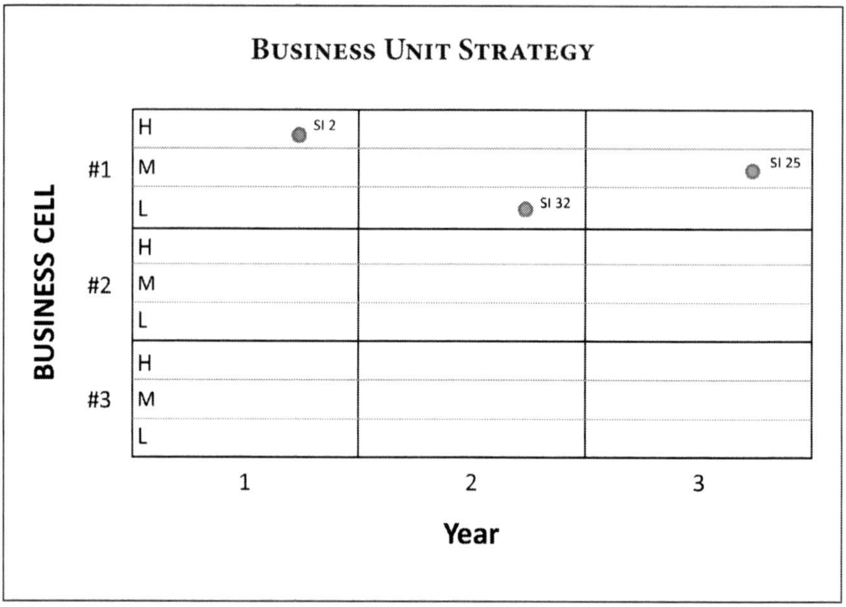

BUSINESS UNIT STRATEGY

"In reality, each of the three business cells had about fifteen different strategic issues. For simplicity, this slide is showing only three strategic issues for Business Cell #1. It summarizes the strategic issues by business cell over short-, medium-, and long-term time horizons, and by criticality levels. Although time horizons can vary in length, we found that in the short term, employees tend to focus well on what needs to be done within one year, and managers can handle projects up to three years in length.

"This map of strategic issues by business cell is the lead-in for the RM. An individual strategic issue is itself the completion event for that strategic issue. The RM, therefore, starts with the end in mind and works backward; it starts with the business cell strategic issues and then maps the projects and critical milestones that culminate in the completion events. Similar to the strategic issues map, we map the RM along a three-year horizon." He showed the following slide:

EXHIBIT 10:

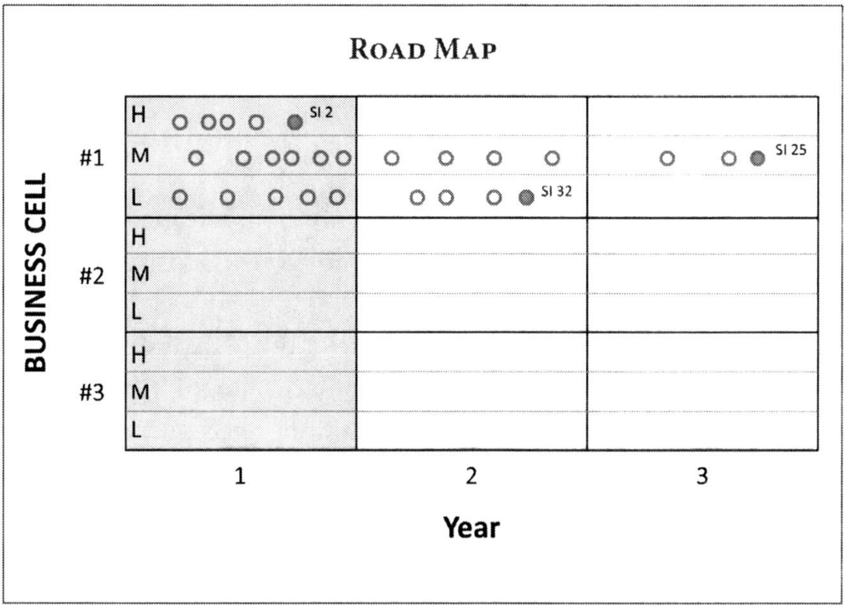

ROAD MAP

"Note that the first year naturally will include more details to tactically manage each business cell and the business unit as a whole. It can also include events like meetings with governance teams, such as a steering committee or a working committee, and the sourcing of critical personnel through human resources. As time passes, the RM shifts, such that year-two items shift into year-one items, and year-three items shift into year-two items, et cetera.

"In summary, change design bridges ideas with purposeful action." Chuck paused, looked at the audience, and said, "This completes my presentation. Thank you for your attention."

The audience applauded, but I could feel there was some tension in the air. The presentation was controversial. Other strategic-planning practitioners, like managers in strategic-planning offices, looked skeptical and preoccupied at the same time. I knew some of them, including a couple of people from my own company.

The symposium chair approached the podium and said, "Thank you, Chuck, for the original and intriguing material presented. The floor is open now for questions." Questions about strategic planning versus the road map process attracted most of the attention. Two short lines formed in each aisle, and the chairman facilitated their questions.

A woman approached the microphone and leaned forward. "Could you please elaborate a little bit more on what is represented in the RM?"

"Thank you for your question," Chuck said. "The RM includes a set of important business milestones that derive from integrating the unit's mission statement, business definition, goals and objectives, business fundamentals, new concepts and strategic issues—whether they are changed, added, or adopted—new business architecture, new organizational structure, and the investment portfolio, or project portfolio.

"The RM improves communications with both upper management and employees. The business unit leader documents the RM, challenges, and progress and presents his or her findings to upper management to gain their support."

The next gentleman in line was wearing a red bow tie and asked, "What are the advantages of road maps?"

"Very good question," Chuck replied. "RM advantages include that they can be tailored to a business unit's needs, or company needs, in less time than strategic planning, especially if the weaknesses and strategic issues analyses are available. It's durable, easy to update, and clear and easy to communicate, both up and down the channel. It's also very low cost to generate. Deriving strategic issues as previously described makes RM maintenance a very low-cost proposition. As well, it involves all the individuals directly responsible for implementing their own plans. A special office is not required to manage this effort. It gives business unit leaders, lieutenants, and employees a true sense of ownership. It also educates business unit leaders on how to differentiate between strategy—what to do—versus tactics—how to do it.

"In addition, it leverages one hundred percent of the work done during the diagnostics phase, thereby providing a very valuable byproduct."

The next audience question was, "What are the limitations of strategic planning, and how does the RM overcome these limitations?"

"While the business consulting world often considers the notion of strategic planning as the game plan for the goals and objectives of an enterprise, establishing a strategic planning office to handle such functions has not always proven fruitful. Several reasons prevent traditional strategic planning from being considered a practical and effective tool. It's oftentimes extraordinarily expensive. It's presented in large reports that are rarely read. It demands that top management invest far more time than is practical. By the time the process is complete, the strategic plan can be obsolete because the business terrain has already changed. It's often difficult to update and reissue.

"RM overcomes all these deficiencies by leveraging the analysis of weaknesses and by identifying strategic issues at a very early stage."

"What will the road map provide?" a man dressed in a business suit asked.

"The RM provides direction by specifically emphasizing the strategic and tactical efforts the unit's management needs to deploy," Chuck said. "It states expectations while recording accomplishments along the way to success. It can be exposed to the hierarchy as well as the lieutenants and employees in a timely manner. It's a powerful tool to share with the hierarchy. It takes only a few minutes for them to understand how the unit is progressing in both its short- and long-term endeavors."

"Does the RM need to be totally complete before starting to implement it?" the next person in line asked.

"Not necessarily," said Chuck. "Business life is too dynamic these days, and many of the elements required to land a major achievement may be conditioned to other events that cannot be anticipated at any particular stage. Nevertheless, as the process continues and the road map becomes updated and robust, the path will be made clear to all decision makers in the hierarchy."

"How long can a road map last?" the next woman asked.

"Contrary to strategic planning, the road map is a relatively short document that gets constantly updated. The initial version is not a guide for the whole year. Once the initial investment is made, it's a very dynamic document. In a way, we can draw a parallel: RM is to strategic planning as CAD/CAM was to design by hand."

"When should a road map get updated?" the next man asked.

"Strategic or tactical elements can be included or changed every time there is a new and important piece of information. It goes through numerous updates at a frequency dictated by internal and external environmental change, including milestones accomplished, newly discovered additional challenges, and so on," Chuck replied.

"What happens between updates?" a smartly dressed woman asked.

"Between updates, the business unit management team proceeds with the last approved road map's instructions."

At this moment the chairman reached the podium and said, "Okay, only one more question. The gentleman with the blue tie, please."

The man reached the microphone and asked, "How many elements does the road map include?"

"The RM includes milestones of all major events that the unit believes are required for success," Chuck explained. "These elements are a small portion of all the issues the unit is dealing with, but they represent the most critical ones. The RM can be made as detailed as necessary to satisfy the needs of the hierarchy and the unit. Presentation time length, executive availability, and the need to focus are also parameters to be considered. It's all about effective communication."

The chairman added, "This concludes the presentation. Chuck will be around, since we have a fifteen-minute break before the next session." People applauded. Several people surrounded Chuck and bombarded him with additional questions. Obviously, for different reasons, there was a lot of interest in the concept of the road map. I tried to catch Chuck's eye to wave good-bye, but he was completely engaged with his small audience. I left the symposium and drove back to the office.

- 11 -

Diagnostics Revisited

Upon my return to the office, I summarized the main points the best I could. I attached the summary to my notebook files. I had questions of my own and was eager to discuss them with Chuck. I knew this would take place in our next meeting.

I stayed longer at the office to prepare the homework I had been given for the next meeting. It was the last homework for the diagnostics phase, and I was happy to complete this assignment. I read my notes and read the white binder reports for the third time. I realized that I had already learned a lot. I was starting to see the big picture and how the diagnostics phase and the change design were connected.

In order to prepare the homework, I decided to summarize what the diagnostic process was about. I felt I had mastered this portion, and I wanted to test myself. I grabbed a legal pad and wrote:

Diagnostics: 12 Steps

1. Preliminary meetings with stakeholders
2. Requests for materials
3. Analyses
4. Preliminary weaknesses

5. Confirming weaknesses

6. Translating weaknesses into strategic issues (short- and long-term)

7. Formulating business cell strategies (short- and long-term)

8. Business fundamentals (hierarchy-dependent issues)

9. New concepts (intra-unit issues)

10. Mission review

11. Business definition review

12. Preliminary goals and objectives

In addition, I added at the bottom of the page what I learned at the symposium a few hours before.

COMPONENTS OF CHANGE DESIGN

1. Business architecture

2. Organizational structure—functional and transitional

3. Investment portfolio

4. Road map

That evening I e-mailed my list to Chuck to confirm. I wanted to be sure that I had the right sequence. When I checked my e-mail the next morning, he had already responded.

From: Chuck

To: Dennis

You passed the theoretical test (the 12 steps) with flying colors.

Time to work on the practical side of it—specifically, the assignments I gave you.

This will complete our diagnostic process. Once we check your "homework" and confirm that you have finished reviewing all the white

> binders, things will change. From then on, we will need to work together on change design, starting with business architecture.

I finished Chuck's assignments and called him to schedule our next meeting.

We met again, and Chuck was very pleased with my work. We spent three hours reviewing the material. He made some suggestions and corrections, and I felt good. Being able to think more about the business realities and possibilities gave me the confidence to participate more actively in my discussions with Chuck. Our interactions started to shift to true dialogues. That gave me a wonderful feeling. Before I left, Chuck said, "Dennis, I'll e-mail you tonight the content of my presentation. Look it over and see if you can draft a new business architecture?"

"I'll do my best, but I'm not sure I'll be able to translate your lecture into something practical."

I went home. Cheryl had seen me working nights and early mornings for the last week to prepare for this meeting. "How did it go?" she asked.

"It went very well, and I'm feeling better." I was happy, and she was happy too.

That night, I went to sleep early. I knew that I was entering a critical stage and that I had to start by reviewing Chuck's lecture about change design. The next day, I planned to spend a couple of hours at work thinking about the subject of business architecture. It didn't work.

I had to face too many crises. I'll never forget one of our customers, James, who called and yelled at me, "I've been calling you guys nonstop for the past month and a half, leaving messages, getting the runaround. You guys haven't fixed this darn problem, and you still have the nerve to invoice us for services you never performed?!"

"James, I understand where you're coming from, and we're looking into this problem. I've recently taken over BLM and am working diligently with my team on just these types of issues," I said. "I know you've heard other colleagues at my company promise you things that never materialized, and I'm not going to do that to you. What I can do for you is to call you next week with an update." Although the air-conditioning was on, I was still sweating through my shirt.

These conversations were painful and humiliating. The pressure was intense, and I didn't have time to really manage. It was a continuous bombardment by customers, the press, and later my own hierarchy. The gap between expectations and reality was substantial. Going back home was the worst part. There was not much I could share. These were all bad stories. I knew that my time was limited, and I had to come up with concrete solutions. I thought I could do it, but I would need some help.

- 12 -

MANAGING ACCOUNTING

It was Saturday. I was tired from a very stressful week. In the morning, I took the girls to ballet. Cheryl would pick them up later, so I would have at least the morning hours to prepare for the next meeting with Chuck on Wednesday.

Chuck had e-mailed me the transcript from his presentation at the society. As I reread it, I focused only on business architecture and finding the right meaning for my unit's situation. I selected certain excerpts, changed their font to italics, numbered each accordingly, and added my comments in normal font so I could discuss them with Chuck:

---

1. Business architecture usually requires drawing block diagrams that connect the major components of business functionality.

Comment: I need to draw a diagram that will represent my current business unit's functionality and then explore what changes I would like to implement.

2. Most of the business units we review in our consulting practice have several business cells, or lines of business. It's important to review how each business cell is performing and how it will contribute to revenues and earnings.

Comment: Well, before I came, there were two people running the unit. One was a half-timer, and the other was a full-timer. Everybody in the unit reported to Charlotte. The business unit collapsed. Pressures came from customers as well as the hierarchy. It is worthwhile looking at the business from a different perspective. My accounting information is not detailed enough. I need to meet with the accountant before I draw any definitive conclusions.

3. Occasionally we find business cells that sell dollars for fifty cents. Sometimes these business cells operate within other business cells, and their performance isn't easy to follow.

Comment: I have a feeling we're losing money on certain activities. If we're losing money and the customers are so unhappy that the media is attacking the company, it doesn't seem unreasonable to consider eliminating this unit. This is probably what the executives have in mind. I need to review how the financial reports are being constructed and how I can better understand what is going on financially.

4. Some business units are serviced by other internal company service units. Sometimes this can result in an economic benefit because it's less expensive than hiring an outside vendor. However, many times these internal services are actually more expensive and/or deliver subpar quality services. If the leader has no control over these service units, their subpar services will negatively affect the leader's business unit.

Comment: This is absolutely correct; we are getting certain services from other units, and they are very poor. This was made worse when the unit was transferred to Peter's division. Jack's division includes certain services that once supported BLM; obviously, he will not give up on these services because he needs them to serve his own units. We're more dependent on other service units, and they're giving us a lower priority than their own units' needs. This is the case with accounting, reporting, and the services that we need so badly.

I'd like to bring some of these services inside my unit, but we don't even have enough personnel to do the basics we need, let alone the budget to add those service personnel.

5. All business cells are not created equal.

Comment: I have the feeling that bunching all activity under one individual lieutenant was neither fair to the individual nor to the unit. That explains why Charlotte decided to leave. She felt she was going to lose if she stayed, either because the unit would be outsourced and she would lose her job, or if the unit remained in the company, she would fail in spite of working extremely hard and probably lose her position. I need to think more about this.

6. Sometimes management focuses on the weakest lines and forgets that the main lines are the ones that require most of the resources, both managerial and financial, to grow revenues and earnings.

Comment: Looking over my conversations with customers and the list of complaints, this is so true. I'm spending most of my time with issues that affect a small portion of the business. I'm not paying enough attention to the main activity.

7. *Therefore, it's important to organize the business building blocks from the point of view of optimizing the value proposition. Later, we'll see that reviewing and changing the nature of the business will have a tremendous impact on how the organization is restructured.*

Comment: Chuck has a lot of experience. I'm starting to better understand the details of our business. Is this the right moment to change the ongoing approach to better accommodate our different activities? I remember what Chuck told me in one of our meetings: "Pay attention to segmentation. The more you segment your customer base, the better the analysis will be."

Every sentence in Chuck's presentation contained a message. It was my responsibility to mine its content and apply its lessons to my business unit and personal situation. I started to feel that if I embarked on a new business architecture, the whole approach to management would change, resulting in both opportunity and challenge.

8. *Please note that while there are many demands, they can't all be done. Provided that the analysis is thorough and the leader is absolutely convinced that the change is doable and beneficial, it is critical to follow the sequence presented here as quickly as possible.*

Comment: OK. I have to move faster. The faster I react to Chuck's stimuli, the faster I can implement quality decisions.

9. *To design the optimal new business architecture, it's important to first understand the "as is" definition of the business unit and clearly identify the:*
- *business cells;*
- *transaction volumes for each business cell;*

- *necessary functions to operate the business;*
- *information requirements; and*
- *dependencies of the business cells with the business unit and with the remainder of the company.*

Comment: This confirms that I need financial and operational data that hasn't been available. Although this issue was identified during the analysis of weaknesses, little has changed in the way BLM gets information, in particular from the other units. I'm missing basic and reliable operational information as well.

---

10. The key is to integrate all the business architectures developed for each business cell into one business architecture for the business unit as a whole. Every business can be structured differently. Without exception, after completing the diagnostics process, we always found a better business architecture than the existing one.

Comment: I'm sure there is a better way to design BLM's business architecture, but I need ideas. I'll start by calling Julie, the previous accountant, on Monday.

On Monday, I reached out to Julie. She was on vacation. Without the numbers, it was impossible to make good decisions. I decided to call Chuck and let him know I had to cancel the next meeting. I couldn't develop the new business architecture without the numbers.

He picked up the phone and surprised me again by saying, "Okay, Dennis. Now that you've said that, I know you are going in the right direction. Please come see me anyway. When I was working on the weaknesses last year, I met with the accountants, and I have an old report. It will be enough to understand what the issues are. I wrote a lot of notes on those reports. This may be enough to get you going."

I was very pleased with Chuck's approach. I was beginning to understand that this unit didn't have a future without major change. I had to dig into change design as soon as possible. I felt that the basic transfer of a portion of Chuck's managerial technology (the one he had developed prior to my coming to BLM) was coming to an end, and we were entering a new working relationship. This process would evolve from him teaching and me learning to a process of design, creativity, and decision making with mutual involvement. I had the feeling that this would be both exciting and tough.

I arrived at Chuck's place at the usual time. We went through the same greeting routine. He had the financial reports on the table. They were covered with notes in red ink.

Chuck said, "Look, Dennis, this format has been used for a long time. In my humble opinion, your predecessor digested the info as it was presented by the accountants. With this level of detail, your predecessors didn't have a chance to save this unit. The data is all mingled; there is no proper business segmentation. They could not do better if they were not told how the data should be compiled and presented. Although it doesn't change the bottom line, segmentation provides greater clarity regarding the profitability for each segment. Expenses could be better understood, and priorities could be defined differently. It's impossible to take action with the current presentation format."

We exchanged ideas and concluded we needed a new approach to the accounting reports. I left the office feeling like I had just taken one step forward and two steps back.

The next day, I met with Julie. Based on the conversations I had had with Chuck the previous day, I detailed how we wanted the accounting reports to look. Her expression turned wide-eyed, and she explained that she had a lot of work and that this was not her main priority, nor the second, nor even the third. She was working in Jack's division, and priorities had changed, but not in our favor. A few days later, and as a personal favor, she provided some raw accounting data that I immediately e-mailed to Chuck.

Chuck called me on the phone and asked, "Dennis, have you considered segmenting the operation and accounting reports into the business cells you have in mind?"

"That's my next assignment; I was preparing to do exactly that. I'll see you on Wednesday."

I was ready to work on business architecture. I concluded that there were three distinct businesses buried under one umbrella: each business cell addressed specific and different issues, was of a different size, and housed different processes. I started to build my own business cell P&Ls, trying to match the true expenses to the recorded revenue. At least one business cell was losing money. Chuck was right again!

The following Wednesday, I came to see Chuck with a large rolled sheet. I unrolled it on his desk. There they were: several alternatives on how to reorganize the business. I felt that one was superior to the others. I explained how I'd derived the alternatives and which one I preferred. I wanted Chuck to know that I was committed.

He looked at my unrolled sheet, held his chin with his right hand, and said in a very low voice, "I agree; let's go for it." I was making progress. For the first time, I understood what business I was really in. The next step was to translate the new business architecture into an organizational structure.

Chuck and I continued to meet and exchange ideas. We had many lunch meetings and after-hours meetings until we came up with an organizational structure with which we both felt comfortable. It was obvious now, after completing the organizational design, that I needed three lieutenants to run my new business. Charlotte's departure meant we could budget for one replacement, but I needed additional budget for two more lieutenants. I knew that Chuck could not help me on this one. I needed help from the hierarchy.

It was the end of summer. Our next meeting took place outside Chuck's office on his deck. The deck was surrounded by beautiful trees. There was a nice breeze blowing. Chuck said, "Dennis, over the last months, we've worked on your unit's diagnostics. We've discussed strategic issues, mission, goals, objectives, fundamentals, and new concepts. We then addressed the change design elements of business architecture and organizational structure.

"For our next meeting, we are both going to prepare a comprehensive list of all projects that have been identified, based on all the elements we've already discussed. Please attach the name of the person you would like to lead each project. Whenever you feel you don't have the right candidate, please write 'NA.' We'll convert this list into our investment portfolio. The investment portfolio is the list of all the projects we need to complete to get stability first and success later."

It took us several meetings at work and at Chuck's office before we agreed on how to classify the portfolio, what projects to launch first, and how to develop the road map according the principles presented in Chuck's lecture at the Society of Practical Business Management. "By the way," Chuck added, "not only is this road map a living document, but you'll use it later when we discuss the alignment concepts."

SECTION 2

TEAM BUILDING

- 13 -

CHANGE DESIGN DASHBOARD

The next Wednesday, we met again to discuss the list of projects and the road map. I prepared a draft of the road map, and we fine-tuned it during the session. It looked reasonable and doable, but we also realized that we couldn't get very far without the help of the hierarchy.

Chuck said, "You should feel good. Look at where you were a few months ago and where you are today. We have achieved another very important milestone. It's time to think and talk about governance."

"What do you mean?" I asked.

"Your bosses gave us some hands-off time, because I asked them. They understood and agreed that you needed time to absorb the situation as well as the new materials. Now they are anxious to hear about the unit and your personal progress. The truth is that so far, the unit doesn't show much progress, but you are progressing, and this is what's important to me. No unit can achieve success without the business unit leader progressing. You are getting smarter and more knowledgeable every day. Nevertheless, you still have a long way to go."

I started to get concerned. I was getting close to "judgment time" without having much to show for it. Chuck continued: "It's like launching a rocket. At launch, the booster engine burns a lot of energy, and the rocket moves slowly. We're still at the booster phase. Soon, the booster engine finishes its job, and the sustainer engine takes over. That's when the rocket achieves target speed, without burning too much energy. That's where we're heading.

"I talked to Peter last week, and he agreed to my suggestion of forming a steering committee to interact with us, discuss ideas, and find solutions where we need the hierarchy to be involved. He's going to invite Paul from the corporate finance department, and Andrew who's in Jack's division. BLM has many inter-unit dependencies with these two groups."

"When BLM was transferred to Peter, some vital functions remained with Jack's division," I said. "This is an inter-unit dependency that has to be addressed too."

"Absolutely," Chuck answered. "The steering committee will serve as your business unit's board of directors. We will be five people overall: you, me, Peter as committee chairman, Paul, and Andrew. Remember, steering committees can be your lifeline. However, their members will initially be very cautious because they're concerned with the unit's performance and don't want to be identified with a losing situation. Plus, they haven't had enough time to absorb what you've already learned and what you're trying to accomplish."

"Do you see this as a positive event?" I asked.

"You may feel uncomfortable at the beginning, but remember the reason for these meetings is that they can be very helpful! As things progress, and they perceive light at the end of the tunnel, the executives will become more favorable to the point that once they feel they have made a contribution, they are ready to 'retire' and claim victory. I suggested the effective frequency for these steering committee meetings to be about every two months. A higher frequency is not recommended, since preparing for each meeting is very laborious and detracts from your ability to focus on the rest of your obligations, like learning new things and managing the ongoing business. But too few meetings may slow us down, since we may need important decisions from them to get us going."

I listened carefully to what Chuck had to say and reflected. I knew he was working hard to make me successful. With all the materials I had already prepared, we were now getting ready to face the hierarchy. After all these months, the preliminary change design had been completed. I thought I understood the material. But now I had to explain it to others, who happened to be my bosses, and that's not always easy. I would have to present by myself. I would face a lot of questions, some totally unexpected. Chuck was preparing me for this event.

Chuck added, "The upcoming steering committee meeting will be here sooner than you think. One of your biggest challenges will be to accurately and effectively communicate with the hierarchy by providing enough detail within the limited time the executives will allot for such presentation."

"I agree, Chuck. Do you have any suggestions?"

"Yes. One of the tools I use under these circumstances is the change design dashboard."

"What's that?"

"The dashboard is a graphic representation tailored to your business unit. It uses symbols to express progress trends and accomplishments to date." Chuck opened a binder and retrieved a colorful table and handed the page to me. "This is a draft I prepared for another client," he said.

EXHIBIT 11:

CHANGE DESIGN DASHBOARD

Business Cell	Business Architecture	Organizational Structure	Project Portfolio	Road Map	Inter-Unit Dependence	Staffing	Supervisor Expertise	Employee Performance	Overall Performance
#1	✓	✓	✓	↑	⇔	✓	↑	↑	↑
#2	✓	✓	✓	⇔	↓	↓	↓	↓	↓
#3	✓	⇔	⇔	⇔	⇔	↓	⇔	↓	↓

"Check marks indicate that the items have been completed. A green up arrow represents a positive trend, a yellow horizontal double-arrow represents an unclear trend, and a red down arrow represents a negative trend.

"The horizontal axis includes many of the items we previously discussed regarding change design, including business architecture, organizational structure, investment portfolio, road map, inter-unit dependencies, staffing, supervisor expertise, employee performance, and overall performance."

"What do you include in the vertical axis?" I asked.

"The vertical axis includes the names of all the subunits, or business cells, which compose your business unit."

I looked at the table. "What's the benefit of doing this?"

"It's a powerful tool with four major benefits. First, it forces you to systematically examine your entire business, to understand the significant achievement milestones, to see what's been completed, and to recognize the different progress trends. Second, it helps you manage up and better communicate with the steering committee.

Third, it guides you in your own operational management efforts. Fourth, it helps you manage down and better communicate with your lieutenants; it can be used for coaching the internal hierarchy."

We spent the rest of the session talking about the specifics of the dashboard, and I started to realize that I wasn't investing enough effort to cover everything the dashboard was requiring. The day had only twenty-four hours, and I had a lot to do.

"Well," I said, "I think the dashboard is a great tool. I'll try my best to prepare dashboards for BLM, and we'll see what happens," I said.

I left with mixed feelings. On one hand, I was starting my journey; on the other, I feared the steering committee would grill me.

- 14 -

Decision Making (Q_{DM})

I knew that Chuck couldn't meet on Thursdays because he taught a business management class at the local university. "I haven't suggested that you participate," he said, "because of your very heavy schedule, but now I think you could benefit from some of the lectures. You may also meet very interesting people who are experiencing similar situations."

After hearing Chuck's presentation at the Society of Practical Business Management and after absorbing the material he presented, I understood that business management theory had a lot of value. Good theory guides you toward promising tactical solutions. I had always been a tactician, but tactics without a strategy have limited value, and a strategy without proper execution is worthless. So I enrolled in the local university to attend Chuck's lectures and complement my learning curve with some theory.

Chuck taught an advanced short course for graduates. Most were new business managers who knew Chuck from the previous semester, and most had tried to make progress in their respective companies by using Chuck's methods. They were all impatient and intrigued to hear what he had to say about tactics. That was my element. Having learned from Chuck about diagnostics and change design, I was ready to acquire additional knowledge in this next phase.

Chuck was not very charismatic, but once people knew him, they respected him. I observed that his logic was better than the typical consultant who had come through our company; I attributed this to his background in engineering, chess, and other vast experiences. I entered the room and passed the time by talking to several people. Chuck arrived on time and immediately approached the podium. He opened his briefcase and removed a binder. We took our seats, and he greeted us.

"Welcome. This is Business Management 703. As a reminder, the prerequisites for this course are an undergraduate degree and to be a current or aspiring business manager." A few of my classmates were not business managers but were dreaming about a potential business management opportunity. The others were managers and wanted to be better prepared for the next step. They knew that Chuck would teach them what they couldn't receive from their own organizations. I was one of the oldest students in the class, and I was realizing that I should have been more proactive about my own career.

"My goal for each of you in this course," Chuck added, "is that you pick up at least one thought or even one idea, take it to your workplace, and implement it in your particular business environment. Understanding management is simple. It's about understanding five phases: problem finding, problem solving, implementation, monitoring, and control.

"In Business Management 702, which most of you took last semester, we reviewed the process of diagnostics and change design. Diagnostics is the process of quickly gathering information, thoroughly analyzing it, identifying and summarizing weaknesses, transforming these into short-, medium-, and long-term strategic issues, grouping them by business cell, and deriving a comprehensive strategy for the business unit. Change design is finding and designing the new business architecture, organizational structure, and investment portfolio to implement the business unit's strategy.

"During diagnostics and change design, you often learn a lot more than your subordinates know about your business unit and processes. This is good because your subordinates will recognize your knowledge-based authority, and you will gain professional respect for solving challenging situations when they come up. And whereas diagnostics is about problem finding, change design is about problem solving—a lot of it.

"I would like to introduce you to a new concept called Q_{DM}. It relates to the decision-making power of any organization at all hierarchical levels. If all things are equal between two competing companies of similar size, the company with the higher Q_{DM} wins. Better Q_{DM} improves performance, which increases the company's value." He had our undivided attention.

"So how do we define Q_{DM}?" he asked rhetorically. "Q_{DM} is a function of the quality of decisions made." He flipped to the following slide:

Exhibit 12:

$$Q_{DM} = \Sigma Q_i = Q_{i(avg)} * N, \text{ where}$$

Q_{DM} = quality of decision making overall

Q_i = quality of individual decisions

N = # of decisions

"Q_i is linked to the quality of the analysis or the quality of the combined efforts of the leader and the consultant during the diagnostic process for every decision. Good and comprehensive analysis leads to excellent decisions. We can assign good decisions a positive value and bad decisions a negative value according to the following scale." The screen now showed a new slide:

Description	Grade
Good	+1.0
Fair	+0.5
Neutral	0.0
Poor	-0.5
Bad	-1.0

"$Q_{i(avg)}$ is simply the average grade of all those decisions.

"N relates to the quantity of the decisions made. This is linked to long hours, hard work, and interaction with those contributing to the decision effort. Most of these decisions occur when implementing the investment portfolio.

"In reality, some decisions are more important than others. However, to simplify this concept, assume that decisions are equally weighted. Let's go through a few examples. Consider the sum approach: business unit A made five decisions whose quality of grades was +1.0, +1.0, +0.5, +0.5, -1.0; so its Q_{DM} equals +2.0. Business unit B made the same five decisions, plus one more fair decision. The quality of its grades was +1.0, +1.0, +0.5, +0.5, -1.0, **+0.5**); its Q_{DM} equals +2.5. Business unit B has a higher Q_{DM} than business unit A and therefore contributed more to its end valuation.

"Consider the average-grade approach: business unit C has a $Q_{i(avg)}$ equal to 0.65 and N equal to twenty; its Q_{DM} equals 0.65 times twenty, or 13.0. Business unit D has a $Q_{i(avg)}$ equal to 0.65 and N equal to thirty (ten more than business unit C); its Q_{DM} equals 19.5. You can see that by making more decisions of comparable quality, business unit D is increasing its value more than business unit C.

"Q_{DM} is a novel concept because it means that business is about making good decisions—and a lot of them. Once the implementation phase starts, a lot of interested parties will be watching how the new decisions impact the business and its business relationships. This can range from the CEO, senior VPs, lieutenants, employees, suppliers, and customers. At this stage, a consultant can be very helpful in objectively monitoring and supporting the business leader's decision-making process. Together, the consultant and business leader can determine how to monitor this progress."

John, who worked for a local company and had been recently promoted to run a business unit, raised his right hand and asked, "Chuck, could you please tell us how that works?"

"I would be more than happy," Chuck answered. "There are different types of consultants. There's one type who makes sure that all important elements are brought to the table for consideration and then empowers you to make decisions. Another type of consultant will not let you make a mistake and will challenge you until you both completely agree with the decision to be made."

"Based on your experience, which method is best? Which method would you use?" John asked.

"Good question. I prefer a hybrid method. At the beginning, during the embryonic phase, we cannot afford to leave any land mines that could explode behind us. So the business unit leader and I will debate a situation and decision until we are both convinced that it's the right thing to do. As time goes on and as the business unit leader demonstrates better decision making, we engage in less of these conversations. Eventually, the business unit leader has to fly solo."

"Thanks," John said.

"Business is about ideas, decisions, and execution. If all of them are good, you are positioning the unit toward a winning situation," Chuck added. "Coming back to the Q_{DM} concept, one interesting benefit of such an approach is that this process can be quantified."

John appeared to be very much into this subject. He raised his hand again and asked, "How would you do that?"

Chuck smiled. I suspected that he was satisfied that the class was following his lecture and that there was participation. He said, "The importance of each individual decision is classified into A, B, or C—A for the most important and C for the least important. The consultant helps you do two things: grade the quality of the decision made on the scale we discussed previously and count the quantity of decisions the leader made in each category—A, B, or C—in a certain time period.

"The main benefits of this quantitative approach include the ability to build benchmarks, such as the quality of decision making for A-type issues—or for less important ones—and the quantity of decisions, measured week to week or month to month."

John looked intrigued. He asked, "Could you please provide an example?"

"Assume that for each type of issue, the decisions are graded.

"We can figure out the sum of all grades for a certain type of issues—A, B, or C—over a given unit of time, such as day, week, month, quarter, et cetera. The sum of all the grades corresponding to each time period, ΣQi, emphasizes the *decision power* of the business leader in the period of time selected.

"You can also figure out the *average quality of decisions* for a given type of issue—A, B, or C—by summing all the individual quality grades by issue type and dividing that by the number of decisions made." Chuck flipped through his presentation until he found the right slide, which showed the following formula:

Average Quality = ΣQ_i / N , where

Q_i = grade assigned to each decision

N = number of type A, B, or C decisions made during any defined period of time

---

"You can further plot them per unit of time and get a feel on how your average changes over time."

We all took notes; it was a novel approach to an old subject. The concept of being active and being right in your decisions was presented well. Whether I would be able to implement this in my situation was a different story. During the remainder of the lecture, we played around with some numbers and learned that there was substantial room to improve our performance as business unit leaders.

"You've heard of 'be careful what you wish for'? Well, decisions lead to execution. So be careful what you decide on," Chuck joked. "Most of you are here because you decided to take on a new challenge or are looking forward to it. Deciding on that new job is just one decision.

"Change design assumes that an ideal team is ready and available; however, this is rarely the case. In reality, your team may be incomplete; every person is different, with different skills and behaviors. Implementing change design is about *tactics*, or the art or skill of employing available means to accomplish an end. It's about linking you, your lieutenants, and employees in the transitional organizational structure.

"During this delicate period of potential managerial chaos, you need to step back and check your own strengths and weaknesses. Under the circumstances, your first big decision is to answer these questions." Chuck flipped to a new slide with the following questions:

NEW MANAGER: SELF-ASSESSMENT

- Am I really able to succeed in performing these newly defined challenges?
- What are my probabilities of failure, and what will happen to me—and my family—if I fail?
- What are the probabilities of success, and what will happen to me if I succeed?
- Now that I know how challenging the situation is and how high the expectations of the hierarchy are, should I quit and look for something else or continue the journey?

"This can be a real crossroads for you. It's as difficult to say no to a new assignment as it is to say yes. In most cases, your hierarchy is not aware of all the challenges facing your unit. If, after your diagnostic phase or change design phase, you don't feel good about following up on the assignment, look for a new position that will match your skills and leave the legacy of the diagnostics phase or the change design to a newcomer. He or she will find a more promising situation to handle than the one you confronted.

"Even if you accept the new opportunity, you may still act with hesitation. This may be the first time you're facing such a personally demanding challenge. You're trying to impress the bosses and not make mistakes. However, you may act more assertively if you're working with a senior consultant. We've seen many managers take on a new business challenge not because of any understanding about the business challenge, but because of the consultant's past performance, quality of work, and reputation. Trust develops later. Developing true trust between you and a consultant is very empowering.

"So once you accept the challenge, you quickly move to implementing the change design conclusions. It's extremely important to make good decisions quickly and to make a lot of them. In next week's class, we'll continue our discussion with personnel issues."

- 15 -

MANAGING DOWN

I was delighted that I had been able to attend Chuck's class on Thursday in addition to our weekly meeting. It gave me time to think about the material and to understand it in depth. Whenever I came up with related questions, I wrote them down so that I would have a list ready for our next meeting.

The weekend was nice. On Saturday I took Cheryl and the girls to lunch at Cheryl's favorite restaurant. The girls also loved it. This place had the best ice cream in town. After we returned home, I did some more homework and started preparing for the steering committee.

On Monday, I went back to work to face more of the same. Most of my time was split between putting out fires with furious customers and trying to find the correct operational data. I found I was doing a lot of work myself and that I didn't have the right team to face the present challenges.

I was so happy when Wednesday came around. I arrived at Chuck's, took my seat, and I said, "Chuck, in class you mentioned that managers have to make a lot of good decisions and that many of these have to do with their personnel. I have several issues with my lieutenants, and I'm currently dealing with a very difficult situation."

"One of the reasons business units don't perform well is the lack of quality lieutenants," Chuck said. "Another is not having enough of them. Sometimes it's an issue of both. We'll talk more about this in tomorrow's class, and I'm preparing notes specifically on this subject."

"Peter's having an all-hands meeting tomorrow, and I know it'll finish well after hours, and I'll miss class—I apologize."

"I understand. It's important that we discuss more about this topic in the meantime. You will typically reflect on the following questions." Chuck flipped to a slide from his class notes and read aloud:

PERSONNEL DECISIONS

- Do my lieutenants have the right skills to implement the road map plan?
- How many new positions does the new organizational structure require?
- Do I have enough quality personnel to fill the new positions?
- Do I have the right personnel for the unchanged positions?
- Who can I trust with the most important projects?
- Can I promote from within the unit, or should I recruit employees from other units?
- Should I recruit from inside the company or from the outside?

"There are three issues to consider when you're building your team. The first issue is reviewing the qualifications of your unit's lieutenants and key employees, and assessing their strengths and weaknesses against the challenges defined. It's not unusual for underperforming business units to have three categories of personnel: the *good*, the *bad*, and the *average*.

"The second issue is dealing with each category of personnel. Good performers will start to lead with conviction in their assigned areas according to the new strategies. These individuals are usually overloaded and very soon reach saturation. You have to ensure that your lieutenants' quality of work isn't sacrificed because of the quantity of work. In addition, a lieutenant or another employee who was expected to perform well may not fulfill expectations. These surprises occur often.

"The bad performers are not suited for more demanding assignments. They soon recognize the fact that it's better for them to seek a new position than to increase their stress load. With underperformers who don't leave, it's more than just letting them go. There are always other issues to consider such as performance improvement plans, matching their skills to a different job, compliance with federal and state law, et cetera.

"Your main problem is dealing with average performers. It can be extremely costly, time-consuming, and even dangerous. You have limited alternatives. You can either:

a) Train them, coach them, and hope they become
   independent and perform better, or
b) Replace them.

"Several decades ago, a legendary venture capitalist told me that if you try to help the marginal performers and still have mixed feelings about the progress made, start looking for stronger candidates. Based on my experience, that advice was right. The key is to measure the marginal performer's momentum, his ability to absorb the new methods and tools, his decision making (Q_{DM}), and his execution capability.

"The third issue is selecting new personnel and being confident that they'll succeed. In any new transitional organization structure, for each position already identified as vacant or needing replacement, you can either *promote* or *recruit*.

"Promoting is both an opportunity and a gamble. Good performers who worked under mediocre lieutenants now have the career growth opportunity they've wanted for so long.

"Recruiting for a business unit under pressure is both critical and difficult. Candidates are reluctant to join a 'loser' unit. An outsider may have the right skills but not know your corporate system. In contrast, an insider may know your system but may not be equipped with the right skills to succeed on the job.

"Always consider the company's hiring rules or policies. The larger the company, the less effective this process can be and the longer it can take. Based on the project you develop, you know exactly which skills are needed for your unit. Focus your interviews exclusively on matching specific unit needs with candidate skills.

"Do not rush to recruit without thoroughly checking the candidate's past performance and the opinions of others—internally or externally—who know how that candidate may react under the present delicate business scenario. Use simulation techniques when interviewing candidates. In other words, describe to the potential candidate a real situation at the company and see how the candidate reacts. For example:

- What types of questions does the candidate ask?
- How does the candidate analyze the information?
- What conclusions does he/she derive from information provided?
- How does the candidate plan to execute some of his/her own suggestions?

"Sometimes, because of your sense of urgency and need to delegate, you can afford minor compromises in who you recruit. However, never hire someone who is unlikely to succeed because that's a guaranteed losing proposition for everyone. Give yourself a fighting chance.

"In summary, your goal is to assemble the best team possible in a short period of time to support, execute, and successfully implement what has already been decided. This is the time to change gears and speed up. At the beginning of the implementation stage, people in the unit are likely going to be stressed. They know that something has been brewing for months, they know about the meetings and the consultants, but they don't know exactly what it means and how it will affect them personally. On the other hand, you know that you're making everybody on your team successful and not holding back.

"Okay, we've made good progress today. Keep working on your presentation for the steering committee and let's keep the dialogue going this week."

"Will do." I packed my things and we exchanged good-byes.

- 16 -

Managing Up

Over the next several days, Chuck and I exchanged information, data, questions, and answers related to the material I needed to present to the steering committee. It covered most of the change design elements. Unfortunately, neither Paul, from the finance department, nor Andrew, from Jack's division, had the opportunity to read all the material that Chuck had prepared last year to really appreciate the situation I was facing.

Our meeting was scheduled for a two-hour block, which wasn't nearly enough for all the material I had accumulated. But I knew I had to squeeze in as much as I could, so I planned to focus on five main subjects:

1) Unit's performance
2) My actions
3) Unit's challenges
4) Possible questions from the steering committee executives, and
5) Help required from those executives

Chuck was very clear and precise in leading my preparations. He said to me, "Dennis, remember that the presentation is the price you have to pay to get the help that only the hierarchy can provide."

We did a dry run the day before the meeting and further fine-tuned the presentation. Finally the day came. The meeting was scheduled from 9:00 to 11:00 a.m. Chuck met me at my office. I wore a blue suit, and Chuck wore a darker color. By coincidence, we were both wearing white shirts and red ties.

We strolled down the corridor, took the elevator to the fifty-fifth floor, went through security, and entered a medium-size conference room. Paul and Andrew arrived on time. We chatted about the Bulls basketball game the night before.

We waited fifteen minutes for Peter to show. He finally walked in and said, "Hi guys, sorry, I was on the phone with Senator J., and I see that I'm a little late. Let's get started." We all greeted him, and I started my presentation. I was very well prepared.

The other steering committee members basically knew about BLM's negative reputation. They knew that frustrated customers had reached out to company executives to find a solution to their problems. That even a senior executive had personally gone to visit one customer, and whatever he had promised to do on behalf of the company had not been delivered.

We discussed BLM's ongoing poor performance. Paul and Andrew grilled me with so many questions about BLM and eventually realized that I was handling fires all the time. Paul added, "BLM's poor performance is already eating up a lot of budget that I could use to support other units in the company. It's stressful enough managing requests every week from somebody else, and I'd rather funnel more budget to a unit that's growing, not one that's struggling like BLM." I understood he was trying to dissociate himself as much as he could from BLM. Andrew was singing a similar tune. The unit was not fundamentally built to succeed. And without major change, it was destined to go under.

I finally took a deep breath and presented the change design dashboard. I introduced the concepts that Chuck and I had used during the change design process, including business architecture, organizational structure, investment portfolio, and the road map.

Some of the steering committee members seemed to have issues with the new nomenclature I presented.

Chuck intervened several times to mitigate the pain, but it was obvious that none of the three executives was interested in identifying with my unit. By now, I was confident that if it weren't for the conversations between Chuck and Greg several months ago, BLM would have been dismantled by now.

Toward the end of the meeting, I brought up the issues that were the most important to us regarding getting more qualified lieutenants and temporary senior help. I explained that our approach would include borrowing them from other company units, and that we were committed to returning the temporary personnel to their original units once they completed their assigned projects.

To our surprise, we got some positive reactions to that idea. Peter had a candidate from another business unit who was up for promotion. He nominated her and it was a done deal. I didn't even have to interview her. Paul, the financial executive, offered a senior accountant to straighten out the financials. I guessed Paul probably didn't have enough work for him. Andrew, the other executive, said he had someone with experience; she was between jobs, and she could take some of the load. It was for me to decide.

At 11:00 a.m., the committee wrapped up. Chuck and I talked about reconvening later that week, and then we parted ways. Overall, I felt beaten. I went back to my regular routine, mulling it all over. I had to think.

- 17 -

SELF-EVALUATION #2

I left for home earlier than usual. I was tired. The long days and the meeting that morning finally had taken a toll.

"How did it go?" Cheryl asked anxiously as she greeted me.

"Well, not exactly as I had hoped, but close to what Chuck anticipated. I've been working so hard for so long, and I haven't received any recognition. I have grown professionally so much since I started to work with Chuck, but it's like he said: people only see the tip of the iceberg. The truth is I didn't have a lot to show. I was working hard, but there's not enough progress on the surface."

"Dennis, I have to tell you, this is getting to be a bit too much for me and the girls. I feel like a single mother. You're working all the time, and on the rare occasions when you are home, you are tired, grumpy, and distracted. I'm doing everything around here, and I need a break. I don't know how much longer we can continue like this."

"I know, I know. I miss being with you and the girls. I feel terrible about missing so many of their recitals and after-school events. Cheryl, nobody knows the future, and you are right, this might be too much to handle. Today felt like it was raining on my parade, and I need to rethink if there is a future for me leading this unit. There is too much visibility, too much discontent from the outside world, and I don't have the full support of my boss or even my employees. I'm meeting Chuck tomorrow, and I'll raise this issue." I hugged her.

"Are you and the girls hungry?" I asked "How about I order in our favorite pizza?" I called for delivery, and it was so pleasant spending time with them again.

After dinner I went to bed, but I couldn't sleep that night. I couldn't find the right position. My forehead was sweaty. I must have fallen asleep around 4:00 a.m. When the alarm clock rang at 6:00 a.m., I woke up exhausted. I took a quick shower, and then I prepared some buttered toast and poured a cup of coffee. Meanwhile, I checked my e-mail. I had several unimportant messages and one important message from Chuck, dated yesterday. It said:

From: Chuck
To: Dennis

Dennis, congratulations on the presentation; it went well. I'll be in your building tomorrow. Can you join me for lunch in the cafeteria at noon?

I answered affirmatively, put my cup in the dishwasher, and drove to work. While I drove, I was thinking that I needed to organize my thoughts and papers. Practically speaking, Chuck was the only one I could talk to about my professional life.

It was a quarter to twelve. I was anxious to meet Chuck. I wanted to have the whole hour to talk…about me.

I gave Jennifer some direction regarding two reports requested by HR. These reports were useless and had come at the wrong time. I was not going to fight the system at this juncture, however. I had other fish to fry. She asked me questions about how to fill out the forms. I looked at my watch: it was 11:55 a.m. I took the elevator down to the cafeteria.

There he was, in his suit and tie, waving at me. He had saved a nice table for us. We went quickly for our salad bar selections and came back to the table. I realized that Chuck was waiting for me to go first. I said, "Chuck, yesterday was not a good day for me. I followed all your rules. I work seven days a week. I've basically abandoned my family. We worked hard for months, prepared rigorously, did the dry run in your office, and the steering committee still beat me up because they think BLM's a lost cause! Taking this job was a mistake. I'm just a puppet in someone's drama of corporate politics."

Chuck was silent. It was an invitation for me to continue venting.

"I'm at a crossroads. I ask myself, should I quit or not? I'm not happy going to work every day to deal with angry customers, and then I get called to my boss's office and have to listen to his critiques about the same stuff."

Chuck was very serene.

"Dennis, let's calmly analyze the situation. Let me ask you a few questions."

"Go ahead," I replied.

"Where were you a few quarters ago in comparison to where you are now? Do you feel you made any progress?" he asked. I started to think but remained silent.

"Tell me, are you personally better equipped to deal with these issues?"

I reluctantly nodded my head.

"Do you know now what has to be done to make this unit successful?"

"Yes, I know," I said, with a mix of pride and sadness.

"As a result of the steering committee meeting, did you get some help that you didn't have before?"

"Yes, I did." It was a fact.

"So what's the problem?"

"I don't know. I feel that in spite of my efforts, I was grilled pretty badly."

"Listen," Chuck said, "you have to differentiate between your individual progress and all the rest. There is a rumor that Greg may be leaving his position, and the fight for who replaces him at the top has already started. Peter wants BLM to succeed, and we are not there yet. I was not surprised at all about what happened in that meeting. The meeting was…well, it was what it was supposed to be.

"We're entering a very delicate phase that bridges what you've learned and execution. You need to make a decision. Can you do it? Are you ready to fight until the last bullet? Or are you ready to look for another job? I will respect your decision either way, but you need to make a decision for your benefit, your family's benefit, and the company's benefit. I need to know, too. I have a meeting with Greg next week, and I need to know what to tell him."

I hated it. The ball was once again firmly in my court. The remainder of our lunch session was extremely quiet. I went back to the office. I realized I was in a volatile situation, but all of what Chuck had said was right. Although I was feeling beat up, I had also gotten help.

The rest of the afternoon was filled with mostly administrative meetings. It was really a waste of time.

After work, I went home. I looked at my girls. They had grown during this last year. I had missed most of their events like skating, ballet, and orchestra. The situation wasn't getting much better. I had been struggling for almost a year. I trusted Chuck, but I didn't know if I could trust myself.

I called Chuck.

"Hi, Dennis, what's up?" he asked.

"I have a question for you."

"Go ahead, my friend."

"You have followed my work for the last several months; you know more about me than I know myself. How long will it take me to show results that will satisfy the stakeholders?"

There was silence; Chuck was thinking. He was usually very fast in giving answers, but this time he was processing. I figured he was either thinking about how to articulate his answer, or he was thinking about how to give me the bad news, or both.

"If you invest a little bit more than usual, it will take about a year. We have still a lot to cover," Chuck finally said. "I don't know enough about you on the execution side, so it's not easy to extrapolate how well you'll deal with team-building and implementation."

"What do you mean by investing more?" I asked. "You know that I still have all these problems with the customers, and they call me all the time. I don't have too much free time at work."

"Dennis, you need to make more time to invest in our process, so we can move faster."

I replied, "I have too many fires every day."

"So, *let them burn*," Chuck said in a firm and convincing voice. "You need the time to accelerate our process."

I remained silent for some time. I tried to understand the meaning of what he had just said. Chuck didn't add anything else. So I said, "Thank you for your views and answers, and thank you for your honesty. I'm going to think a little bit more, and I'll get back to you."

"Sounds like a plan," he said.

I concluded that this was the deal. I would have to work even harder for one additional long year to have a chance at making the needed changes. I reflected on this for hours.

- 18 -

WHY PROCESSES FAIL

Thursday arrived, and I went to hear Chuck's next lecture at school. Outside our classroom, I saw John. He started telling me about his analysis of his lieutenants and how he was going to apply the material he learned to his specific situation. Just as I was getting interested in John's discussion, Chuck showed up and said with a smile, "Let's go inside—it's time to get started."

We took our seats, and Chuck continued: "Good evening, everyone! Today we are going to cover a new issue: processes in oligopolistic industries. The past century will be remembered as the century of industrial expansion, especially for industries related to oil, roads, electricity, and automobiles. Many start-ups competed fiercely. Those that perfected production processes, discipline, and efficiency grew over time. They built huge enterprises that matured and consolidated into oligopolistic institutions.

"Because they achieved excellent production results, these organizations believed processes were the panacea for every business effort. They created corporate cultures based on manufacturing processes and applied these to nonmanufacturing activities. Here is where problems started."

John asked, "How can the processes that were so effective in manufacturing pose so many problems to nonmanufacturing environments? What's taken so long to identify their failures?"

Chuck responded, "Great question! When there's no competition, monopolies *resist efficiency* and they foster nonchange—'since things have worked well for fifty or a hundred years, we don't need to change.' Fifty years ago, American manufacturers had matured and consolidated to the point where there were few domestic competitors and less, if any, foreign competitors. As foreign countries developed, their companies expanded their footprint in America. American companies continued to apply the same manufacturing-based processes that brought them success decades before. But with new foreign competition, American companies have been losing market share, revenues, and profitability. So, from this perspective, it's the increase of foreign competition that's created these new challenges.

"By the way, some say that monopolistic organizations don't need as much active management because there's enough demand for their products or services. This explains why these organizations love processes. They think they can turn the key and look away. In reality, what happens is that when enough customers get upset, customers and regulators become the de facto management."

I took the opportunity to ask, "Chuck, what's your definition of a process?"

"Anyone else want to try to answer?" Chuck offered.

John raised his hand and said, "A series of actions or steps taken to achieve an end."

"Nice," Chuck commented.

Maria offered, "A series of actions, changes, or functions bringing about a result."

"Yes," Chuck added. "You are both right; let me provide you with a definition that's a little more comprehensive. A process is a series of actions or procedures that consume resources at different stages. Each stage converts inputs into outputs, until the main objective is achieved.

"Note that processes are a critical part of monopolistic cultures. In these cultures, some executives think that processes are equivalent to 'autopilot management,' and that it doesn't matter who's running the operations, how good management is, or what's the experience level of the current employees in their particular roles. Executives expect that the process will take care of all that.

"In a purely competitive environment, technical knowledge is 'king' in developing a career. But in monopolistic or oligopolistic cultures, other factors are key. These cultures don't perpetuate the importance of developing technical knowledge and technical competitiveness. Some nontechnical executives consider technically skilled employees incapable of managing others because they're simply 'too technical.' They feel threatened by technical employees who might replace them. Instead, they reward and promote based on a candidate's verbal ability, appearance, and perceived energy.

"All things being equal, management knowledge and technical ability should be the major elements when selecting a new manager. Having these attributes means better decision making. Better decision making favors everybody. Processes do not make decisions."

"So what are the needed characteristics for these types of companies to be successful?" Maria asked.

"Maria, the ability of monopolistic or oligopolistic cultures to stay in business and be successful depends on several basic elements, such as threats from competitive forces; the ability to improve service or product quality based on actual customer satisfaction measurements; and the internal balance between discipline and creativity. Business management is about making plenty of high-quality decisions. It's an art and a science, and not everybody who speaks well can make the right decisions.

"Okay. Let's take a break. When we come back, we will discuss the process of 'building a process.'"

During the break, John and I talked about process building. We realized that the challenges Chuck had presented existed in our own companies. We came back from the break, and Chuck said, "Many of the changes to be implemented in any business unit may be linked to current processes. Processes are needed. They are part of the business management discipline. Okay, let's do a class exercise."

"Will this be graded?" Felicia asked.

"I haven't decided yet," Chuck answered. "This is the game. Please write twelve considerations for making a process successful."

We spent most of the remaining time writing our views. At the end of the class, Chuck collected the material and said, "As we agreed last week, remember that we're meeting tomorrow, instead of next Thursday. Tomorrow, I'll provide you with a summary of the best answers from today's class exercise. We'll also have an additional class exercise, so please read the next chapter in the booklet. I'll present the last topics related with the process chapter, and I'll entertain your questions on everything we've discussed on the subject of processes.

"Enjoy the rest of the day!"

I went home and had dinner. I asked the girls how things were going. They were growing up, and I was torn between the man I was and the man I wanted to be. The girls went upstairs, and I stayed at the table with Cheryl, talking about trivial things. I watched the news. The economy was looking shaky. I read the material for tomorrow, and I went to sleep.

Friday went by quickly. As usual, I had more meetings and more problems in the field to resolve. After work, I went to class. Chuck started class by distributing a summary of yesterday's materials. "Please take a few minutes to read this material before we proceed," Chuck said. I looked at the paper.

From: Chuck

To: Business Management 703 students

Subject: Considerations to make a process successful

The following are the best answers from everyone's responses.

1. Purpose

Not all activities can be encapsulated in a process format. If a process can be avoided, it should be.

2. Goals and Objectives

Whether the effort is to build a new process or review an existing one, the first step is to understand the goals and objectives of the activity and its implications.

3. Process Definition: Boundaries

Process definition lists what happens between the start and end points. It includes all the activities performed by each department, group, or employee who will be involved in the process. Activities transform an input into an output. The beginning trigger starts when someone performs an action on an input that he or she receives from another work group, vendor, customer, or employee.

4. Process Flow

When listing the activities, do not analyze the process, just describe it. One effective way of doing this is to first create a matrix on a large board. Label the vertical axis with the major steps or department names and the horizontal axis with time. Then list each activity performed by each group, department, or individual. Many processes do not stay in one department but may span across several.

5. Resources Needed

Envision every process as a group of boxes. For every box, there are three parameters to define: time per unit, cost (the total cost of completing a unit in each step), and quality standard (the definition of what is acceptable and what is not).

6. Inputs—Outputs

For each step, the input and the output should be stated in detail, including how time was allotted for the particular step.

7. Dependency Analysis

Not all steps are created equal. Steps to be performed by other units (beyond the control of the business leader) require special attention, including discussions and agreed-upon written summaries between the participating units. This analysis should include the activity's expected duration, cost, and quality.

8. IT (Information Technology)

Many companies have corporate or central IT services. They control all initiatives regarding new IT projects. It is important to know if the IT services needed in every step of the process can be satisfied internally by the business unit employees or if they depend on central IT. Many central IT units are booked in advance for very long periods; others have a cost structure that makes any new initiatives prohibitive.

9. Monitoring and Control

Monitoring and controlling has to be designed within the process, including:

- How will the reports look for each step of the process?
- Who is going to prepare the reports?
- What content will be reported?
- Who will receive these reports?

10. Financial Implications

The cost of each step has to be calculated. Getting things done is one issue. Getting them done below a certain cost is another.

11. Finding the Right Skills

Process designers usually idealize all employees and job descriptions for every step. This seldom happens. Whoever is or will be in charge of a process needs to specifically compare the job descriptions with the available personnel skills.

12. Training, Communications, and Launch

Once the skill gaps are identified, training design is mandatory. Simulation is the best technique for training each individual in his/her responsibilities. Once everyone is aligned, it is time for 360-degree communication about the major goals and objectives and the highlights of the process, including how it's expected to work. The most important piece in the communication plan is to share comprehensive information with those units outside of the business manager's control.

In an attachment to the list, Chuck wrote:

Sometimes processes are needed as part of the business management discipline. They look simple when they work. But what happens when something goes wrong? Processes require a continuous search for individual excellence, since it is the only way to achieve success and avoid crisis.

Process success is defined when every step of the process is completed on time, at cost, and with acceptable quality. Business units' leaders should realize that when more steps are included in any given process, the probability of failure increases. The ratio between the number of employees and number of steps in a process should also be considered, since, in certain processes, redundancy assures satisfactory results. Possible bottlenecks should be specifically analyzed. In any process, a step that is not performed or partially performed will have a negative impact on all the subsequent steps (even if all the rest of the steps are conducted reasonably well), resulting in poor overall results.

In spite of the hierarchy's expectation that work be performed in 'autopilot' mode, managing processes is not a trivial task, and processes often become extremely inefficient. Processes have a natural tendency to be unstable. To be continuously successful, they need to be *changed and updated frequently* to achieve cost reduction, time reduction, or quality improvements. Sometimes they also require a change in the number of steps. This has a direct impact on the need for training or upgrading certain employee positions that may require different employee skills. Dependencies on other units make process management even more complex, lowering further the probability of success.

"Okay," said Chuck, "now to our class assignment: Why do processes fail? Go ahead and write your thoughts."

I felt I had an unfair advantage over my classmates. I had been working for months with Chuck on the issue of weaknesses, and I was very aware of the process problems in my unit. I wrote:

PROCESS FAILURE REASONS:

1. Goals and objectives of the activity
- Goals and objectives are not clearly defined
- Corporation is indecisive on the subject

2. Deciding if the overall activity is appropriate to be included in a process
- Utilizing a process as a substitute for sound management

3. Management weaknesses
- Lack of definitions (roles, responsibilities, and authority of the "process owner")
- The selected process owner has no authority to control the process
- The process owner has no control on the outcomes of other linked processes
- Lack of managerial capabilities to lead, guide, and mostly coach the process members
- Lack of incentives (monetary and nonmonetary)
- Lack of recognition, in particular when "good things" happen
- Individual mandates are not clear

4. Process definition: boundaries
- Process boundaries were not specifically planned

5. The process flow
- The process flow wasn't properly designed or changed

---

6. *Resources needed*

- Required human resources were not properly allocated, or not allocated at all
- Equipment was not provided

7. *Inputs-Outputs*

- Inputs-outputs were ill defined

8. *Dependency analysis*

- The process is distributed among several departments, and some are not devoting the resources required

9. *Poor environment*

- The process is not effective
- The process is not documented
- The activity cannot be expressed by a single process; instead, it's a mixture of several intertwined processes (often operating under different umbrellas)
- The process conflicts with another process
- The process doesn't enable its members to be more proactive
- Every process member disregards the overall process and tries only to make the most out of his/her specific job
- Recent changes in the business environment were not recognized or partially recognized
- When changes were recognized and responsibilities were assigned, they didn't budget for necessary resources
- The process doesn't track critical parameters

10. *IT*

- IT systems were not incorporated in full during the design
- Central IT did not participate in the design review of the suggested process
- Operational information is not properly recorded

- Operational information is recorded but not transferred to those who can make decisions
- Systems or tools required to properly process the information are not available

11. Monitoring and control

- The process is not monitored
- Conflict-resolution mechanisms are not available
- The hierarchical decision-making process doesn't exist or ignores the subject
- The first hierarchical layer with conflict-resolution jurisdiction is too high in the organization
- The individual responsible for conflict resolution lacks enough authority to solve the problem
- The process owner cannot provide the resources needed
- The ongoing process has been overoptimized, and there is no practical way to deal with unexpected events or new demands
- Basic IT resources and managerial decision making are not available.
- Note: quality decision making requires the existence of three major elements:
    o Understanding the detail of the activity
    o Having the information necessary to understand trends and changes
    o A clear and agile managerial flow of decision making
- Making continuous improvement a priority; achieving minor gains on obsolete processes

12. Individual competence

- Individuals cannot do the job for different reasons (new technology, changes, more volume)
- A process member leaves, and there are no succession plans or instructions available for the remaining personnel, thereby weakening the team to a level of incompetence

- Adequate training is not available
- People don't know exactly what to process and/or deliver
- Poor decision making

13. Financial and operational information

- Very vital financial information is missing because the process didn't include transactional tracking
- Operational information is not recorded
- Operational information is recorded but not transferred to the decision makers

14. Communications

- Communications between the members of the unit in question or communications with the other departments are weak

"Okay," Chuck said, "it's time to finish. I'll start collecting your notes now." He walked from one student to the next, collecting our papers. I had a good feeling that I did well. "Here are some common life examples." Chuck showed the following slide:

PROCESS FAILURES DUE TO GAPS

- *Operator Gap*—Somebody is not at work (retirement, vacation, position vacancy)
- *Quality Gap*—Somebody makes a mistake
- *Strategy Gap*—Somebody does not know what to do overall
- *Tactics Gap*—Somebody does not know how to do a particular step
- *Process Revision Gap*—Changes in an IT system may require revising the existing process to sometimes eliminate certain steps and/or introduce new ones
- *Training Gap*—Lack of appropriate, custom-tailored individual training

"I'll be posting the grades online by end of tomorrow, Saturday," Chuck said. "Let's take a five-minute break, and when we return, we'll move onto what happens when processes fail."

- 19 -

PEOPLE MANAGE PROCESSES

"Welcome back class. Before the break, we were talking about *why* processes fail. Now, *what* are the main consequences of a failed process?" Chuck asked.

Several hands went up.

"Failure to deliver on time," John answered.

"Failure to deliver the required quality," Felicia added.

"Failure to deliver within the planned costs," Mary responded.

"Right, all of the above," Chuck said. "Process effectiveness is measured against the contract terms, which is what the business unit leader and upper management see."

Felicia raised her hand and asked, "What do you mean by contract?"

"That means either an outside business obligation or an internal commitment. It's the function of cost, timeliness, and quality. You need to have the ability to constantly benchmark the process you're interested in, which means getting into the numbers.

"Let's run through an example. First, assume a 20.0% probability that the process will be internally managed at or below the budgeted cost, including internal personnel hours, dollars, and outsourcing needs. In addition, assume a 90.0% probability that the transactions in this process will be delivered per the contract's on-time terms, and a 50.0% probability that the process will be delivered according to the contract's quality standards. What's the process *effectiveness* value of the whole process?" Chuck asked.

John was already plugging the numbers into his smartphone. He said, "The result would be equal to 20.0% times 90.0% times 50.0%... that's 9.0%. Seems like an awfully low number to me."

"Well," Chuck said, "why do you think the effectiveness value is so low?"

I raised my hand and said, "There are two possible causes. Either the process designer missed something, or the execution is very poor."

"Good answer, Dennis," Chuck said enthusiastically.

"How are these probabilities derived?" Felicia asked.

"Based on past performance, the process designer can establish the standard costs of each step and of the whole process. Often, changes that weren't budgeted for can take place and impact the process, making it less effective.

"You should also evaluate the number of steps in any given process. Let's focus for a moment on timeliness." Chuck displayed the following chart:

EXHIBIT 13:

TIMELINESS COMPLETION PROBABILITIES		
1 step $(N\%)^1$	10 step $(N\%)^{10}$	50 step $(N\%)^{50}$
99.9%	99.0%	95.1%
99.0%	90.4%	60.5%
95.0%	59.9%	7.7%
90.0%	34.9%	0.5%
80.0%	10.7%	0.0%

"Assume that a process has ten steps. Ten individual steps each performing at 99.9% timeliness means the whole process will be timely in 99.0% of the cases. But if every step is performed timely only 95.0% of the time, the whole process will be timely only 59.9% of the cases. Quite a difference," Chuck said. The class started to murmur. It was an eye-opener.

Chuck continued: "If all steps are each 80.0% timely, the whole process will be timely 10.7% of the cases. What can we learn from this?"

John was the first to respond. "That a successful process requires delivering at levels not seen before, at least in my place."

"Correct, John," Chuck said. "For a fifty-step process, it's even more dramatic. Fifty individual steps operating timely at 95.0% results in 7.7% timeliness, and fifty individual steps operating timely at 80.0% results in almost 0.0% timeliness. The shorter the process, the better the chance of achieving success; the longer the process, the more demanding the process manager must be to achieve the quality required.

"This analysis regarding timeliness also applies to the other contract terms of cost and quality. This is very powerful. Now, you can analyze a process that was budgeted based on past performance or experience, measure current performance variances, and assess future performance and effectiveness. Think about ways to shorten a process, identify critical process steps, and include the right ones in a list of metrics. Does anyone have more questions on this topic?" Chuck asked.

"What about when companies recognize that a process isn't working as expected because of inter-unit dependencies and they introduce a new process owner function?" asked Felicia.

"Good question. What's your definition of *process owner*?" Chuck answered.

"An individual held accountable and responsible for the workings and improvement in the process," said Felicia.

"The person responsible for process throughput and quality of output," said Maria.

"The person who coordinates the various functions and work activities at all levels of a process," added John.

"Interesting," said Chuck. "Although these are appropriate, the common denominator of your answers relates to the process owner's responsibilities, or duties. What about his rights? Theoretically, this person should have the authority or ability to make changes in the process as required, and to manage the entire process cycle to ensure performance effectiveness. Practically, the concept of process owner in a multiunit setup may not work if he's responsible for improving performance but lacks the adequate authority to enforce the needed changes. It's no wonder why many process owners become highly frustrated employees.

"Important inter-unit processes require a *process manager* with the authority to manage change, make real-time decisions, enforce business discipline, and formally involve the hierarchy of the different business cells or units."

"Chuck, this is just like a situation I'm facing. What about conflicts between different units when they both work in the same process?" John asked.

"Conflicts in inter-unit processes exist and are natural and shouldn't be avoided. Process conflicts are an excellent vehicle for finding problems. When resolution is possible, conflicts should be treated at the proper level and in a timely manner. Governance is also important. Depending on the importance of the process, forming a small group or committee of directors or senior managers from different units can be instrumental in finding rapid, practical solutions to conflicts. It accelerates the process of decision making, releases stress, and ultimately improves the performance of the process.

"Business units should aim for full independence, including the control of critical business processes. It's an important factor to changing performance. The business unit leader and some lieutenants will probably be measured, among other things, through the metrics of process performance. When possible, bring inter-unit process functions into your business unit to simplify those processes and improve effectiveness."

"But what can we do when political situations dominate?" Maria asked.

"Developing the skills of your own employees sometimes allows you to take on certain activities that are currently in the hands of other units and which you haven't done before. Then senior management will see that you are capable and will be more likely to move these process elements to your unit," Chuck answered.

"We're running out of time, so let's briefly touch on our last topic of this chapter, or process bottlenecks. What is a *bottleneck*?" Chuck asked.

John raised his hand and said, "In the context of our topic, a bottleneck is a phenomenon where the performance or capacity of an entire process is limited by a single event or limited resources."

"Excellent answer, John. Assuming we have only one bottleneck in a process, who can tell me the cost of an hour of a bottleneck?"

Nobody answered.

"Maybe Mary would like to share her thoughts," Chuck said.

Mary was hesitant. She finally answered, "I would calculate all the costs incurred by the particular step and then divide that number by the number of operational hours for that particular step."

"Who agrees with her?" Chuck asked. Several hands went up. "Any other opinions?" I knew Chuck well enough to know when he felt that the answer was not correct. This was one of those moments. There was something else we were all missing.

The silence was deafening. Chuck finally revealed the answer: "Please write this down in your notes. The cost of an hour of bottleneck is worth the cost of an hour of the whole process, not just the step. It's not the cost of one hour of the person or costs incurred by the step representing the bottleneck. It's the cost of the whole process. Think about that when you evaluate whether the bottleneck has to do with cost, timeliness, quality, number of steps in a process, or inter-unit issues."

I had never thought of it that way. That was something! The murmuring among the students continued for a while. The lessons were overwhelming, and everybody was thinking about how to apply the new findings to their particular situations.

"In summary, processes fail when managers incorrectly assume that life will always follow the designed process. Processes don't manage people. People manage processes. Ultimately, it's all about teamwork and mutual respect among the team members. Thank you. See you in a couple of weeks," Chuck said.

As I was leaving the building, I was feeling good. I realized that I had learned a lot during these last months. I decided to take a break on Saturday. I called my brother, Jim, and he invited us to visit him at his summer home in New Buffalo, Michigan. Even though it was a two-hour ride from home, it would sure be worth the effort.

That morning was beautiful, and I was relaxed. But from time to time, my mind kept tugging at me, reminding me that I had to make a decision and let Chuck know what was next. As soon as we arrived, the girls went for a swim. Cheryl was happy. She had a great relationship with Jim's wife, Jane, and both liked to walk through the trails and talk. I also went for a swim. I hadn't done so for a long time. It sure felt great.

As I walked back to the cottage, I suddenly remembered that Chuck had mentioned he would post the class grades online. I got to my computer, logged in, punched in my code, and yes—I got an A! I stepped outside with a sense of pride. As I took in the natural beauty of the trees, the lake, and the boats, I decided, "I've got to succeed. I'm going for it."

In the afternoon, I invited Cheryl for a walk. "Cheryl, I'm going to continue with BLM—I don't have other options right now. But I want to be on the same page with you."

"Dennis, you know I love you and support you. Do you feel in your heart that this is the right move for you?"

"Yes!"

As soon as I got back into the house, I left a message for Chuck on his cell that I needed to talk to him. He had been very patient, and he deserved to know. That night Chuck called me back, and I let him know about my decision.

"Okay," he said. "Next Wednesday, we will talk about the investment portfolio. Bring a complete list of potential projects. We need to get rolling. One year isn't a very long time. Keep me posted on your assessment of the new recruits."

That was classic Chuck. He always brought me back to reality; he always made me face the necessities of our business situation. I spent most of Sunday working on the project list and the questions for the new recruits.

- 20 -

TIME MANAGEMENT

It was Wednesday. I arrived at Chuck's place totally energized. We briefly discussed my decision. He was one hundred percent behind me, and I felt good.

He didn't waste any time in bringing me back to reality, though. "Before launching any project, ask and answer the following questions:

- What will be the tangible benefits upon successful completion?
- Who is going to run it?
- What resources are needed to complete it?
- How long will it take to complete?"

"Chuck, I've concluded that, although I know what has to be done, I don't have the budget to run all these projects."

It was ironic that a few days prior, I had made the critical decision to stay on, and now I was asking myself if that decision was right. Should I be doubtful again?

"Could you please provide me with some direction?" I asked.

"Don't despair. My experience shows that many of the projects in the list of 'potentials' are doable internally, within the existing and available budgeted resources, under the business leader's control.

This is the time for real leadership; you will have to take on as many projects as you can on a personal basis. This could be a temporary assignment until you find a 'parent' for each project on the list. Until then, you're the leader who needs to manage the most critical projects."

"Are you giving me *more* work?" I asked.

"I'm not your boss. I'm only your coach, and I'm not giving you more work. I'm only suggesting how to use your time differently. Consider that there will be a need for managing *simultaneously* a substantial number of projects. Some will be large; others will be relatively small. Some will be very difficult, and some will be light. You may delegate portions of these most important projects to other employees, but crucial projects at this juncture require your undivided attention, since those projects will make or break your unit's future performance."

I felt as if I were under a thousand-ton press. I asked myself why Chuck didn't tell me exactly how he envisioned the next steps. I hadn't considered such a load when I decided to continue the journey.

Chuck read my body language and said, "Relax, I'll provide you with some ideas. First, as long as you don't complete these projects, you'll continue to have dissatisfied customers, and I'm sure you know that by now. So delegate the handling of unsatisfied customers to your lieutenants and other employees, and use that time to run the projects."

"Okay."

"Second, use the remainder of this week to record how you're using your time and send me your 'time pie' by the end of Friday." I nodded and took notes.

"Third, there are a few other important projects that require out-of-pocket dollars beyond the original budget and some that require unique resources, like specialized IT skills. They need to be exposed to the hierarchy for additional support, but we have to know precisely how much they are going to cost. The hierarchy will ask questions, a lot of them. You have to be able to clearly articulate the economic benefits of each project. This is of prime importance—it's a major test for you as a business unit leader. It's a sales job, and its success will ultimate determine your future and the future of the unit as a whole.

"Detailed background material, proper preparation, and eloquent presentation are really important. The issue of who is going to manage the projects to be funded by the hierarchy may or may not come up. As a business leader, you should be prepared and open to discuss the available options for selection."

I listened silently. I felt a lot of pressure, but I also felt that Chuck was doing his best in finding the right path. He continued: "Only if this 'test' is successful, and the hierarchy has good vibes about the benefit of the project, can you discuss the issue of needed resources. Hierarchies can make great contributions on the tactical side by facilitating that which is beyond the reach of the business unit leader."

"But where am I going to find the time to prepare this presentation? It feels like additional work, and my 'time pie' is already maxed out," I said with a worried tone.

"Not really; it isn't more work. The fact is, you have to prepare a presentation for the steering committee every two months. You just have to figure out the topics you need to prepare and how to promote your cause. I'll help you."

"Sorry, I don't mean to complain. I hope you understand where I'm coming from," I said.

"Okay, the third suggestion is to pair the newcomers' and the key employees' names to each of the projects identified in the project list, and to match their skills to the individual challenge the best you can."

"I promise I'll think about all these issues. Can I contact you on Friday after hours?"

"Sure you can. You know that I'm available to you twenty-four seven."

"Can I tell you something else?"

"Sure. Go ahead."

"I'm a little concerned about managing all of these projects almost simultaneously. It's a massive undertaking."

"We have up to one year to make this happen. I've seen time and again that there is something special and very positive about addressing simultaneous projects. Progress in several projects simultaneously results in synergistic effects that facilitate the solution of other pending projects and challenges in a business unit.

"You and your lieutenants have never faced so much work. But it all makes sense. The need for this concerted effort is irrefutable. It simply has to be done, because by now we know it's the right thing to do. It's impossible to predict *a priori* all the effects that each solved problem or project completed will have on other projects, but we have confirmed that there is a synergistic effect that helps accelerate the overall problem-solving process. Simply said, it's magical."

I thanked Chuck and left.

The next day, I started recording how I was spending my time at work. I looked back at my activity during the first part of the week, and I recorded every activity I was involved in on Thursday and Friday. I counted the hours I dealt with unhappy customers, the hours I spent on administration, the hours I spent in "unwanted meetings"…and I was shocked. After drawing the pie, I realized I was doing a lot—except leading and managing my unit. I felt embarrassed.

It was the end of Friday. I called Chuck and told him about my findings. He listened to me, and then surprisingly he said, "Congratulations. You have just recruited the best person to help you."

"And who's that?" I asked and immediately realized I had spoken too soon. I understood that I had to change my routine. I could see Chuck smiling on the other end of the line. "Well," I added, "this has been a very convincing exercise. Any other things you would like to tell me?"

"Yes, I'd like to bring up a very important principle in business management."

"What's that?"

"It's called the principle of *action-reaction*."

"Sounds like physics," I said, smiling.

"For many years," Chuck added, "I observed that the occurrence of an unexpected event in a business unit usually triggers a quick reaction from its manager. Many times, these quick reactions result in serious mistakes. Sometimes these unexpected events are complex. School has trained us that every problem has one unique solution."

"That's true."

"But a complex problem usually requires multiple elements, which once integrated can constitute a good answer. This requires looking at the problem from different perspectives. Sometimes creating an interdisciplinary team to discuss these unexpected events can foster the creativity to come up with several ideas, filter them down, and finally yield a solution to the problem. This is an important concept to study and understand because it goes against the training you had at school.

"Usually, when a negative action has occurred, a manager's initial reaction is very different from the solution he would've reached after a careful reasoning process. When looking for a comprehensive solution to an unexpected problem, mitigate risk and convert negative energy into positive. Never reply immediately to a new, unexpected problem you haven't already solved before. Take your time, take a step back, and carefully analyze the potential damage this event could really produce. Although this may cost you a little more time on the front end, it can save you much more time down the line."

I jotted down this very practical advice in my notebook.

"Anything else I should know?" I asked.

"Yes, a couple of additional issues. First, from now on, instead of meeting at my office, we'll meet at one of your three facilities. You are going to launch a lot of projects," Chuck said. "Obviously, there will be exceptions, like when we're preparing a presentation for a steering committee meeting or analyzing a major topic. Otherwise, we'll work in the field. Second, I need to better understand what kinds of project-management tools you have available. As a business unit leader, you will face two types of needs: data availability and management, and project scheduling."

"Chuck, I'm aware that data management is the base for good quality and timely decision making. All along, I've been struggling with the lack of data and data integrity. I found that operators have been collecting incomplete information and generating reports that make little sense. Without someone to proactively question them, the quality of their work hasn't improved. My predecessors didn't process the right data for far too long, and any information feedback is currently misleading. It's costing me time to identify which important data is corrupted and needs to be immediately investigated and repaired.

"Not only that, but the hierarchy forces us to use the central IT department, which unfortunately doesn't even have some of the data we request. The hierarchy also communicated that units shouldn't develop any homegrown systems and won't support any new software unless central IT blesses it. Well, guess what? Central IT is migrating to a new enterprise system, and they've estimated that it may take up to two years before they get to me, since we're not the largest unit in the company. This concerns me, and I don't want to get called out for not really following orders by trying something on my own."

"Listen, the reason you don't currently have the right data is because none of your predecessors defined what was needed. If they couldn't define it, they couldn't request it. Would you agree?"

"Yes."

"We can't make progress without the right data. We can't afford to wait. We need to start an initiative and get the information we need by ourselves. You need to know what's going on right now to better manage your time later. Project success depends on this. It's important to use any tools available, even if they're primitive.

"In most cases, the information we need can be generated by using spreadsheets. By developing the spreadsheets and generating the needed data, you're also properly developing specifications for central IT."

"I received a transferee a few days ago," I said. "His name is Tom. He's very analytical and a spreadsheet wizard. I'm thinking he may be the best option to help us with this endeavor."

"Well, you know my answer."

"I'll put Tom on it right away," I said.

After a few months of work, the new and accurate data proved crucial in identifying the magnitude of the operational weaknesses in my business unit. We didn't have anything like this before. We changed existing processes, made more operational decisions, and improved the overall quality of our decision making. Several times, it helped us be more responsive and better prepared to address customer needs. The days of feeling like a headless chicken chasing in all directions were coming to an end.

And two years later, when central IT finally called me because they had time and were ready to help us, we had our specs all ready. We didn't have to waste any time in getting them on board and on track. I really appreciated this new approach to better time management.

- 21 -

PROJECT SCHEDULING

It was Thursday and time for Chuck's class again. Chuck came into the room, greeted us as usual, and then said, "Today, ladies and gentlemen, we will discuss a subject that many of you have asked about: project scheduling. Please raise your hand if you have been involved in project management in the past."

Without exception, everybody raised their hands.

"So why are you interested in project scheduling?" I got the feeling that Chuck wanted to make this session a little more interactive.

Felicia said, "I'm interested because, from talking to my colleagues and from my own experience, it's very difficult to finish a project on time."

"Thanks, Felicia. Who else?"

John said, "My problems were related to project costs. I found it difficult to complete my project within the financial constraints."

Other students chimed in with similar examples.

After a few moments, Chuck summarized, "Your interest in project scheduling and project cost comes from the fact that finishing a project on time and on budget is almost 'mission impossible.' Is the process of project scheduling needed?" he asked rhetorically.

I raised my hand and said, "Absolutely needed, although I'm struggling with the question of which is more important, managing time or managing cost?"

"Dennis, thank you for a very good question," Chuck said. "Managing time is much more important than managing cost. Experience shows that managing time properly helps control costs, while controlling costs ignores the value of time. Many governmental organizations manage projects by controlling costs. It's so rooted in the American system that it's very difficult to modify. The results: almost all projects managed based on cost end up with substantial cost excesses and dramatically longer times to complete than planned."

Chuck continued: "In general, project scheduling is necessary, but it can become expensive, not only because of the absolute cost but mainly because of the opportunity cost. Never forget what else you might accomplish with the same resources involved in project scheduling and monitoring.

"Business units in need of change don't have 'free' resources to schedule and monitor. It's generally the opposite: the main contributors are very few, and they are already overwhelmed. In addition, new decisions and changes take place every day. It's important to prioritize them in such a way that the scheduling process doesn't hurt the project progress.

"What programs are you using to schedule and monitor projects?" Chuck asked the class.

"PERT...Microsoft Project...Gantt charts," some people responded.

"Okay, okay," Chuck said, raising both arms. "Scheduling programs range from the most sophisticated, like PERT—short for Program Evaluation and Review Technique—to Microsoft Project to Gantt charts. PERT was originally developed by the US Navy in the 1950s and is commonly used to define the critical path of relatively large and interdisciplinary projects. The critical path indicates the minimum time needed to complete a project. Although PERT is a very powerful tool, many users of these programs fail in their endeavors. Projects take much longer and costs run much higher than the project schedule indicates.

"Let me tell you an interesting story related to these facts," Chuck said. "When I was a young engineer, I worked with a superb mechanical engineer named Seth. He was very bright and very optimistic. Seth assumed that everybody working with him was as capable as he was. He was given the responsibility to run an important project. He prepared and provided a schedule. The schedule was approved by his boss, and the project started.

"A short time after launch, the monitoring process started. Initially, he made a lot of progress with a great design, but the people on his team couldn't keep up with the expected pace, and after a few months, when it was clear that his project was behind schedule, his boss decided that Seth could not manage projects, that he was a very good engineer, and that he should go back to doing only design. He was removed from the program and carried the stigma of failure for the rest of his career.

"A few days later, a new project manager named Aaron was selected. He came back to the boss and claimed that the project was previously ill-conceptualized, and therefore the schedule was not realistic. He came up with a schedule that was almost double the time and the cost provided by Seth. The project was important, and its continuation was approved. It took twice as long and twice the cost to complete this project. The project was successful. At its conclusion, Aaron was acknowledged as a great project manager.

"The truth is that Seth would have eventually finished this project in less time and at less cost than Aaron did, and he would have provided a better product. But he lost his opportunity. What can be learned from this story?"

John was the first to raise his hand. "The hierarchy doesn't like deviations from plan. They like matching plans to execution."

I added, "True. Also, too much optimism is a negative characteristic for a project manager."

Felicia said, "In my experience, even if we follow the essence of the plan, usually the tasks take longer than expected. Should the plan be modified as the project progresses?"

Chuck responded, "Reasons for project management failure are attributed to poor time or cost estimates by the participants. For example, events with unexpected outcomes—like unfavorable test results in an R&D project—can bring a whole program to its knees. In addition, the reason for failure in completing the project on time could be linked to the way that the estimates provided by the program participants were interpreted by the scheduler.

"For those of you who use PERT—or who plan to use it or something similar—let me describe for you some of the tool's failure mechanisms. Schedulers ask project participants to estimate the minimum time, T_1, a most probable time, T_2, and a maximum time, T_3, to complete each of the tasks in which they participate. Schedulers rarely explain how participants should properly estimate these times.

"Certain project participants offer very optimistic times, while others provide very pessimistic ones. If the project manager and the project scheduler had substantial scheduling experience, they would be able to better estimate T_1 and T_3 and define how many standard deviations these values were from the most probable time, or T_2.

"Each set of three times—minimum, most probable, and maximum—for each task is the simplest representation of a Gaussian distribution. The PERT program combines the individual Gaussian distributions for all the tasks into an overall project Gaussian distribution.

"When all the tasks are finally computed, a PERT program provides the *most probable expected completion time* for the whole project. It's common for presentations to upper management and to internal teams to include this expected time of completion. Everyone remembers this number and expects it to come true. Unfortunately, it's the wrong approach because it inevitably underestimates the right amount of time. The project manager is in trouble before he's out of the starting gate."

It seemed that Chuck's statements hit John pretty hard. John jumped from his seat. "So what's the right approach?"

"Theoretically, while the program calculates the most probable time for project completion, it's not enough for presentation purposes. Remember that the most probable time indicates that there is only a fifty percent probability of completing that project on time—only fifty percent. You still need to include an additional time component beyond the expected most probable time for completion."

John appeared eager to understand this subject at its roots. He had told me that he'd failed to complete projects a couple of times in the past, and these failures had cost him a promotion. He asked, "What's that additional component?"

"Depending on how nearly accurate you want your estimate to be, you would add a time value based on a multiple of the distribution's standard deviation," Chuck said.

"And from your experience, how much additional time do you need to add to the new expected time for project completion?"

"In a Gaussian distribution, a one-sigma standard deviation secures a sixty-eight percent probability of success; a two-sigma standard deviation secures a ninety-five percent probability of success; and a three-sigma standard deviation secures over a ninety-nine percent probability of success. I remember a one-year project where one sigma was three months. For that same project, if you wanted a higher probability of success, you needed to budget more than three months. Once you explain these types of details to the hierarchy and the employees, you'll be fine."

The room was silent. Many now understood the errors that they had made in the past, and most had learned a very valuable lesson. I was sure that they would apply these concepts in future endeavors.

"Does anybody have any questions on this subject?" Chuck asked.

Felicia said, "Thank you, Chuck; this is fascinating. Do you have any more secrets like this that we should know for our next project assignment?"

"Yes, Felicia. For those of you considering PERT, please realize that it's a complex, time-consuming, and costly tool. So if a project justifies using PERT, you have to have very clear criteria. Microsoft Project is a simpler alternative. It has certain weaknesses, particularly regarding task relationships. Also, as the product has become more robust, it's also become more complex to use. Regardless of which scheduling program you use, be cautious about how much time it takes to keep them up-to-date so that it doesn't negatively impact the actual project work you need to do."

"Are there any benefits to using these types of tools?" I asked.

"Absolutely. I estimate that seventy percent of the benefit of these computerized tools is in the project design phase. Project schedule design helps clarify relationships, responsibilities, and other critical tasks previously overlooked. It provides an idea of a project's time frame. Some projects may require this initial effort to better understand the magnitude or complexity of a proposed project."

"So what would you recommend for simpler projects?" John asked again.

"For most business unit projects, a Gantt technique with a time base could be sufficient," Chuck responded. "A Gantt chart can be very useful because it gives a 'panorama' of who the main players are and what is expected from them."

Mary asked, "Could you please describe what a Gantt chart is?"

"Yes, Mary," Chuck responded. "Henry Gantt developed a type of horizontal chart to illustrate a project's schedule. These Gantt charts illustrate the start and finish dates of the project activities. Sometimes they also show relationships between these activities. Gantt charts can be also used to show the project's current status by using a vertical 'now' line. The best bet for a business unit leader's action-item system is to complement it with a Gantt chart and with frequent meetings headed by the project manager. Okay, that's all for today. See you next week. Have a good night," Chuck said.

I felt very happy to have Chuck as my personal coach. To me, it seemed like he knew everything. John approached me before he left and murmured, "You're lucky that you can work one-on-one with him. He's a great asset. See you next week."

I approached the podium and said to Chuck, "Thanks. These classroom discussions have been very helpful to me. As soon as I come back from my customer visit, I'm going to begin scheduling meetings to launch the projects."

"Why are you visiting a customer?"

"Peter asked me to. This customer is a longtime friend of his, and Peter asked me to do anything I possibly could to calm him."

"May I join you? I really would like to see why your customer is so upset," Chuck said.

I was surprised for a moment. I regained my composure quickly and said, "Sure, I'm leaving tomorrow at 6:00 a.m. I can pick you up. The plant is a two-and-a-half-hour drive from your place."

- 22 -

Business Philosophy

The next morning I picked up Chuck, and soon we were on our way to the client meeting. It was going to be a long drive. We started to chat, and the conversation delved into the meaning of change.

"Change is about making something different from its current state," Chuck said. "Every change requires the direct and indirect collaboration of three different types of individuals. First, there are the stakeholders: their expectations drive change in an organization. Then there are the transformation agents: they establish the organizational framework for the adaptation agents to implement. Last, there are the adaptation agents: they implement what the transformation agents recommended. This takes place even if it means going outside their comfort zone, since new skills need to be acquired for successful process completion.

"Before launching and deploying a project, a manager needs to understand why change is needed, the stakeholders' expectations, and what problem will be solved. What's the *here*, the *there*, and the necessary transformation that gets you from *here* to *there*? Sometimes the hierarchical lines of management know what's needed. Other times, they can't precisely articulate what change is needed."

"That is exactly where I am," I said.

Chuck continued: "Sometimes the need for change takes place in larger companies because units are managed by budget alone. Managing by budget and being satisfied with budget-only performance guarantees failure because it ignores other operational issues, the importance of developing an intrapreneurial environment, and new opportunities.

"Sometimes change is needed to offset precedents of retaliation for failure. Fear of failure results in a lack of ideas and innovation. When doing nothing is the preferred policy in a company, there is no motivation to take risk…and the business falls behind.

"In the modern world, taking some level of prudent risk is necessary to maintain leadership. A culture needs to welcome novel ideas and make these ideas work. Otherwise, doing nothing brings failure; it's just a matter of time.

"The need to improve a decaying unit sometimes requires the participation of an external force, like a high-quality and experienced consultant, who's less influenced by internal politics and is better positioned and better suited to handle the complex and interdisciplinary issues. Oftentimes, it's the consultant who brings in a crucial needs-based perspective and solution framework. It's the consultant who develops the theory of 'need' and gets approval, through initial meetings, from the relevant hierarchical authority. Of course, there may be other times when a call for transformation starts as soon as a new leader is appointed to do the job."

"That's exactly our situation," I said.

Chuck was on a roll. "And then there are times when the current leader gets to be in the hot seat and is given a new chance to lead. In doing so, the macro-objectives for the business entity in question are clarified and shared among all main stakeholders and decision makers. Examples of macro-objectives could include more revenue, more profits, and more efficiency; or, as in our case, prevent negative headlines in the local newspapers about your unit's lack of performance.

"We are experiencing different times. Change is in the air. People change, markets change, technology changes, competition changes, customers change, performance changes, and expectations change.

Change in all these parameters may and will trigger changes in practices. Dynamic change is now part of corporate life, and speed of change becomes critical."

"It seems that corporate values are more important than I thought," I said.

"Since we're driving over two hours to your customer, let me tell you a story that I know pretty well. I think it'll help you better understand the importance of values and business philosophy in corporate culture."

"I'm intrigued."

Chuck took a deep breath. "It's the role of the corporate leadership as well as the board of directors of successful companies to ensure that the basic corporate principles that lead a company to growth and success do not change. It can take several decades to build a great company, but only months to start a destruction process. It's quite a challenge when corporate leadership gets confused about the meaning of change and bundles change in *practices* with change in *principles*."

"Give me an example. I have a personal interest in this area."

"A good example is the Hewlett-Packard Company, or HP," he said.

"Weren't you involved with HP in the past?"

"Yes, that was more than three decades ago," Chuck said. "Here's a bit of high-tech history for you. HP went from having very long-tenured CEOs to having three different CEOs in a one-year period. As you might know, HP was founded in 1938 by Bill Hewlett and David Packard. It started in a garage. Their first product was an oscillator for Walt Disney's movie *Fantasia*. The paint for that equipment was baked in Packard's kitchen oven. David Packard and Bill Hewlett successfully managed the company for thirty-eight years and made it a multibillion-dollar company.

"Hewlett and Packard handpicked John Young to follow as CEO; he held the position for sixteen years from 1976 to 1992, and the company's stock improved continuously during that period. He was succeeded by Lew Platt, who was CEO for seven years, and the company's stock continued to grow.

"In 1999 the board of directors concluded that HP was not properly addressing the opportunities provided by the Internet and decided to recruit from outside the company. Valuation declined, and many employees lost their jobs.

"In 2001, conflict developed regarding the acquisition of Compaq. Many perceived that this was an investment in 'old technology.' The company became distracted with internal politics and lost the momentum of the web revolution."

"Chuck, how do you recall all this stuff?" I asked.

"HP was my favorite American company, and I took every opportunity to read and learn about it," he said.

Suddenly, my phone rang. It was Jennifer.

"Dennis, I received a call from Mr. Pitcher's office. They are running late regarding an important negotiation meeting, and they would like to know if they could reschedule your 9:00 a.m. appointment for 10:00 a.m."

"Sure," I replied. "Please let them know I'll be there at ten." I disconnected the call. "Sorry for interrupting you, Chuck—please, proceed."

Chuck had overheard my conversation with Jennifer and said, "Why don't we stop for a cup of coffee?"

I took the first exit, and we pulled up to an old diner. I parked. Chuck took his briefcase with him, and we went in.

We sat close to the front window. I asked for decaf, and he asked for herbal tea.

While waiting, I said, "How does the rest of the story go?"

"Here comes the interesting part," he said. "In the 1970s, Dave Packard and Bill Hewlett composed a document that later became a famous piece of corporate literature known as 'The HP Way.' The HP Way described their corporate creed—the set of values that were to

permeate throughout HP's corporate culture. I always carry a copy
of this document in my briefcase. It's a good example of a company
constitution. Since we have plenty of time, would you like to read it?
It's not long, and it's very educational."

"Please," I said. I was intrigued. I started to read.

THE HP WAY

We have trust and respect for individuals.

We approach each situation with the belief that people want to do a
good job and will do so, given the proper tools and support. We attract
highly capable, diverse, innovative people and recognize their efforts and
contributions to the company. HP people contribute enthusiastically and
share in the success that they make possible.

We focus on a high level of achievement and contribution.

Our customers expect HP products and services to be of the highest
quality and to provide lasting value. To achieve this, all HP people,
especially managers, must be leaders who generate enthusiasm and
respond with extra effort to meet customer needs. Techniques and
management practices which are effective today may be outdated in the
future. For us to remain at the forefront in all our activities, people should
always be looking for new and better ways to do their work.

We conduct our business with uncompromising integrity.

We expect HP people to be open and honest in their dealings to earn
the trust and loyalty of others. People at every level are expected to
adhere to the highest standards of business ethics and must understand
that anything less is unacceptable. As a practical matter, ethical conduct
cannot be assured by written HP policies and codes; it must be an integral
part of the organization, a deeply ingrained tradition that is passed from
one generation of employees to another.

We achieve our common objectives through teamwork.

We recognize that it is only through effective cooperation within and among organizations that we can achieve our goals. Our commitment is to work as a worldwide team to fulfill the expectations of our customers, shareholders, and others who depend upon us. The benefits and obligations of doing business are shared among all HP people.

We encourage flexibility and innovation.

We create an inclusive work environment which supports the diversity of our people and stimulates innovation. We strive for overall objectives which are clearly stated and agreed upon, and allow people flexibility in working toward goals in ways that they help determine are best for the organization. HP people should personally accept responsibility and be encouraged to upgrade their skills and capabilities through ongoing training and development. This is especially important in a technical business, where the rate of progress is rapid and where people are expected to adapt to change.

I looked over to Chuck.

"These principles seem to be as relevant today as they ever were," he said. "Even though they may have been revolutionary back then, HP was committed to practicing what they preached."

"This is fascinating," I said. "How did you get involved with HP?"

"I was involved with high-tech management for many years. In the late seventies, I met John Young, president and chief executive officer of the HP Company, and was inspired to join HP for a sabbatical. The first day I was invited for a full 'welcome day.' I received a copy of the HP Way, and I became a fan of it. For years, I had a copy of the original HP Way. I cherished the document. I called it 'the HP constitution.'

"That year, I had the unique opportunity to see John Young in action. I admired his talent, his clarity, and his solid decision-making process. He promoted and mastered the delicate balance between freedom and discipline. He's probably one of the best technology CEOs in the history of America. He noted how HP's core values didn't change, although practices might. Young used to say that what was fundamentally important was doing something you can be proud of, satisfying customers in the process, and that profits followed that.

"Young was loved and well-respected by his employees. I remember him sitting, having lunch and mingling with the employees on sunny days at Page Mill Road in Palo Alto. HP had a clear business model during John Young's tenure. In those days, managers and employees were highly motivated. The business management monitoring and control process were also high-quality—this stemmed from the fact that John Young visited all fifty divisions in 1979, on average, one division visit per week. Each local division made a presentation about its own sophisticated area of expertise. Mr. Young was always prepared with sharp questions to the presenter, who was usually the head of the division. Open discussions followed. In those days, there was a great balance between decentralized operations and centralized monitoring. For a company that was growing very fast, HP remained very agile."

"I'm curious—in such a fast-growing environment, how did they manage R&D?" I asked.

Chuck knew this story very well. "Every business division manager had his own R&D budget to improve the new generations of existing products as well as to adopt new technologies. The central R&D facility was within walking distance from the office of the president and CEO. Their seven hundred members at that time were supposed to do practical research—invent new breakthroughs and help the divisions adopt the new technologies. The R&D budget, as a percent of revenue, was the largest in the industry. Three-quarters of the total R&D budget was distributed to all divisions and provided the division managers with independence. The last quarter of the R&D budget was invested in a central R&D

facility and provided the division managers with direct support and the possibility to 'acquire' new technologies."

"Did the divisions grow quickly?" I asked.

"Divisions grew very quickly because the division managers were 'quasi-CEOs' who got a lot of guidance and support from headquarters. John Young was instrumental in helping them perform their function successfully. In 1979, there were numerous divisions in the United States as well as overseas, where some HP products were manufactured in countries like Singapore and Malaysia. This was happening long before the concept of globalization was recognized in the United States.

"In 1992, John Young left HP and was replaced with Lew Platt. Mr. Platt followed John Young's school of management: he adopted the HP Way based on respect for the individual. Likewise, he was focused on winning, and most of all, Platt was a principled leader.

"In 1999, Lew Platt left, and the HP Way was replaced with the 'Rules of the Garage.'" Chuck turned over the page on which the HP Way was printed and read:

RULES OF THE GARAGE

- Believe you can change the world.
- Work quickly, keep the tools unlocked, work whenever.
- Know when to work alone and when to work together.
- Share tools, ideas. Trust your colleagues.
- No politics. No bureaucracy.
- The customer defines a job well done.
- Radical ideas are not bad ideas.
- Invent different ways of working.
- Make a contribution every day. If it doesn't contribute, it doesn't leave the garage.
- Believe that together we can do anything.
- Invent.

"When comparing the HP Way with the Rules of the Garage, notice that the spirit of 'we' changed into 'you.'"

"Chuck, in your opinion, how important is this?" I asked.

"Are you asking me about losing the HP Way?"

"Yes."

"In my view, this is crucial."

"And how did that affect HP?"

"Well, I expected a dramatic deterioration, although I couldn't predict exactly when. A few years later, in May 2012, HP did announce the release of thirty-thousand employees."

We finished our drinks and headed to my customer. When we arrived, my customer provided us with more information. Over lunch, he brought up additional issues he had, and I addressed them. In the back of my mind, though, I knew things would only change for the better after my new projects were completed and our services improved. I summarized the next steps BLM would take and specific issues we would attempt to solve. We finished lunch, said our good-byes, and Chuck and I drove back.

The drive back was uneventful. Chuck and I were both a little tired. Chuck said, "I think you should compose a document called 'The BLM Way' for your business unit. You will never regret it. Although you are not a company, you can compose a set of rules that will help you establish a new culture."

"And then it'll be time to launch the projects on our list?"

"Before you call any project meeting, let's first take a couple of days to work together on certain topics and disciplines that will be very important in performing your job. Can you meet with me tomorrow—Friday?" he asked.

"Sure," I answered. "If we need more time, we can continue on Monday."

"Or Sunday?" Chuck suggested.

I understood his meaning. I said, "Okay, let's start tomorrow morning, and let's decide at the end of the day how many more hours we'll need."

"You got it."

"What's the main subject for tomorrow?"

"Blocking and tackling."

"I'm not a football player," I said, smiling.

"Don't worry," he said. "From now on, you will become one. I'll see you in my office at 8:00 a.m."

SECTION 3

OPERATIONAL MANAGEMENT

- 23 -

MANAGING MEETINGS

The next day was a sunny, beautiful morning with blue skies. I drove my Taurus to Chuck's office. I had planned to work on issues related to launching projects. While driving, I called Jennifer and asked her to cancel and reschedule the few things I had on my calendar.

I arrived at Chuck's office, and this time we went directly to work. I started the conversation. "I was intrigued by your comment yesterday about 'blocking and tackling.' What did you mean by that?"

"There are three elements I would like to cover in the next few days," Chuck said. "You can call the following subjects 'blocking and tackling' for business management: the art and science of conducting quality meetings, handling action items, and training and coaching. We may not cover everything today, but we'll highlight the main points."

"Sounds like a plan. Now I understand why you wanted to do this before launching projects."

Chuck looked at his notes and said, "Although we don't have a lot of time for the material we need to cover, we don't like to leave business landmines behind us. As usual, it's crucial that you understand these concepts, so let me know if you have any questions or comments."

His message was clear: *Pay attention; we can't afford mistakes.*

I took out my notebook and tried to capture as much as possible. Chuck continued: "Many of the *decisions* pertinent to any business unit are made or communicated in meetings. Project progress is made through meetings. Meetings are one of the most effective ways *to communicate change.* They provide the opportunity to present ideas, discuss them, and, many times, emerge with decisions that may be different from those the leader considered prior to the meeting. Business success relies on quality meetings. To reach that quality and to make meetings successful, they have to be addressed by you, the leader, very seriously.

"How many meetings have you attended in which nobody came prepared, including the person who called the meeting, or a substantial portion of the meeting was outside of the initial scope of the meeting, and when you left it, you realized that nothing of value was accomplished?"

"Most of the time," I answered. "It's extremely frustrating."

"Frustrating and demotivating. You can spare your lieutenants and employees some of this frustration by communicating that you plan a series of serious meetings to address the execution on most issues, challenges, and problems identified. This is a significant investment of time from you, the lieutenants, and employees as well as the opportunity cost of not doing other tasks. However, it's worth it if employees have been focusing on the wrong tasks. Nothing will be more important at this stage than your own discipline in conducting these meetings.

"Think about your meeting-related efforts in the following context: prior to the meeting, during the meeting, and after the meeting."

"Okay. Let's start with efforts prior to the meeting," I said.

Chuck looked at his notes and said, "Initially, for the critical projects for which you'll be directly responsible, you shouldn't delegate:

- Preparing the agenda;
- Defining meeting objectives;

- Selecting discussion topic(s);
- Selecting participants (all relevant stakeholders);
- Specifying who will present analysis and materials; or
- Allotting time for presentation and discussions."

"The meeting agenda should include all of the items on this list, especially the meeting objectives. Confirm everyone's attendance and that those presenting are clear on their assignments. Please ask Jennifer to help you coordinate this."

I took notes and then asked, "What do you suggest regarding efforts during the meeting?"

"From your perspective, effective meetings have multiple purposes:

- Finding solutions to the identified challenges;
- Learning about the participants' contributions;
- Assessing these individuals' future potential;
- Getting 'buy-in' from those who need to contribute to a possible solution;
- Establishing clear and well-defined action items; and
- Recording what was agreed to be done, who's going to do it, and when the action will be complete."

I got concerned. "Am I running these meetings alone or will you also participate in these meetings?"

"I'll participate, as long as you'd like me to be there," Chuck said.

"Could you help me document the follow-up actions?"

"I could, but I have a better idea. In these types of meetings, when challenges are discussed, I like to diagram possible solutions on the whiteboard. I'll ask one of my associates to join us and take notes so that we can maintain the momentum and avoid derailing the process.

"It's normal to have a negotiation between you, the leader, and the person assigned to an action item. It's like a contract between parties, with many witnesses present. Therefore, it gives the participants a sense of urgency and importance about the subject at hand. In addition, you need to consider that during the same meeting, you'll be going through a test too."

"What type of test?" I asked with concern.

"The test is about the fairness of your demands from the meeting participants. In their minds, questions will come up, like:

- Is the assigned task needed and important?
- Is the time given to complete the task reasonable?
- Is the leader prepared and knowledgeable?
- Does the leader's decision consider all aspects of how to execute a particular action?
- Is our leader's decision-making process logical and reasonable?

"These first meetings set the tone for the long haul—just like when students measure up their teachers at the start of a new school year. After three to four meetings, you'll know all that you need to know about your employees. It will also show how 'human' and talented you are in their eyes, setting the stage for months and years to come."

I was trying to digest the importance Chuck was placing on these first project meetings.

"Any questions?" Chuck asked.

"No, it's very clear. It makes a lot of sense."

"All the elements we've discussed so far have related to preparations *before* and *during* the meeting. Let's now talk about issues *after* the meeting."

"I'm ready to take notes," I answered.

"Within twenty-four hours after the meeting, review all the action items that were assigned to the meeting participants. Distribute summary reports—with any changes highlighted—to each participant who was assigned action items. If there's a substantial change in content, you may need to renegotiate a corresponding change in scope or completion date. We can help you manage the action item dynamics."

"This is all clear. I see that you take meetings very seriously."

"Remember, meetings are important to you since you are going to spend most of this year in meetings. Meetings will become the key to your success."

"In the past, I had some discipline challenges. Do you have any suggestions for those?" I asked.

"Well, let me share a few rules that can help you, particularly under the present circumstances:

1) If somebody is missing, particularly a presenter, without preapproval from the leader, the meeting is cancelled and rescheduled.
2) If all presenters come to the meeting but someone doesn't bring the agreed-upon material, the meeting is cancelled and rescheduled.
3) If incomplete work is presented that doesn't address the particular action item under discussion, the meeting is stopped and rescheduled."

"How many meetings will end up cancelled, and how will employees react to that?" I asked.

"At the beginning of the process, you will cancel a few meetings. People will learn very quickly that you mean business. After a few surprising incidents, nobody will come late or unprepared unless they have your preapproval. The quality of the presentations, both in format and content, will substantially improve. In the subsequent months, you'll become very familiar with the strengths and weaknesses of your personnel.

"You may also have to invest in some of your lieutenants and employees by coaching them, training them, changing their roles, or even replacing some of them."

"This will be a big change by itself," I said. "Discipline in this unit has eroded with time. The leaders have lost the employees' respect. Without respect, collapse is sure to follow. What's the right environment for making a meeting the most productive and the most effective?"

"That's the sixty-four-thousand-dollar question. The right environment for a meeting is the one that frees the participants from fears."

"Interesting, but what kinds of fears limit participants from expressing their opinions and beliefs?" I asked.

"Fears are based on personal experience, either directly or indirectly. Precedents leave lasting impressions. We've witnessed three main types of fear: fear of retaliation, fear of being overloaded, and fear of criticism."

"Okay," I said. "How can those fears be eliminated or mitigated?"

"Let's review them individually," Chuck said. "Fear of retaliation: avoid punishment of any kind for people providing opinions. You should be clear that there will be no retaliation to those expressing their opinions, and you personally will have the moral and practical obligation to respect your promises."

"I can do that," I said.

Chuck continued: "Fear of being overloaded: avoid overloading a lieutenant or an employee with more work than the person can digest or by immediately asking him or her to implement a good idea he or she suggested.

"If every time somebody suggests an idea, you ask him or her to deliver the work associated with that idea, people will not suggest ideas, and you will lose an important source of contribution. Creative people are mostly busy in their own activities and shouldn't be penalized. Leaders like you should be hesitant to use this failed policy. In addition, you need to consider that people are different. Those who tend to be strategic may not have the right skills to execute the ideas they propose. These good ideas should be encouraged and shouldn't be lost. A good idea is a very valuable asset, and it should be channeled in a way that has the largest probability of success."

"Okay, what is the last category?" I asked.

"The last type," Chuck said, "is fear of criticism: avoid criticizing a person who presents a suggestion that may be perceived as irrelevant. The leader will not criticize any employee, nor will he or she allow any member of the team to criticize a colleague for trying to contribute. The recommended behavior is to add the suggestion to the list of alternatives and compare it with the other suggestions. Ultimately, the most promising alternative will be selected."

Chuck paused and then continued. "Many organizations were and are still based on the *yes-man* and the *good-ol'-boys-club* concepts. Others avoid delivering bad news to the hierarchy at any cost. It's not the lack of product demand that brings them down—as some claim—but rather the atmosphere of intellectual oppression and fear, the lack of investment in new ideas, and the ignorance and disregard for what the competition does. Those who practiced these cultural elements have failed, and those using them now will soon follow.

"Some top executives become victims of their own cultures. There's too much to lose—such as pensions, interesting work, and so on—to publicly express their opinions. Management positions in these companies get filled not by the most competent personnel, but by people whose communications skills and personal looks seem to better fit the organization's preconceived notions. In other words, a manager wouldn't need technical expertise to be promoted.

"These companies develop a failing dual-ladder system— managerial and technical. The managerial ladder has seemingly limitless potential. Without access to the managerial ladder, the technical ladder limits techies to a few opportunities. These corporate politics and policies are fueled by the notion that you're either technically oriented or managerially oriented, but not both. Techies can't possibly possess sufficient high-quality interpersonal skills to qualify for managerial-level positions. This is a big fundamental mistake."

"Was this typical of the auto industry, for example?" I asked.

"Auto companies typified these values. Their cultures were obsolete. The effects of these policies carried over into how cars were designed, manufactured, and marketed. Chrysler's CEO, Marconi, brought about change by destroying an obsolete culture. It started at the top. With virtually the same group of employees, he achieved completely different results.

"After taking over the Chrysler Group in 2011, Fiat CEO, Sergio Marconi, closed Chrysler's executive offices, including the one that he was supposed to occupy. He moved his office close to the young engineers who were contributing to changing the character of the company."

"How can such a strong culture be changed?"

"Cultures can be effectively changed by a new CEO. Even in the midst of a pervasively stubborn culture, business unit cultures can likewise be changed by business unit leaders. The errors of the leaders of the auto industry not only pushed talent out of the ranks—displacing technologists and forcing early retirement, among other things—but they also brought the state of Michigan to its knees, making it rank number one in unemployment in the country for a long time. Many other states were negatively impacted by the auto industry culture and collapse as well.

"Apparently, business leaders who foster a dysfunctional and misguided company culture while unfittingly occupying key positions can prove devastating to their communities, their state, and the entire country. The same applies to any company, business unit, business cell, and so on. One poor leader can bring down a whole unit and make it collapse. Some companies under financial stress reduce headcount with demotions and honorable terminations. Fear of retaliation turns people into yes-men or silences them at best. Yes, the leader may get his or her way, but at what price?

"Executives who foster this type of culture miss out on new and creative ideas. They miss out on the opportunity to learn from experienced personnel who can constructively discuss their ideas based on scientific evidence. Today, technology and technologists play a significant role in any business. They are an essential means for any company's survival in light of our place in an increasingly competitive global economy. Competition requires high-quality decisions that do not leave behind minefields full of potentially destructive surprises. Technologists should be provided the opportunity to make important contributions."

"What else can I do in addition to removing fears?" I asked.

"Clearly, eliminating fear is not enough. Leaders need to encourage and motivate their employees to contribute and feel like they're part of a winning team. Dissidents should be welcome. Their contribution can be major. Leaders should listen to them by encouraging legitimate disagreement and teaching everybody mutual respect. Playing devil's advocate is one of the strongest methods to foster creativity."

"But if there are many opinions and I select only one, how will others feel about it?" I asked.

"Once you hear all opinions and weigh the different alternatives, you should be ready to clearly articulate your decision and present a matching rationale for it to the meeting participants. There is one rule for the leader to explain and for the lieutenants and employees to remember: once you listen to everybody and you make a decision, the whole team needs to support that decision until all tasks related to the decision are complete."

I listened and realized that I was still learning a lot, just in time for my next moves.

My conversation with Chuck had made me realize that the meetings I had conducted had been unstructured and unproductive. I knew that people grumbled about having to attend them. So I communicated a new plan to everyone at BLM. I told them that, in the future, I would plan a series of meetings to address the execution of our business solutions. I added that I would define the objective of every meeting, select the discussion topics, decide who would participate in each meeting, specify who would make presentations and how much time they would have, and prepare an agenda well in advance of every meeting. My meetings would be on time, short, based on one-page agendas, and have no side discussions.

I also realized that Chuck was right about BLM's culture. It was uncanny how accurate his assessment was. The people I managed were indeed afraid of retaliation for stating their opinions, afraid of being overloaded, and afraid of being criticized. By asking a lot of people a lot of questions, I discovered that previous managers had created a culture that resembled tyranny.

I gathered my lieutenants, and together we wrote guidelines that communicated our desire to create and maintain a culture of honesty, excellence, and transparency. Then we called an all-employee meeting, and I explained to everyone that the culture at BLM was changing right then and there. I asked them to contact my lieutenants or me about any concerns, complaints, or ideas they had about absolutely anything—from their workload to employee activities. I also let everyone know that retaliation against any employee who voiced an opinion was no longer acceptable and would incur consequences.

After the meeting, my lieutenants and I received numerous e-mails from employees who thanked us for recognizing the unit's long-term morale problems and for being open to suggestions. We also received some extremely helpful ideas on a variety of topics, including the division of work and job sharing. The exercise had a huge impact on me. I began to know individual employees and learn their needs, desires, and aspirations. I could feel morale lifting. I loved it.

- 24 -

TARGET AUDIENCES

The next day, I was back in Chuck's office, settling down to business with our mineral waters and granola bars. Chuck said, "Selecting the right target audiences for the meetings is also a key ingredient in making progress."

"What does that mean?" I asked.

"As the business unit leader, you should have initial meetings with the following target audiences." He showed me a list:

MEETINGS WITH TARGET AUDIENCES

1) Leader's lieutenants
2) Key employees in individual business cells
3) Project managers and internal project participants
4) Project managers and external project participants

"The purpose of redesigning a business unit's organizational structure is to better define what every business cell has to deliver. Meeting with every one of the lieutenants individually every two weeks is a good idea. Agendas for meetings with the lieutenants should be treated with the same rigor as described before. Discussions regarding controversial issues should be reserved for one-on-one meetings with the lieutenants.

"It's important to meet with key personnel of new or restructured business cells as well. They have the opportunity to present their ideas to you. You have the opportunity to better understand the business cell situation in the process. Sometimes you, your lieutenant, and his or her key employees may have different opinions. So handle these situations with finesse.

"Projects that include different cells within the business unit require integration. Meetings involve many participants, including the business unit manager, the business cell lieutenants, and the project manager. So you have to motivate the participating lieutenants to work together and direct these meetings to helping the project manager succeed.

"Some projects depend on external business units, or those that are outside the scope of control of the business unit leader. Unattended, these dependencies can negatively impact your unit's performance. So the first objective when meeting with these external business units is to understand the details of the other unit's process and how this affects your unit's performance. External units have no cause to alter their level of service if they don't understand the impact of their actions. We have witnessed this anomaly too many times.

"These types of meetings may have special challenges for you, because the lowest common managerial denominators in the hierarchy who can address the problem are VPs, senior VPs, or, in some cases, the COO or CEO himself, depending on how 'silo-oriented' the company culture is."

"Well, that certainly explains why units reporting to different organizations don't resolve conflict in a timely manner. This is exactly the scenario I'm facing now," I said.

"After properly diagnosing how your business unit is impacted by an external unit's actions and what their process is, you can prepare a compelling case to present to upper management. Usually, well-presented logic prevails, and if the claim is right, the other unit will try to avoid conflict escalation and will settle to avoid the possibility of a losing situation. When done right, they will accommodate your needs. A small change in a service group can translate into a positive impact on the performance of your unit," Chuck said.

"I often discover that the people doing the work in these service units don't understand BLM's goals and objectives, and they don't have the authority to make changes. Do you have any suggestion on how to handle these situations?"

"Identifying the right champion with the right power in the specific service unit is usually the most effective way to proceed. Look for them and find them. Informal meetings with the service unit champions are very helpful. Every time you reduce your dependence on other units, either by solving the problem or by bringing that particular service into your own business unit, it's beneficial. Either approach often secures better timing, quality, and cost."

Chuck paused, took a sip, and continued: "To complete the list, let me mention a couple more types of meetings for you to consider: first are meetings regarding projects that involve subcontractors outside the company. These meetings are different in nature from all the previous types of meetings I've described, since they require accommodating two distinctive cultures. The relationship in this case is mostly based on economics. The other type is meetings with the hierarchy. We will discuss that subject as we continue to prepare for the steering committee."

"Thanks, Chuck; I took notes," I said. "This will be very helpful in designing my meetings schedule for the whole quarter. Do you have any suggestions regarding meeting frequency?"

"Having regular internal meetings with a certain project audience on a predetermined day of the week, every week, or every two weeks, is not always a good idea. Those who've tried that approach realize it doesn't work. The frequency of target audience meetings depends on the time it takes the assigned employees to complete the most critical action items.

"However, don't wait too long between meetings. If the work will take substantially more than two or three weeks, your action items should be revised and decoupled into smaller assignments. The danger with long spacing between meetings is that work progress can veer in the wrong direction, wasting precious energy and time in the process."

"Okay, I think we covered everything about meetings. I feel better equipped now to prepare a meeting master schedule," I said.

"Let's spend ten more minutes discussing meetings," Chuck said.

"Okay."

"Meetings are the best place to evaluate lieutenants and employees—to discern between those who can play ball and those going down to the minor leagues. Meetings can be used for individual practical evaluation, especially when the agendas are properly developed and managed. It's the best stage for real interviews. There is no better way to assess the value of an employee than to observe him or her during a meeting.

"Have a clear expectation of each of the participants in the meeting. These expectations include content as well as format."

"How can I compare the abilities of my lieutenants?" I asked.

"You can use simple tools to differentiate between individuals, such as lieutenants and employees. For example, use a three-by-three matrix with one axis related to *content* and the other to *format*. This mechanism has also been used to help define succession plans." Chuck quickly sketched a grid:

EXHIBIT 14:

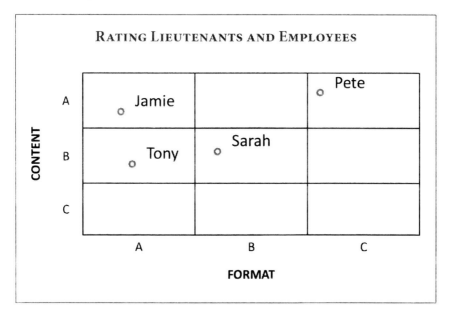

"*Content expectations* relate to the way the lieutenant or employee prepares for the meeting, the quality of his or her work, the depth of his or her analysis and knowledge, the way he or she articulates ideas, and so on. *Format expectations* relate to behavioral components, like being on time, how he or she interacts with other members of the team, and his or her acceptance by others.

"Once all these characteristics are observed and studied, match the unit's needs against the present strengths and weaknesses of the individuals working in your unit. You, as the leader, need to promptly identify if there are any problematic individuals in the group and decide if the problematic individual can grow or not and how long it will take to raise his or her level of competence. You'll reach the point when you decide if the individual is part of the solution or part of the problem. If the individual is part of the problem, it's important to find a way to accomplish two things: remove him or her from the critical paths, and look for a replacement."

"What do other companies do under these circumstances?" I asked.

"Companies have different policies on how to deal with unwanted personnel, either by finding a new home for the employee or by following disengagement processes. In any case, you'll reach a point in which it's time to make the move. The worst scenario for you as a leader is to invest in somebody who cannot and will not be able to keep up with the new unit's pace. This scenario is a bad deal for both the leader and the employee. We've seen employees get sick on the job when they struggle with the assignments, and we've also seen leaders lose their jobs for not having the right team at the right time."

"By the way, I'm not sure I can absorb much more today."

"I understand. We'll reconvene tomorrow."

"Can we do it in the afternoon?" I asked.

"Sure. Tomorrow, Sunday afternoon, we'll tackle the next blocking and tackling topic about handling action items."

- 25 -

ACTION ITEMS

On Sunday morning, Cheryl, the girls, and I went to church. Afterward, we went to our favorite restaurant on Grand Street, close to Michigan Avenue, where they served a fabulous brunch. After a great meal, we returned home. Cheryl took the girls to visit her parents by the Indiana border and I drove to meet Chuck.

Neither Chuck nor I was happy to work on a Sunday afternoon, but we both felt that we had to accelerate the pace of progress. I parked in the circular drive. The flowerbeds were full of vivid colors, which was nice. After our routine greetings, we took our positions, and Chuck said, "Dennis, this week we covered the subjects of managing meetings and target audiences. Today, we're going to discuss how to handle action items. Action items are a very important piece of the process. Please remember that they are the bridge between diagnostics, change design, teamwork, and execution.

"Although the process of strategic planning has failed too many times as a valid and effective corporate tool, many of the structural elements included in the strategic planning process are very valuable, including:

- strategic issues;
- long-term strategies;
- short-term strategies;

- tactics;
- policies;
- et cetera."

As I was listening, I thought, "Who doesn't know about action items? This isn't the best way to spend my Sunday." But if Chuck was bringing this up, there was something else that I probably didn't know about.

Chuck continued: "Action items not only are the way to make things happen, but they are the platform for unraveling additional unexpected challenges during their execution. The process of seeking action-item completion frequently provides new ideas that may result in additional strategic issues to consider. Newly developed strategic issues can have an impact on long- and short-term strategies, tactics, policies, and additional new action items. It's a never-ending process. We used to say, if a business leader is not tracking a hundred action items at any time, he is not managing."

"Many of my bosses never followed action items very closely; nevertheless, some of them were promoted. How?" I asked.

Chuck didn't waste time in responding. "During my career, I've visited many executives. I was puzzled by those who had a neat, paperless desk. It was as if they perceived their role as waiting for something to happen in the future. They acted as if nothing was going on. When I inquired about their management style, they would say, 'My management style is about delegation. I delegate. If my guys have a problem, they come to me, and I facilitate the process; I remove the roadblocks.'

"Since everyone in any organization is very busy, imagine if all levels in the hierarchy applied the same corporate delegating: the accountability ball constantly rolls, passing from one hierarchical level to a lower hierarchical level, until the lowest basic level in the organization is reached. This basic level, by definition, is not equipped to deal with these new challenges and therefore has no chance to solve the problem that was originally delegated by an executive in the first place."

"So what happens?"

"The problem reverses course and, over several months' time, creeps back up the hierarchical ladder to the top executive. As the problem travels down and up the hierarchy, its context also keeps changing from the original challenge. By the time a solution is offered, it's too little, too late, and nobody has learned anything from the yo-yo experience. Under these circumstances, what do you think the executive who initiated the process should do?" Chuck added rhetorically.

I remained silent. Chuck continued: "When later I asked about the whereabouts of the managers who managed by delegating, I learned that the vast majority failed in the eyes of their superiors and were later relegated to side jobs. Promoting them exposed their incompetence. Managers who overdelegate reach their level of incompetence much sooner than those who solve the challenges by being active."

I had asked a question and had gotten a long answer, but I had also learned my lesson. It was time to refocus.

I said, "Chuck, going back again to the subject of action items, could you please review some of their failure mechanisms and also provide me with some concrete examples?"

"Absolutely. Decades of experience have proven that, in handling action items, there are numerous failure mechanisms that weaken management intentions and jeopardize the quality of the results. The following are some examples of failure mechanisms. I printed this page for you to keep."

"Thanks, let me quickly review it while I'm here." The page stated:

ACTION ITEMS—COMMON FAILURE MECHANISMS

a) Before the action items are selected:
  i.   Lack of focus
  ii. Lack of business experience
  iii. Lack of creativity
  iv. Fear of stretching the cultural envelope
  v.   Weak decision making

b) Capturing and documenting:
  i.   Lack of a good documenting mechanism
  ii. Lack of tracking capabilities

c) After the action items have been completely defined:
  i.   Lack of evaluating tools
  ii. Not reviewing properly the time to completion
  iii. Not reviewing the capabilities of the responsible party to deliver
  iv. Lack of support to help the employee succeed
  v.   Leaders' inabilities to grade, evaluate, and provide constructive feedback (including confrontation)

"Chuck, who should—and who can—originate an action item?"

Chuck reflected for a moment. "Anyone in the organization can originate the idea or suggestion for an action item. It's both a right and an obligation. Whoever has the authorization to launch an action item is responsible for that action item. Therefore, it's critical that you develop a very specific set of rules for your subordinates to follow about what they can or can't authorize on their own. Otherwise, they'll create a lot of waste and problems that you'll have to clean up."

"If action items are so important, what's your recipe for managing them?" I asked. "I've seen meeting participants get summaries of the meeting, but they usually only follow through on any actions on a volunteer basis."

"Professional action-item capturing is very seldom seen in industry. The key is to capture the action item during the meeting. Use this form to capture them." He showed me a sample form:

EXHIBIT 15:

MANAGING ACTION ITEMS

Project Name: _____

Project Manager: _____

Employee Name: _____

#	Action Item	Issue Date	Due Date	Status	Actual Completion Date	Content Grade	Timeliness Grade
1							

"The top of the page includes the names of the project, project manager, and employee. It also includes these eight fields: action item number; action item description; issue date (or the date the action item was recorded); due date; status; actual completion date; content grade; and timeliness grade.

"At each different project meeting, the project manager creates or updates the page for each project participant. This also means that every lieutenant and employee who works on multiple projects ends up with multiple *Managing Action Items* pages, one for each project in which he or she participates. The project manager fills in the final four fields and grades as each action item is completed. It's easy enough to view these pages on a projector system every time there's a meeting on the subject."

"Will you be able to help me this year, until things become better?" I asked.

"Yes," Chuck answered. "Richard, one of my assistants, will be present at every project meeting. Slowly, you will become so accustomed to seeing this format that it will be natural for you to do it yourself in the future. Consider also that the number of pending projects you will have to manage by year-end will decrease to a lesser number. Richard will capture, edit, and review each individual action item upon your real-time decision to activate an action item. The same day, after the meeting, he will send you all the relevant pages corresponding to each of the participants for your review—one page for each participant."

"Coach, could you please walk me through the details?" I asked.

"This is the first time you've called me *coach*. What happened?"

"Well, aren't you my coach?"

"Sure," he replied, "but what caught my attention was that this was the first time you referred to me that way."

"Okay, do you prefer me to call you *Chuck* or *Coach*?" I asked.

"Either is fine. I owe you an answer regarding the details. Once you receive all the pages from Richard, you will carefully review the language and the content of all the action items recorded during the meeting. Once you review the details, you can highlight changes in different colors: leave old action items in black, new additions in blue, and cancelled items in red. Then send the files back to Richard. He will review your modifications and comments and professionally edit the final list and details. Richard will then send you the final copy for your final approval and distribution to the 'troops.' Are the details clear now?"

"Very clear."

"You'll be the first to use it, Dennis, and later you'll teach your other project managers and lieutenants how to do it. Remember, precise action items save time, money, aggravation, and conflict. There are a few more things that Richard will do for you: first, he will update every individual project master file in three distinctive sections. Section one will include all pending action items for the project, both old and new. Section two will include all completed action items for the project. That will help you track the chronology of achievements. Please make sure this section has the two additional columns to grade performance timeliness and content. Section three will keep all those action items cancelled for historical record keeping. In all cases, maintain the original action item numbers as originally stated."

"Okay, I think I'm clear now. I never considered this level of detail before. Could you please expand on the issue of grading?"

"Listen, how many times at year-end have you had to evaluate your employees, under time pressure, following an HR request, and then you do your best, knowing that it's not good enough?"

"You're right; unfortunately, it happens every year, and I don't always feel okay with the job I do. Sometimes I felt that I didn't communicate with my guys often enough during the year, and sometimes I realized that problems were delayed until the annual review took place. It wasn't helpful."

"Grading the action items will help you overcome all the difficulties you mentioned. There is no better evaluation method than following how the lieutenants and/or the employees perform the jobs you requested through the completion of the action items. You may consider separately two main areas: content quality and timeliness. The content grade relates to the quality of the employee's end product. Usually, you can use a scale of one to ten or one to one hundred, whatever is convenient to you. Once you select the scale, you should maintain that scale for the rest of the year.

"The end products for review may be different for different people. They could include elements such as detailed reports, analysis, decision making, and quality of implementation. This list of deliverables should cover the full range of the employee's expected activity, according to the updated job expectations, not job descriptions.

"Grading timeliness is as important as grading content. Two employees delivering the same content quality can be extremely different in the value they provide to the team, depending on the original time for submission and the number of cycles it takes them to complete the assignment.

"Once the two key parameters are graded for each action item, you are ready to very accurately calculate individual performance. The most effective approach is to group all action items issued during a period of time—either monthly, quarterly, or semiannually—for the particular individual in certain 'buckets' that you'll select. The 'buckets' can be sorted by project or by professional characteristic. For example, all action items linked to sales visits to customers could be grouped in one category."

"Why is this better than using the HR forms?" I asked.

"Very simple: the benefit of this method is that the evaluation corresponds to the real value provided by the individual to the company. In this case, you represent the company."

"Coach," I said, smiling, "this is extremely interesting. This will force me to be more direct with my employees, helping them to focus in their areas of contribution. I think that both sides may feel better. There will be no surprises at year-end. My employees' successes will be a function of my personal behavior as a manager and the amount of time I want to spend in making them successful."

"Yes. I'm proud of your remarks," Chuck said.

- 26 -

SENSE OF OWNERSHIP

We finished the session, and we chatted a bit. I told Chuck that Cheryl and the girls were visiting the grandparents, so I was home alone. Chuck looked at his watch and said, "You know, my wife is out of town. Would you like to join me for dinner? I know a place downtown I think you'll really enjoy."

"Okay, sounds like a great idea," I said.

We decided to drive separately, so I could go home directly from the restaurant. Chuck made the reservation. One hour and fifteen minutes later, we met there. It was one of those well-known, prestigious restaurants. Jim, the maître d', welcomed Chuck with a hug. It was obvious that Chuck was a regular. We were seated in a large corner booth that seated five. It was very private, and I knew we would end up talking about business again.

"Hi, Mark," Chuck greeted the waiter. I was surprised he knew every waiter by name.

"Hi, Chuck," Mark responded. "It's great to have you back. I thought I saw you in here last week with your wife. Why didn't you ask for me?"

"You know I follow Jim's orders. Wherever he seats me is okay with me. I don't interfere with his rules."

Mark laughed and asked, "What would you like to drink?"

I asked for a glass of red wine, and Chuck, as usual, asked for water with no ice. A few minutes later, Mark was back with the drinks. "I recommend the crusted halibut. It's absolutely delicious," he said.

"Okay," Chuck answered. "I'll have it, with a green salad and a baked sweet potato."

"And what can I do for your guest?" Mark asked.

"Mark, this is my friend Dennis." I introduced myself and took a few more seconds to explore the menu. It was unbelievable. The last time I had had stone crab was years ago in Miami, and I was excited to repeat that experience.

"Are you ready?" Chuck asked me just as I was finishing making my selection.

"Yes, I am. I'll go with the crab," I responded.

"Excellent choice, sir," Mark answered. "Would you like to add a soup or a salad?"

"What soups do you have?"

"Today I have minestrone and clam chowder."

"I would prefer the clam chowder, please," I said.

I felt good. It was a nice place, and the service seemed excellent so far. We had a great dinner. To my surprise, Chuck didn't talk about work, but just before coffee, he said, "Dennis, this restaurant is extremely successful. Do you know why?"

"Probably the quality of the food," I answered.

"The food is excellent, but it's not only the food."

"Well, what is it?" I asked impatiently.

"These people have a great sense of ownership!" Chuck answered. "All weak business units have something in common: the lack of a sense of ownership. As long as the business unit leader feels more of a victim than a leader, the unit does not perform well. There is one element in the process I outlined to you that can change the character of the unit completely. This element is the moment at which you, as the business unit leader, acquire a true sense of ownership."

"How do you get there?" I asked, intrigued.

"Although this element generally evolves gradually, you will perceive the period in which it happens. Once you really feel that this is your unit, your ship—that you are the captain people accept and respect—your confidence grows and subsequently propagates through the ranks. When this confidence reaches the bottom of the organizational pyramid, folks feel a sense of ownership, which soon converts into a sense of pride. What a feeling for an employee to belong to a unit that has direction and has a captain who navigates according to known charts, with ambitious objectives and a sense of purpose at the same time. That's when the unit starts to gain praise in a three-hundred-and-sixty-degree environment.

"This is the moment when employees come home, and instead of lashing out at their loved ones with frustration, they kiss them. Their jobs are more secure, so they experience fewer illnesses and less depression. Motivation takes over, and these employees wake up willing to be a part of something successful. Nobody goes to work to become part of a failure, and those who find themselves in that position sometimes don't know exactly what to do. In this economy, nothing is guaranteed unless you can achieve exceptional performance."

He got me thinking. I would never forget this restaurant, not just because of the food and the service, but because of the lesson I'd learned. It was a magnificent lesson, learned close to the Magnificent Mile. I had a cup of coffee, and Chuck had a chamomile herbal tea. Several servers greeted Chuck as we were leaving the restaurant: "See you soon. Please visit again."

We gave our parking stubs to the valet. While we were waiting for the cars, Chuck said, "I'll see you next Wednesday; you can start now to develop your project launches and schedule reviews. Please coordinate with me ahead of time so I can let Richard know when and where we are going to meet. By the way, please make all security arrangements necessary for him to enter the building."

"Will do," I answered.

The cars arrived; we shook hands and walked away. As I began my drive home, I said to myself, "I went for an excellent meal and ended up, once again, with a great lesson."

- 27 -

COACHING AND TRAINING

The next Wednesday, I went to visit Chuck. He briefly explained that we were going to finish the "blocking and tackling" preparations. Then he added, "Dennis, now we're going to cover two more concepts: coaching and training."

"What's the main difference between the two?" I asked.

Chuck answered categorically, "There is a major difference between coaching and training. Coaching relates to a one-on-one relationship, in which the manager teaches and guides the individual to the best of his or her abilities."

"But my bosses never had the time to teach me."

"This is common. In many organizations, managers don't even know how to coach their people. This can break down whole processes. In other places, coaching is limited by the manager's available time; because of the massive demands on any leader, time becomes a scarce resource. Nevertheless, on critical subjects, both functions of coaching and problem solving can be combined. Another very effective way to do this is to delegate this function partially, or totally, to a senior consultant, as your company is doing now.

"Training, on the other hand, may be mandatory and relates to short courses delivered by internal staff or training companies. Training exists in every company and is mostly conducted through the HR department. The materials are mostly generic in nature. This activity has some merits since knowledge is always valuable. Some of these initiatives are triggered by mandatory budgets dedicated to this purpose. Most training efforts are topical, like project management, or helping participants know themselves better, or how to better use Excel, et cetera. Training is not an alternative to coaching."

"What impact does training have?" I asked.

He replied, "I have never seen general training dramatically change the character of any business unit. The only training that can really change the character of the unit is multidisciplinary training on the job. This approach has a strong coaching component embedded. Life is continuous, and business management is part of life. It's the combination of all disciplines: finance, accounting, marketing, sales, R&D, engineering, production, quality control, customer service, and others that make a difference in achieving sound decision making. The manager not only has to know enough to ask the right questions, but also has to learn the art of integrating all of these disciplines.

"Integration is the key to sound management. Companies that built organizational silos experience very low effectiveness. They are destined to decline. Some survive—like in the utilities, education, and health-care sectors—because government regulations convert these organizations into reimbursement-plus-profit centers. This approach is extremely ineffective and often creates inflationary pressures as well.

"Fostering silos in a company is a political decision, not a managerial one. Although silos are based on a 'divide and conquer' policy with the intent of simplifying things, they can actually end up cannibalizing the organization itself. Employees are so immersed in their narrow profession that they don't understand the company for which they work. They get limited learning and growth opportunities, which impacts their professional development. Some organizations utilize management rotation, but this cannot compensate for the negative effects of a silo culture.

"Integration, on the other hand, is much more effective, can overcome the effects of the silo culture, and requires continuous learning."

"When you say 'continuous learning,' are you referring to continuous improvement?" I asked.

"No. Continuous learning is very different from continuous improvement. Continuous improvement is very tactical and focuses on how to squeeze another marginal percentage in efficiency. Continuous learning is the process that enables people to learn and integrate new disciplines.

"This is one of the objectives of our effort to provide you with additional tools that will show you how you can learn by yourself and teach others through the coaching process. The more disciplines that are integrated in a decision, the higher the probabilities of success."

We continued to talk a lot about coaching and training. I understood the importance of both, but I also understood the difference. I knew I still had a lot to learn to become an effective coach.

- 28 -

SELF-EVALUATION #3

A few days later, Chuck and I got together for lunch. He said he wanted to talk to me about an important issue. When Chuck said something was important, I knew it was important.

"Hi, Chuck, how are you?" I asked.

"I'm fine," he answered. "What about you?"

"Hanging in there," I answered with a smile.

He dove right in. "Okay, Dennis. The best way for you to continue to grow is to inspire you to further build on your primary talents—most importantly, to identify specific personal management areas that require further development."

"That sounds great! How do you plan to do this?" I was intrigued.

"I think we can do this by following a sincere process of personal evaluation."

"Okay," I said. Then I added, "My bosses do this every year, but I don't gain much from those evaluations."

Chuck looked at me and said, "Truly valuable evaluations need to be custom-tailored to you as an individual. I recommend not using generic templates or methods that use them. The maker of the generic forms doesn't know you or your boss or your lieutenants. They don't know the type of challenges your business unit is wrestling with, and especially the unique culture of the unit. In general, these forms include several dozen leader characteristics, which after closer review lack many more personal characteristics to explore and improve. While some of those characteristics may appear in the forms, many may be irrelevant to the current situation. In my experience, the benefit of relying on generic forms is limited and may translate into a loss of a unique opportunity to improve the quality of an individual leader."

"What are the main benefits of this custom-made approach?" I asked.

"Dennis, when you take one of your girls to a music competition, you know that her final ranking is a function of the number of mistakes she makes during her performance," Chuck said.

"Yes, I've seen that too many times," I acknowledged.

"This is similar," he said. "Skill-improvement efforts produce much better leaders and maximize return on investment for the company. The first step is to specify a set of leadership characteristics that are important to track and evaluate. I'll help you identify these based on careful observation of real-life situations. We'll discuss and agree upon the list of characteristics and parameters."

"Have you already selected my parameters?"

"During your interactions with others—like Peter, the steering committee members, and your lieutenants—I observed and identified certain parameters related to your behavior that I'd like to present to you. You can self-evaluate these, think about them, tell me if you agree, and work on them to improve your managerial abilities."

"This might be too embarrassing."

Chuck was quick to address this subject. "The purpose of self-evaluation is to achieve genuine results. This process is confidential. I will not share this document with anyone in the company."

"Okay, then let's proceed." I was eager to know where this effort would lead me. So far, I had gone from one learning experience to another.

"If you ever want my opinion regarding the grading of these parameters, ask me and I'll gladly let you know my views, and then you can compare them with yours for further analysis. For every parameter under evaluation, you can determine the degree of difficulty and, in addition, indicate the grade corresponding to the previous period. Adding examples could be an additional feature. For grades, you can use an A, B, C system with the addition of a plus or a minus. Once you're done, we'll establish one or more actions to support your continuous personal improvement on each specific skill. I'll use simulation techniques to recreate the same real-life situations, emphasizing the actions that will improve your chances for better results."

"Okay, are you ready to share your list with me?" I asked anxiously.

"I've prepared a list based on several months of observation." Chuck handed me a couple of pages. "I identified more than a dozen parameters and then grouped them into eight categories. For each parameter I've added a short description to help you interpret the meaning of each category. Please read the document aloud, and let me know if it's clear."

I started to read:

EXHIBIT 16:

SELF-EVALUATION CATEGORIES

1. Content

Understand the complexity, challenges, and "nuts and bolts" of the business.

2. Tools

Design and define methods, programs, templates, checklists, work methodologies, and files that can be utilized to facilitate the work of an employee or lieutenant to satisfactorily complete their assignments.

---

3. *Management*

Achieve goals while managing the business the way you think it should be, in the absence of cooperation or agreement. It includes two major situations: managing up and managing down.

3.1 Managing up

3.1.1 Managing requests
Satisfy or decline requests.

3.1.2 Avoiding/inviting pressure
Avoid being pressured by upper management (comments, character, etc.).

3.1.3 Controlling meetings
Achieve preestablished goals for a meeting.

3.2 Managing down

3.2.1 Evaluating employee performance
Fairly evaluate the employees (i.e., balance fairness between the company and the employee).

3.2.2 Supporting employees
Support the employees in their development and provide them with success opportunities.

3.2.3 Monitoring employees
Constantly monitor the performance of the employees by utilizing existing reports or new reports when necessary.

3.2.4 Motivating employees
Excite employees to perform to a new level.

4. *Time Management*

4.1 Self

Protect your own time while maximizing your effectiveness.

4.2 Others

Be conscious of and make the best use of other people's time (e.g., running effective meetings).

5. *Controlling Emotions*

Take time to understand why you as a leader react the way you do regarding different events or stresses.

6. *Decision Making*

Before making any decision, have a set of logical rules to ensure a high probability of being correct (prudent decision making). Gain experience and knowledge to increase the likelihood of being right (enhance one's prudence).

6.1 Strategic versus tactical items

Differentiate between a strategic and a tactical issue (what to do vs. how to do it).

6.2 Action-reaction versus multiple variables

Avoid action-reaction (immediate response to unexpected situations) and consider multiple variables when resolving any challenge.

6.3 "Patching decisions" and reversibility

Avoid implementing an inadequate short-term solution at the expense of a major problem; understand the reversibility of temporary solutions.

6.4 Defending your own logic

Articulate the rationale of your own logic to the hierarchical levels (above or below) to rationalize and defend the soundness of a decision or proposal.

7. *Discipline*

7.1 Self-discipline

Address issues thoroughly and decide in a timely manner

7.2 Unit discipline

Encourage a culture in which the behavior of every member corresponds to a given set of rules that were well communicated to the parties involved

8. *Fighting Power*

Build a strong desire to win

I was a bit overwhelmed. That was quite an evaluation document. I had never gone through such a process before. It sounded scary at first because Chuck had selected those parameters based on something he had seen or heard. Still, I was eager to learn more about me. I was ready to go home, sit down by myself, and start the process.

I followed Chuck's recommendations and started to write my self-evaluations following the parameters and the guidelines that he had selected. I wasn't always sure about the degree of difficulty, so in some cases I left it blank.

SELF-EVALUATION

TOPIC	DIFFICULTY	GRADE
1. Content	High	C
2. Tools	Medium	C
3. Management		
3.1 Managing up		
3.1.1 Managing requests	High	D-
3.1.2 Avoiding/inviting pressure	-	C-
3.1.3 Controlling meetings	-	C
3.2 Managing down		
3.2.1 Evaluating employee performance	-	B-
3.2.2 Supporting employees and deciding if they can contribute	Medium	C
3.2.3 Monitoring employees	-	C
4. Time Management	Medium	C
5. Controlling Emotions	-	C
6. Decision Making	-	C
6.1 Strategic versus tactical items	-	C-
6.2 Action-reaction versus multiple variables	-	D
6.3 "Patching decisions" and reversibility	-	D
6.4 Defending your own logic	-	C
7. Discipline		
7.1 Self-discipline	-	C
8. Fighting power	-	C

In general, the low grades were telling me something about the degree of difficulty. I looked at the grades and felt uncomfortable. I started to think about how I would react if my girls brought home such a report card from school. How would I feel as a parent? Thankfully, nobody except Chuck would see these grades. I realized that, for far too long, my company had neglected to help me develop the real skills I needed now to face my ongoing challenges.

On the one hand, with these grades, I knew I couldn't go very far. On the other hand, I realized how lucky I was to have somebody to help me develop better skills. I felt closer to Chuck, and my trust in him was as high as it could be. I had so much work to do for the unit, but I realized that I also had a lot to do for me. I remembered Chuck's words: "The quality of your unit will depend on your ability to grow, develop, master, and ultimately teach."

The week went by very quickly, and soon it was Wednesday again. It was a rainy day, so I drove slowly and arrived at Chuck's a few minutes late. Chuck greeted me as always. After we sat down, he asked, "Did you have time to do your self-evaluation?"

I showed him my grades for the parameters he selected. I was sure that he had known the results before he had assigned the homework. Chuck looked at the list and said nothing.

"Is this for me?" he asked.

"Yes. I printed this copy for you," I replied.

"And how do you feel about it?"

"I'm surprised at my own weaknesses. It was like looking into a mirror for a while and disliking what you see," I said. "I know now, without a doubt, that without me changing and improving substantially, I have little to offer in helping my employees through my personal coaching. Chuck, thank you for your efforts. I now understand you better, and I promise to do whatever possible to continue this journey until we declare victory."

When I said those words, I didn't know exactly what I meant by "victory," but I knew it had to be something that felt better than what I was experiencing at that moment. Chuck smiled. I knew he was pleased to hear what I said. He put the copy of the graded parameters in a drawer and said, "You're welcome. There's a lot to be done, so let's get started. Today we are going to talk about preparing for the next steering committee meeting. Before we start the session, could you please tell me what you have learned in the last weeks regarding project gestation and prioritization?"

I wasn't really prepared to do the talking today; I was still immersed in the results of the self-grading process, but I understood that Chuck was trying to complete a chapter so we could move to something new. I started my short dissertation: "I realize that project gestation and prioritization is a very important phase. Based on the methodology I learned from you, I invested a lot of energy in the process of selecting the right initiatives. I now believe that these initiatives, when integrated, will bring the unit to a new, stronger level of performance. As you taught me, there are several major parameters I considered before launching a project:

- What will be the tangible benefits if the project is successfully completed?
- Who is going to run it?
- What resources are needed to complete it?
- How long will it take to complete?

"Although I didn't think initially that it was possible, I recognize that you were right. Most of the projects are doable internally within the existing resources. It was an issue of changing the current priorities. We have only a few initiatives that require dollars or unique resources, and I'm still exploring how to execute them."

Chuck interjected, "So how do you think the steering committee will react?"

"I expect the steering committee members will ask tough questions in the next meeting, and probably a lot of them. But I think I'm now better prepared to answer all the questions related to my ongoing projects. I feel ready to articulate the benefits of each project. I'm aware this is a selling job. Succeeding during the meeting will ultimately determine the probability of the success of the unit as a whole. Based on the previous steering committee meeting, I realize that proper presentation and background material are of real importance. I know that if this test is successful, and if Peter and the other members get good vibes about the benefit of the projects, I can discuss the issue that interests me the most: the needed resources. I expect they will make good contributions on the tactical side by facilitating resources that are out of my decision range."

Chuck interrupted me. "Please master the issue of who you selected to manage each project. This issue may or may not come up, but you better be prepared."

"I feel prepared. We need to manage a couple dozen projects simultaneously. I've decided to personally manage the most important projects, at least for the time being. For the larger projects, I've selected other employees to be responsible for segments or components."

"Dennis, you'll do very well in this area."

- 29 -

FUNDING PROJECTS

I worked hard over the weekend. I not only had to monitor all the action items I had asked my lieutenants and employees to complete, but I also had to work on those that depended on my personal involvement.

I started to feel what Chuck was insinuating all the time. Everything had to take place simultaneously: hiring, building a team, managing projects, taking action on a personal basis, and much more. I started to jump from one issue to another, from one category to the next. I also realized there were a few projects I couldn't launch. They were very important. One in particular was more than an A-category project; it was an A+, and I had it on my personal action item list.

On Monday, I called Peter. His assistant put me on hold, and a few minutes later, I heard Peter say, "Hi, Dennis, what can I do for you?"

I described the situation and then added, "Peter, this project is crucial, and I need the resources IT is asking for to complete this project."

"What about your existing budget?" he asked.

"You know, Peter," I said, "the budget shrank when this unit was transferred to your division, and the resources presently available to me are not enough to properly run the current operations."

"I'm sorry," Peter said. "We transferred the unit and the unit budget to my division prior to you being selected. Believe me, there were few degrees of freedom to do it differently. Back then I was forced to take the unit 'as is.' How much is this project going to cost?"

"The IT department claims that it's a four-month job for several programmers. They are asking for $300,000, fully loaded." There was silence on the other side of the phone. "Peter, it's just 'funny money.' It's not an out-of-pocket expense for the company; it's only an internal accounting transfer."

"Listen, Dennis, I just came from a meeting with the CEO and COO. Demand for our company's products and services is going down, and they're asking all of the senior VPs and VPs in the company to cut their budgets. That means part of BLM's budget too. Also, corporate is putting a freeze on new hires starting at the end of the month."

I felt like I just got sucker-punched and had the wind knocked out of me. "Peter, I have to turn this unit around, and I feel I'm making progress, but how can I produce serious change without the proper budget?"

"Dennis, it is what it is. I'm sorry, I have an international call to take on the other line." Peter hung up.

I was shocked and somewhat confused. My budget was already insufficient, and now it was getting trimmed even further. My roster was incomplete. I had a few candidates, but I wasn't sure they were the best choice, and my hiring window was closing soon. This was frustrating.

So, I called Chuck and told him about the situation. "This IT project was about building a dedicated web portal that would integrate several existing complex programs and provide direct connectivity to the customers so they could, among many other things, follow up in real time on the status of their particular situations. Although this solution could be a great relief for me, my unit's budget lacks the funds the IT department needs. Ironically, the IT department has staff without a lot of work, but the company's current policies prefer the programmers to be idle than to provide the help we need."

Chuck said, "Dennis, can you send me the last available copy of your unit's detailed financials?"

"You will have it shortly. Please check your e-mail," I said. I asked Jennifer to e-mail the latest financials to Chuck right away.

I went to an administrative meeting called by Peter. When I came back to my office, I asked Jennifer if we had heard from Chuck. Jennifer answered negatively. I asked, "Did you send him the last version of the financials?"

"Not yet," she answered.

I just about went ballistic, but then I remembered that Chuck had told me to "never react quickly to an unexpected situation." I took a deep breath and calmly asked, "Jennifer, this is urgent—what happened?"

"The financials in the file were from last month. I called accounting, and they told me that they were finishing the new version and that I'll have it momentarily."

"When did that call take place?" I asked.

She looked at the clock and said, "More than an hour ago."

"Okay, Jennifer. Call them back, and if you don't get the new financials immediately, let's send Chuck the last version we have."

"Okay, boss." I heard her making a call. After a few minutes, she entered my office and said, "The latest version of the financials arrived, and I forwarded it to Chuck. I also printed a copy for you; it's in your inbox. I also confirmed that Chuck received the e-mail."

A few minutes later, I checked my e-mail, and there it was, a memo from Chuck saying, "Dennis, I have the information. I'm leaving for the airport right now. I'll review the material during my flight, and I'll communicate my findings once I arrive at my hotel. Please have a copy of the material handy so we can discuss it if needed."

A few hours later, I was home. I was ready to go to sleep, but I still needed to talk to Chuck. I was reluctant to disturb him. Chuck was always busy. Suddenly, I heard my phone ringing. I quickly picked it up.

"Hi, Dennis. I hope you're not in bed," Chuck said.

"Hi, Chuck. Thank you for calling," I said anxiously.

"So, I've reviewed the financials and gone through the P&L, balance sheet, and cash flows. There are two numbers in the detailed P&L that I would like you to look into further. Do you have access to your copy of the financials?" he asked.

"Yes, give me a minute." I ran to my briefcase. "Okay, I have them in front of me."

Chuck continued: "Well, this is what I would like you to do. Look at the P&L expense list: item number seventy-nine shows six hundred thousand dollars, and number one hundred four shows four hundred thousand dollars. Their descriptions aren't clear. Please find out more about these. Tomorrow I'm in meetings all day. I can call you at noon your time. Please be ready with your findings. I won't have too much time to talk to you, but I'll do my best. Okay?"

"Thanks, Chuck, I'll be ready when your call comes," I said with confidence. Chuck was right. The descriptions of those items were not clear. During the diagnostics phase, we had identified this weakness regarding the quality of the financial reports. Unfortunately, we didn't have the internal accounting muscle to develop a new specification describing exactly what my unit needed.

The next day, as soon as I arrived at the office, I called the accounting department manager. His assistant picked up and said, "Tim hasn't arrived yet. Would you like his voice mail?"

"Sure," I answered. I heard the voice mail beep and said, "Tim, this is Dennis from BLM; I need to talk to you urgently. Please call me back at 57643."

I started to doubt I would have the answers Chuck was looking for in time. Failure to get them would probably be a great disappointment for both of us. I called Tim's assistant again. She picked up the phone, and I said, "This is Dennis again from BLM. Could you please tell me who is assigned to work on our financials?"

"I'll have to ask around. Let me do so, and I'll call you right back. Oh, wait a minute, Tim just walked in. Would you like to talk to him?"

"Absolutely!" I exclaimed.

There was silence for a while and then: "Hi, Dennis, this is Tim. How are you? I haven't seen you in a while."

"You're right, Tim. It's been a while. Sorry I don't have much time to catch up now. I'm the new manager at BLM and I need your help."

"Please, go ahead."

"I received my unit's latest financial report. I have two P&L entries that we need to further clarify. Could you help us do so?"

"Give me the entry numbers, and I'll see what I can do."

"Thanks, Tim. The entries are numbers seventy-nine and one hundred four."

"Let me talk to Clara. She deals with your unit. She's in a meeting right now, but as soon she is available, I'll address the issue."

"It's 10:06 a.m. now. I need this info at 11:30 a.m. sharp. Can you give us an answer before then?"

"I'll do my best."

"Much appreciated. Thanks, Tim," I said and hung up.

Time passed with no call. I looked at my watch; it was 11:05 a.m. I called Jennifer and told her that I was expecting a call from either Tim or Clara in accounting with some very important information, and she shouldn't leave the office until this phone call came through. I signed some forms, went to the restroom, came back, and asked Jennifer if anyone had called from accounting.

Not yet. I looked at my watch—it was 11:28 a.m. I sat in my chair. Five minutes later, the phone rang. It was Tim. I took my pad and was ready to write down the information, and that's when Tim said to me, "Dennis, this is a courtesy call. Sorry I'm late. I put Clara on the case, and she's finishing her review. She'll call you shortly."

"Thanks, Tim. I'm sure you remember the urgency of this matter," I reminded him.

"Absolutely, Dennis; she'll call you in a few minutes."

At 11:41 a.m., Clara called me. "Hi, Dennis, it's Clara. I have the details for you. Item one hundred four is the last payment to a vendor for ongoing supplies. Item seventy-nine is a payment to a contractor doing repair work in the field on behalf of your unit."

"Do we have a signed contract with them?"

"Yes, it's a five-year contract signed four years ago. In the past, it was paid by Jack's division, but since we realized it was a BLM-related contract, it's recently transferred to your account. The payments are now coming out of your budget."

"Do you have a copy of the contract?" I asked.

"Yes, it's in front of me; it's a relatively short document. I was just reviewing it to make the transfer."

"Clara, please e-mail me a copy." It was 11:47 a.m.

Two minutes later, I was reviewing the document. I immediately called the field supervisor in my unit and asked him to join me. I had questions, and he had answers. The contractor's activity was not critical, and we could partially absorb the work internally. It would demand more efforts from my troops. There was a clause in the contract that after three years, this agreement would automatically be renewed month-to-month, unless the contractor received notification from our company of termination. The contractor had symmetric rights.

It was getting close to 12:00 p.m. I thanked the supervisor.

The phone rang—it was Chuck. "Hi, Dennis. Were you able to find out what those lines were?" he asked.

"Yes, I also think I found the money for the IT project," I responded.

"Congratulations," he said. "That is excellent progress. By the way, I got an e-mail from Greg this morning that they're cutting costs and will freeze hiring at the end of the month. That means you need to put the pedal to the metal and accelerate all processes for recruiting and project launches. We'll talk again. I have to run."

During the coming days, I filled all my open employment slots, and I had enough in my budget to launch the IT project and support some of the cuts. Because of the conversation between Chuck and Greg, the cuts in my unit were limited. I survived one more time.

I was ready to rock and roll. That call to Chuck, the review of the P&L items, and my quick response all paid out. I felt I was in business. In the following weeks, the first projects were launched. Chuck and Richard were at my side helping me with action items, monitoring, and control. During project meetings, from time to time, Chuck would stand up and approach the meeting room white board, where he explained or expanded on a concept, making convincing arguments one way or the other. This was always helpful, because it generated true dialogue. I explained that everyone was entitled to his or her opinion, and there would be no retaliation. I also explained the other elements that Chuck had taught me regarding management of successful meetings. One important thing I decided: there would be no fear in my meetings.

The results of this policy were amazing. Employees who were usually extremely quiet and had never expressed themselves before started to give opinions, and to my surprise, they made very good contributions to the final decision making. We started to make good progress. Project managers were assigned to specific projects, and action items were recorded and implemented as planned. In the following days, we exchanged a lot of PowerPoint graphs and tables with Chuck via e-mail.

The date of the next steering committee meeting was around the corner. We did a dry run for my presentation. I felt more confident now than I had felt in my preparations for the previous meeting. After the dry run, Chuck reminded me, "During the meeting you will first show the achievements and progress made. The dashboard will be very helpful, as well as the detailed list of the projects already launched or about to be launched."

I continued to perfect my dashboard. Chuck was right; I was the first beneficiary of this exercise because it forced me to focus on what was needed. I knew I had to convert the reds into yellows, the yellows into greens, and the greens into check marks.

At the second steering committee meeting, I presented the dashboard. Peter and the other members were positively impressed. They were still struggling with the nomenclature, but they started to understand the value of what we were doing and the value of the words "infrastructure buildup." They liked the check marks and the green arrows, and they started to ask questions to better understand what every square meant. This tool was completely a nontraditional way to present to the executives in my company, but soon they realized that this method was more transparent and achieved better communication.

The stress of the first steering committee meeting was in the past. I knew that Chuck had done a lot of lobbying before the meetings, and that had softened up the members. I felt more support than I had in the previous meeting, and at the end I got some positive comments regarding the changes already made and the results achieved. The committee members decided to temporarily add one more senior employee to support our projects. I welcomed that with open arms. When the meeting was over, I approached Chuck, shook his hand, and said, "I feel much better."

I went home earlier than usual. Cheryl asked me how it went. I hugged her and said, "It was good; now I'm in business, but still there's a long way in front of me."

It was Friday. I wanted to celebrate, and we went out to dinner.

- 30 -

Informal Management

Chuck's course at the university was over, and now I was focusing on the ongoing projects.

I continued with the project management meetings. I applied the theory I learned from Chuck. Richard, his assistant, was very helpful. The book of "action items" grew very quickly as we completed action items and added new ones to do. The teams understood that we meant business, and everyone understood they had a specific role. No more having several people chasing the same ball. All lieutenants and employees started to play their positions.

Chuck, Richard, and I met frequently to ensure that progress was being made on the most important projects. We usually met at one of my facilities, but from time to time, I met with Chuck in his office. I learned that every visit was worth my time and effort, because I was smarter every time I left that office.

The next Wednesday, Chuck started by saying, "Dennis, in the work we've done together, we've covered numerous formal management techniques and methods. There are also informal management techniques that have proven very successful. They can be very effective for you." He paused. "There is a beauty to informality. It's spontaneous; it reaches people whom the leader usually doesn't see, and it usually contributes to the enhancement of the strategic issues list. Please consider that the more strategic issues you collect, the better your chance to continue to progress."

Chuck continued: "One of the most famous techniques of informal management is attributed to Bill Hewlett, founder of the Hewlett-Packard Company. It was called 'managing by wandering around.' I heard about the great results of that approach straight from the source, while I was doing my sabbatical at Hewlett Packard in Palo Alto in 1979.

"One of the most famous stories was told as follows: In one of his wanderings, Bill Hewlett interacted with a couple of engineers. He was exposed to the idea of developing a handheld calculator. Since it was a totally new concept to the company, HP decided to do some studies with one of the best consulting companies at the time. The studies pointed out that there was no future in developing such a device. In spite of the negative report, Mr. Hewlett decided to try anyway, and he authorized the product development. Upon product introduction, HP successfully competed against Texas Instruments, their rival at that time. That personal calculator became the first building block in the multibillion-dollar computer business."

"Fascinating. Any other informal techniques?"

"Yes. Other informal techniques include breakfast programs with employees and impromptu unit visits. Their degree of effectiveness depends on different factors. Some lieutenants may be sensitive about you forgoing the chain of command and talking directly to their subordinates; they may perceive this as a lack of confidence in them. Remember, though, that being seen by the troops has always been an encouraging factor. Carefully manage the information you collect from those experiences."

We took a break. A few minutes later, we reconvened, and Chuck asked me, "Is there any topic you would like to discuss?"

"Yes, as a matter of fact, I wanted to discuss the work we did on organizational structure. By now I've realized that organizational structure design isn't just about drawing squares and trying to fill them out with names. I don't have the same degree of freedom that the CEO or a senior executive may have. If the CEO decides he or she needs a VP, many individuals can get involved, like HR, a recruiting company, or even board members.

"At my level, the hiring process is sometimes more complex, so I have to adapt the functionality to my existing team. Obviously, I'm always willing to improve the team's capabilities. As I become more familiar with the existing personnel, I think there will be room for additional changes."

"Fine-tuning the organizational structure after this period doesn't mean you missed anything at the beginning when you first designed your initial organizational structure," Chuck said. "It means that now you know the organization better. That's why we call the first effort the transitional organizational structure.

"Continuous fine-tuning of the organization is necessary and geared toward the buildup of what we previously called the sustainable organization. A sustainable organization has a very high probability of lasting several years. This provides good stability for business development, but mostly it helps in the process of succession plans. A sustainable organization allows the leader to 'grab' business opportunities along the way and solidifies the future of the team roster.

"Newly recruited employees come into a new environment. Improved unit performance may attract capable employees from outside the unit who are looking for challenges and for an opportunity to work in a place that has a future and good management."

We chatted about various details regarding my business cells. While I was preparing to leave, Chuck said, "Before I forget, I think this is a good time for you to prepare your next self-evaluation."

"Okay," I answered.

Chuck continued: "I would like to add one more element to this next evaluation. After you grade yourself, please add a paragraph explaining your current feelings about each particular skill. This will be very helpful to you in the future."

"Will do," I said.

- 31 -

SELF-EVALUATION #4

I went back home, looked for my previous evaluation, and followed Chuck's suggestions. Working with Chuck for all these quarters had taught me to be tough on myself and to pursue quality and even perfection. I was very far from ideal, but I also knew that I had to progress as much as required to achieve success within company standards. I knew that success in the eyes of the company would be expressed with recognition, a promotion, and even a bonus.

I started to fill out the form. I discontinued recording the degree of difficulty, but I added a few more subcategories to the original list.

SELF-EVALUATION

1. Content

Grade: B (up from C)

I firmly believe in building a solid foundation prior to tackling the multitude of issues. There is a consistency to all the work that we have done. In every case, we have relied on getting the fundamentals right. We have built upon the elementary information. While this approach seems simplistic at first, a solid foundation has been established. The work we spent on building the functional organization is already paying dividends.

---

2. Tools

2.1 Action items (new tool):
Grade: B

I have used this tool, and I find it quite effective, particularly in the way that Chuck and Richard are using it.

2.2 Matrices (new tool):
Grade: C-

Simple matrices, such as level of difficulty vs. impact, are very helpful in prioritizing activity. This is a step often skipped (by me and others) because it seems academic and intuitive.

2.3 Homework (new tool):
Grade: C

This is another area where the time to conduct the homework didn't materialize, but I'm doing better.

2.4 Other Tools
Grade: C

Tools developed during project management sessions with managers have been helpful. These include pie charts of their time use, assessment of employee strengths and weaknesses, challenges and roadblocks, behavior expectations, and content expectations.

3. Management

3.1 Managing up

3.1.1 Managing requests
Grade: D (up from D-)

Do not reply immediately to management requests. Take the time to analyze a situation and determine the best course of action. I need to rely more on my instincts and wisdom.

Don't let management issue a quick order and respond in a knee-jerk fashion. It proves them right and me wrong. Recognize how I make decisions (not immediate; use my intuition) and use this to my advantage.

3.1.2 Avoiding/inviting pressure
Grade: B (Up from C-)

If I invite pressure, I get pressure. Don't invite it.

3.1.3 Controlling meetings
Grade: B (up from C)

Control meetings with my management. Set agenda. Bring up good news first (e.g., accomplishments). Be deliberate in asking for decisions and approvals. Think hard about what I need approval for and what I can go ahead and do without approval.

3.2 Managing down

3.2.1 Evaluating employee performance
Grade: B (up from B-)

Be straightforward in letting people know when they have not performed.

3.2.2 Supporting employees and deciding if they can contribute
Grade: C (no change)

Be aggressive in helping people perform. Looking back, this is a mistake I have repeated over many years as a supervisor (without realizing it). My assumption has been that people will react like me, and that is wrong. They need a lot of direction during the initial project roll-out, and this will pay dividends later.

3.2.3 Monitoring employees
Grade: C (no change)

4. *Time Management*
   Grade: C+ (up from C)

Don't let others control my calendar. Cut meetings short when possible. Delegate some meetings. Set aside appropriate time to finish projects, with adequate time for review. Take a look at my actual time pie chart and compare it to an ideal one. Time and energy are all I have; I must be wise in how I spend them.

5. *Controlling Emotions*
   Grade: C (no change)

Recognize my emotional response to certain issues and individuals. Make sure I understand why I'm reacting in a certain way. Ask myself questions: Am I acting out of fear or intimidation? Am I acting to avoid conflict? Am I acting because I'm angry or my pride has been wounded?

6. *Decision Making*

6.1 Strategic versus tactical items
Grade: C+ (up from C)

I have learned quite a bit about the difference between strategic and tactical actions. I find myself evaluating actions to determine if they are strategic or tactical in nature. In the past, I don't think I was really able to clearly differentiate between the two. I still find that I enjoy the tactical items, mostly because it feels more active to me and results are more immediate. I'm beginning to appreciate the strategic, however. The results are not as immediate but are of a higher quality.

6.2 Action-reaction versus multiple variables
Grade: C (up from D)

I understand the difference clearly. The "patch of the day" will work for that day, but it usually does not anticipate the unforeseen consequences. The multiple-variables approach makes sense and obviously requires a great deal of thought. Chuck says that every problem can have one hundred solutions, but only one or two will really work. I do not understand yet how you can be so confident in the one or two right answers out of one hundred. I enjoy quantitative analysis because there can be only one correct answer. However, if the analysis is qualitative in nature, it is much more difficult to pick the right answer, or the most prudent answer.

6.3 "Patching decisions" and reversibility
Grade: C+ (up from D)

Make sure that any patching decisions are reversible.

6.4 Defending your own logic
Grade: C (no change)

Be able and willing to defend my logic even if I am winning. I can explain why I have proposed to do things a certain way or made a decision.

7. *Discipline*

7.1 Self-discipline
Grade: C+ (up from C)

The one word I keep coming back to in my review of the past six months is discipline. We have tackled all of the subjects with a great deal of discipline. Rigorous analysis has been required to develop the functional organization. The discipline requires a great deal of thinking time, and it is tiring. This has resulted in a change in my behavior. (I do not like to admit this.) It seems like the discipline that was required in my school days has dissipated over the years in the work environment. Because of the discipline required, I feel like I am performing at a much higher level than in the past.

8. *Fighting power*
Grade: C (no change)

Nothing is lost until it's lost. In the past, I gave up on some opportunities that could've been won. Now I'm playing through the final buzzer.

When I finished writing, I realized that I was changing. I was adopting Chuck's excellence principles. I was happy about that, but I knew I had to improve my grades for my own sake.

We kept making progress. After a few months, the IT project was completed. Initially, we offered access to the portal to only a few customers. They provided invaluable feedback including remarks, opinions, and possible changes and improvements. A few weeks later, the web project was formally launched. It was very instrumental in facilitating communications, and customers were extremely happy with this new tool.

Chuck and his team ran a new independent customer survey to compare results with the one they had summarized before I came on board. The change was dramatic and favorable.

Over the next months, we pushed through other projects, and we trained and coached personnel. Things started to happen. Firefighting was reduced. Chuck was right; we were improving by working on the projects instead of directly addressing firefighting and placating the customers. It was a great decision.

Customers started to forward us positive letters. That was good material for the next steering committee meeting, and I started to collect them in an album. At the same time, the bad press that used to appear in the newspapers stopped.

Our dashboards started to change colors, and green became the most dominant color. There were still yellows and a few reds. The chart helped focus my efforts toward the projects that needed more help.

Business cells started to perform better. Every time a project was completed, they had less work, fewer complaints, more effectiveness, and overall a better feeling. Employee attendance started to go up. People felt better. The best signal was that employees and supervisors from outside the unit were interested in joining us. This was a very good sign.

Although I started to feel extremely good, I couldn't lower my guard. I had to invest more and do better.

SECTION 4

MONITORING AND CONTROL

- 32 -

PREPARING FOR GROWTH

It was Wednesday again. It was a beautiful spring day. I entered Chuck's office. He opened by saying, "In previous quarters, we covered in detail the processes of diagnostics and its derivatives, such as identifying weaknesses, strategic issues, and business cell strategies. We've covered the different components of change design, including business architecture, organizational structure, investment portfolio, and road map. We went on to discuss building a team and managing operations.

"During this period, your business unit has solved numerous problems, and, while many issues have been eliminated from the action list, many new issues have been added to the same list. This is expected at this stage of development—the more problems that are addressed, the more new initiatives get developed."

"Chuck, it looks like a never-ending process," I noted.

"Please don't be discouraged. Although good management leads toward a never-ending process, as you progress together with your teams, the situation does reach balance.

"The main difference in the life of the business unit is that the Q_{DM}—the quantity and quality of decisions previously discussed— grows substantially. As you, your lieutenants, and employees make more quality decisions, everyone's motivation and hope will increase and your business unit will perform better. The process we've followed has provided you with tremendous knowledge and substantially increased your personal confidence."

"You're right," I replied.

Chuck continued: "The hierarchy, lieutenants, employees, suppliers, and customers all feel better. They perceive that you're stabilizing the unit and that there is a clear direction toward a better future."

"I agree. The meetings with the hierarchy have changed from being challenging to being cooperative. It seems that when the hierarchy smells victory, they want to have a piece of the action," I added, laughing.

"Now that many of the strategic issues are finally known in detail, your core team has been upgraded; new leaders have emerged, and operational issues have been clarified. It's time to prepare the organization to move from defense to attack. During the next months, we'll discuss the issues of performance, metrics, alignment, and how to use the alignment method to design compensation incentives."

"Okay. Sounds ambitious, but I know we can do it. Please clarify for me—what do you mean by attack?"

"*Attack* means pursuing growth. Growth can be organic by introducing new products and services, or by developing and implementing a well-thought-out mergers and acquisition—M&A— strategy. Controlled growth is good for business. It benefits the shareholders by augmenting the value of the company. It also benefits its employees by providing new opportunities, job stability, and better compensation. A successful sales force needs solid internal support, competitive products and services, and excellent customer service. It's difficult to sell if the company is known for its weak customer service.

"An M&A team can find the right targets to acquire, but if the unit's basic business core is weak, inefficient, or disorganized, it's better not to pursue any acquisition. It becomes an adventure more than a well-planned business step. Remember, Dennis, you don't build a second floor when the first floor is burning. Sustainable growth requires quality across the board, from the business leader to the employees working at the lowest levels of the organization. It requires that everybody develop a sense of ownership. Over time, that sense of ownership converts into a sense of pride.

"Moving from defense to attack also means to precisely articulate both the comprehensive short-term strategy and the long-term strategy in a way that is extremely clear to everyone: you, the hierarchy, and all the lieutenants and employees. These strategies are based on substantially improving crucial success parameters."

"But the more things I complete, the further I get from the original road map," I replied.

"Dennis, that's fine. Today you know your business much better than when you drafted your first road map. In previous quarters, we tackled the issues of problem finding, problem solving, and implementation. Now you can update and communicate changes in the road map and investment portfolio. You can request the budgets necessary to support and accelerate these changes. Your final effort before attack is dedicated to the processes of monitoring and control."

"What's the difference between the terms *monitoring* and *control*? At work, these terms are interchangeable."

Chuck replied, "Monitoring relates to the act of measuring. Control relates to the act of correcting any departure between expected outcomes and real results."

"So, when will the unit be ready for attack?" I asked excitedly.

"Once these two elements are in place and working well, the unit is prepared for attack. Dennis, I want you to know that I can see you're changing, leaving your hesitation behind and looking to the future with some optimism. This is good progress."

I had some urgent operational issues in my unit, and I wanted to ask Chuck about them. We spent the rest of the afternoon in discussions. To resolve my operational challenges, we developed a method by which we both carefully listened to each other, and, after cautious analysis, we selected what we thought would be the best alternative. I liked that we took the time to reach consensus. We didn't want to leave any landmines behind.

- 33 -

MEASURING PERFORMANCE

Peter took a hands-off approach with BLM. He gave me and Chuck the freedom to do what we were doing. Then, one day, he e-mailed me and asked, "How's BLM doing?" I wanted to impress him. In the past, I would have reacted immediately and started to describe the present situation. But this time, I recalled Chuck's lesson about the principle of action-reaction. I paused and remembered that there was a recent corporate change.

Earlier this year, the company hired a new CEO. Like his predecessors, he had asked executives from all the divisions to demand better performance. Over the past five years, most executives would look at their budgets and cut costs by a given percentage. This year, however, budgets were already so lean that there didn't seem anything was left to cut.

I realized that Peter just wanted to see performance that he could report up the corporate ladder. Instead of reacting immediately, I called his office and offered a few dates when I was available to more formally discuss our progress. I let Chuck know that I was drafting a progress report for Peter. I was proud of myself for not jumping the gun. I was gaining confidence personally as well as in my business unit.

That Wednesday, I had a dentist appointment. I left work, intending to go from the dental office to my meeting with Chuck. At the dentist, however, the procedure left the right side of my face ballooned. When I arrived at Chuck's, he looked at my face and said, "Seems you won't be talking much today."

I nodded in agreement. Silently, I entered the office and took my seat. I gestured to Chuck that I was writing something in my notepad for him and wrote, "How can I measure BLM's performance for my upcoming presentation with Peter?"

I handed the pad to Chuck. He read it, looked at me, and smiled. He said, "Let's start from the basics. A performance presentation is based on the parameters you monitor and control. When we design monitoring, we include groups of data that need to be periodically reviewed." Chuck took the pad and began to write:

MONITORING PERFORMANCE

1. Financial performance
2. Unit operational performance
3. Business cell operational performance
4. Operational trends
5. Long-term strategic performance
6. Individual performance

"The first five focus on the performance of the unit itself. They have a 'team flavor.' The last one evaluates individual performance."

I took back my notepad and wrote, "This is a lot of data and it'll take a lot of work to gather it."

"Excellent management requires the constant review of quality data. When properly done, your cautious review of the data will help you zero in on new strategic issues. This and the project meetings you are conducting are excellent sources for 'problem finding.' Every one of the data groups previously described contributes to the process of

monitoring and measuring. Let's review a little more detail for each
of these groups," Chuck said.

"First is *financial performance*. This is one of the most common
sets of data. Financial performance reflects the contribution of the
unit to the company's bottom line. There are numerous ratios that
can be used to determine financial metrics based on the P&L, balance
sheet, and cash-flow statements. These three financial statements
are also used to determine valuation. Valuation is probably one of
the most important metrics in this set, but it's not commonly used
internally to evaluate business units, unless they are facing a sale or
merger. P&L-based valuations sometimes use multiples of EBTDA.
In other cases, balance sheet–based valuations lead to book value
or liquidation value. Cash flow multiples are also used to determine
valuation. Consequently, executives focus mostly on financial data.
Since I know you are familiar with the financial statements and the
resulting ratios, let's move on to the other categories.

"Number two is *unit operational performance*. In a service or
product company, operational performance must also include the
same elements and events by which customers are going to judge
the unit's performance. The ability of your unit to understand the
business and what is really important to the customers on the one side,
and your operations on the other, become the main components of
operational metrics. Customer-oriented metrics are the real drivers
for the product or service provided."

I wrote, "But customers have different opinions."

"Correct, Dennis. Usually, before we define key parameters, it's
important to survey your customers for either services or products
and to better understand what they value. It's your responsibility to
translate the results of the survey into the operational performance
required.

"Number three is *business cell operational performance*. This
section relates to the business cells that operate within your
business unit. Every business cell needs its own set of performance

parameters; for example, the number of post-installation repairs in a given month.

"Number four is *operational trends*. This information is obtained by analyzing historical data and statistics. Trends analysis is a helpful way to understand the evolution of selected parameters. Any departure from trend requires analysis and decision making. Oftentimes, trend analysis is the trigger for process changes. An example would be tracking the number of repairs that took more than five days." Chuck took a sip of his mineral water.

"Number five is *long-term strategic performance*. Previous long-term strategies had projected or forecasted outcomes. Now that time has passed, how do those projections and forecasts compare with reality?

"Number six is *individual performance*. This includes both lieutenant performance and employee performance. We previously discussed in length how to manage action items as well as how to grade timeliness and quality for each individual employee who participates in a project.

"Dennis, your jaw is swelling quite a bit. Would you like some ice to put on it?"

I wrote, "No. Stop for now and continue another day?"

"Okay. Let me know as soon as your jaw recovers, and we'll talk more about metrics and alignment."

I packed my things and left. As I drove home, eager to ice my swollen jaw, the furthest things from my mind were metrics and alignment.

- 34 -

METRICS

It took me a few days to fully recover from my dental work. I was feeling better, though, and I really wanted to feel well before meeting with Chuck again. My unit was progressing, step by step. Some short projects had been successfully completed, and I had more time to spend with the larger and most important ones.

For the first time, I was doing things simultaneously: developing tools, hiring people, improving processes, managing projects, making good decisions, preparing presentations, meeting with Chuck, and even evaluating myself. Thanks to Chuck, I had learned something extremely important: how to be my own boss. I was interested in improving execution. I knew that if I worked closely with Chuck, the quality of execution could be measured.

I gave Chuck a call, and we met. I asked, "Everybody in the company talks about metrics. What's your opinion? How do you define metrics?"

"In principle, a business metric is any type of measurement used to gauge a quantifiable component of a business unit's performance."

"For example?"

"Regarding services—timeliness, quality, and cost are always representative metrics. You can use these parameters to measure the performance of certain critical portions of your own processes linked to the particular service under consideration."

"Okay. What about product metrics?"

"Product metrics can be also derived from the surveys. Questions in the survey have to be carefully drafted. Let me give you an example from the auto industry. TGWs, or 'things go wrong,' are recorded for different types of complaints—wind-noise complaints are a representative example. The total complaints per model per year are reasonable metrics to be included. Type and number of failures under the warranty period is another set to consider."

"Thanks. I understand better," I said. I was wondering how I could design a good set of metrics to evaluate my unit. "Coach, so what's your philosophy on how to approach metrics?"

Chuck smiled when I called him coach. He answered, "In principle, metrics management requires two elements: availability of accurate performance information and the standard against which you compare that performance."

"What should I consider in defining the standard?"

"The success of any metrics system requires respecting one premise: metrics need to be realistic and fair to both the employees and the company. Metrics design is linked to managerial honesty. Achieving a truly fair environment is possible when both the business unit and the employees benefit from achieving the selected metrics. It's a delicate balancing act. The more demanding the achievable metrics, the more they're appreciated. If metrics are too weak, they foster complacency and ultimately defeat. If metrics are too aggressive, they foster frustration, demotivation, and ultimately collapse. So the key factor is finding the right balance."

"This'll be quite an effort."

"Yes, but once you do it, the standards will be valid for a long time. Having said that, you'll need to clearly communicate to those involved what the expectations are."

"Just to recap, can you give me another example of a commonly used metric?"

"Let's see. Take, for example, backlog. Understanding backlog is important for predicting future revenue, for shedding light on other parameters such as delivery time, and for determining materials availability, process balancing, human resources required, et cetera. Here you see how one parameter can have multiple effects. Independent of its direction, it's the gap between the numbers recorded and the standard selected that will push you to act."

"Wow, this is getting interesting," I said. "It seems that metrics relate mostly to collective performance."

"In general, yes, but as soon as you identify someone who's disrupting a business unit or cell's performance, address that immediately."

"Okay," I said, "we've covered performance and metrics. It seems I have everything I need, at least from the data perspective, to monitor my unit and business cells."

"Not so fast, Dennis. Remember we have one more item to cover on the list: alignment."

"Right. You mentioned this at our last meeting, but I was in such pain that day that I forgot about it."

- 35 -

ALIGNMENT

"Dennis, I started writing an article for a business journal. It's about business unit goals and objectives. I think it's the right time for you to read it because it leads into our conversation about the alignment program. Although it's incomplete, we'll pick up our conversation where the article currently ends. It won't take you too long to read. While you're doing that, I have an important call to take in the other room," Chuck said. He had connections all over the world, and people called him for advice, mostly in times of crisis.

I made myself comfortable and started reading the article he had given me.

BUSINESS UNIT GOALS AND OBJECTIVES

In some companies, it is unlikely that the process of cascading goals and objectives (G&O) from the CEO will cover the whole gamut of G&O needed by all the company's business units. Consequently, each layer of management ends up defining the specifics of its own organizational layer. In some companies, a more profound conflict of interest may exist when executives and managers set their own G&O and those G&O directly tie to their compensation. Easy-to-achieve G&O foster stagnant and uncreative environments, and the company suffers over the long run.

Upper management is not always available to investigate and optimize the process of cascading G&O to the lower ranks. In many instances, middle management perceives the integrated cascading process as a threat instead of an opportunity. It all depends on the culture of the place, its history of compensation incentives, recognition methods, retaliation policies, and precedents. It should, however, be one of the most important responsibilities of any CEO and his or her management teams.

Cultures result from how policies are driven by the top of the organization, not the bottom. In many cases, the cascaded G&O are based only on financial objectives. Attempting to achieve a certain number in revenues or profits as a result of cascading corporate G&O can completely ignore understanding the business unit's real situation in terms of present and future needs. This approach is too simplistic and therefore dangerous for the future of the unit and ultimately the company.

In many companies, bonuses are linked to the short-term strategy. Linking them solely to financial results is even worse because it completely disregards long-term investments needed to build a sound business environment that propels future financial success. A generic bonus system often becomes the real enemy of the business unit itself; even worse, it becomes the illness of the corporation.

Weak G&O create complacency, low efficiency, and a culture that is very difficult to change. Strong G&O demand a sense of urgency, productivity, and a culture that is flexible. Therefore, the business unit leader who really wants to succeed and create positive change needs to blend two sets of G&O components:

a) Assigned: long-term and short-term G&O cascaded or assigned to the unit from upper management

b) Self-generated: long-term and short-term G&O

Merging these two components becomes part of a more robust set of G&O that will secure a stronger future for the unit…

As Chuck returned, I finished reading the draft of his article. It was clear to me that Chuck had seen all these things happen in his many years of consulting, and they really bothered him.

"Chuck, this is good stuff. But how does this relate to alignment? I've heard you use that word so many times. And you said that once I master the alignment program, I could move on to the next phase. So what's the general purpose of the alignment program, and why do you put such emphasis on it?"

"It's very simple. Let's start with the definition of alignment. Alignment is the integration or synchronization of aims, practices, and so on, within a unit or company. This synchronization needs to be achieved by precise communication. Its implementation is tailored to the business unit's needs, and its proper execution produces excellent results and ultimately a successful unit.

"The alignment program improves a manager's ability to implement short-term strategies by increasing the focus on the goals and objectives for a given period, usually one year. The process begins by defining the unit's long- and short-term G&O. It then cascades these G&O throughout the organization to every lieutenant and employee. Like my article says, it also incorporates whatever cascades from the top of the organization."

I interjected, "Chuck, you've repeated that every business unit is different. What's your definition of a successful business unit?"

"That's a fair question. For me, a very successful business unit:

- Grows revenues;
- Grows earnings;
- Achieves growth in market share in the addressed market segments;
- Offers quality products and services, as judged by its customers and their level of satisfaction;
- Brands products or services that are recognized by customers and competitors;
- Fosters innovation;

- Provides a desirable place for talented individuals to work;
- Maintains a graceful balance between discipline, freedom, and creativity; and
- Develops leaders who are respected and admired by their employees, hierarchy, clients, competitors, shareholders, board members, and analysts."

"How does a business unit achieve all that?" I asked.

"A successful business unit excels when three managerial elements are properly executed," Chuck said with a very serious tone.

"First is the *long-term business strategy*. It relates to the deep understanding of the future potential of every piece of the business and their impact on the company as a whole. Multiyear budgets should be a derivative of this process, not the other way around.

"Second is *short-term business strategy*. This is a derivative of the long-term strategy. In many cases where companies lack a clear formulation of what the long-term strategy is, they tend to focus only on tactical elements. The short-term strategy has several functional components. These components are mostly captured by the alignment program and require a full and comprehensive coordination. Among them are short-term goals and objectives, plans, and budgets.

"Third is *operational discipline*. The alignment program requires operational discipline to foster and accelerate execution, to achieve top performance, and therefore to reach the desired results," Chuck added.

I carefully listened and took notes. I wasn't skeptical as much as I was intrigued and a little concerned that I wouldn't be able to successfully implement the method. So I continued to grill Chuck. "How does the alignment program improve the unit's performance?"

"Improvement is achieved by optimizing the performance of each and every component of the business unit through the performance of each lieutenant, manager, and employee," Chuck said.

"How do you know that this approach is going to work for my unit?" I asked.

"This approach is based on the principle of fairness. Not only does it have theoretical foundations, but it's also backed up by practical studies, real-life implementation, and constant feedback through a rigorous lessons-learned process. It has successfully passed the test of time, having produced in all cases impressive performance results."

"How many tools are involved in the alignment program?" I asked.

"The system encompasses two tools: report cards and expectation pages. The report cards are provided only to the business cell heads— your lieutenants and supervisors—to evaluate them on the basis of the business cell's performance. This also includes those responsible for internal services, even if they do not have P&L responsibility."

"So who receives the expectation page?" I asked.

"The expectation pages are provided to all employees in the unit, including the cell heads," he said.

"So my lieutenants will receive both?"

"Yes. By providing both tools to each of your lieutenants, you'll learn how to better judge them as business cell leaders and as individual contributors. Those activities are different in nature, and you will also have to learn how to distinguish between the two."

- 36 -

REPORT CARDS

"What are the goals of the report card?" I asked.

Chuck replied, "A report card, or RC, is a managerial instrument that establishes periodic communication between a manager or lieutenant and his or her subordinate supervisor in charge of a team of personnel regarding that *team's performance*. The goals of a report card are to improve unit performance, to align decision making hierarchically across the unit, and to improve performance in each subunit or business cell."

"I assume you've implemented these methods before for other companies and other business units. What's your experience regarding the benefits they achieved?"

"Report cards have benefited all my clients," Chuck said. He stood up, walked to the bookcase, retrieved a binder, flipped the pages, and showed me a listing of the most common improvements:

REPORT CARDS: BENEFITS	
Increases in:	Decreases in:
• Revenues	• Expenses
• Profits	• Losses
• Productivity	• Inefficiency
• Quality	• Employee turnover
• Morale	• Needless operational costs
	• Ineffective training

"There are three phases to managing report cards." He showed me the following page:

REPORT CARDS: 3 PHASES

1. Allocating targets
2. Implementing the tool
3. Evaluating results

Great, more tasks to add to my already long list of to-dos. The learning process was never-ending. However, I was transforming from managing from the hip to managing it right. Someday I would get my reward.

"*Phase one* is about allocating targets, or the goals and objectives, for each business cell," Chuck said. "Recall that a business cell is a group of employees performing a well-defined function and reporting to the same manager. All of your lieutenants who have other employees under their control will receive a report card. The process of building a report card for a business cell starts with understanding the company's G&O.

"It's your role to merge the company's G&O with your unit's and business cells' G&O, and come up with the right blend of targets. Be careful because not choosing the right ones will create major problems that can surface six months to a year later. That's too long to wait just for poor results."

"And I can look to the road map we developed previously to help me identify those key report card targets, right?" I asked enthusiastically.

"Exactly!"

"Can we go over some examples?"

"Targets can correspond to any of the performance components we've already discussed, including financial performance; the unit's operational performance; the business cells' operational performance; operational trends through historical data, statistics, and statistical analysis; long-term strategic performance; as well as selected parameters.

"Financial performance can include total sales, repeat sales, and profitability.

"Operational parameters can include specific internal process parameters or other external parameters, such as a certain level of customer satisfaction or service quality.

"Trends can focus on changes in sales or other parameters that seem important to you.

"Long-term strategy performance can include a partial milestone of a multiyear program or effort."

"Okay, so how do I prepare the RC tool?" I asked.

"*Phase two* is implementation. It's not very difficult, but it does require some discipline. Preparing the report card includes five steps." He showed me the following page:

IMPLEMENTING REPORT CARDS: 5 STEPS

1. Prepare the tool and allocate the targets
2. Assign weights to each target
3. Develop the grading scales
4. Discuss with your lieutenants
5. Sign off and launch

"Okay, Chuck. Can you please walk me slowly through each one of these steps, starting with allocating the targets?" I requested.

"First, you as the manager will prepare a separate report card for each business cell lieutenant. Consider the road map previously developed and allocate targets to each business cell's report card."

"Okay, but how many targets should I select for each report card?" I asked.

"Number and list up to six targets," Chuck answered categorically. "Having more than six targets dilutes the purpose. The purpose is to have your lieutenants focused on what you think is really important for your business unit. Yes, you will make mistakes at the beginning, but you will start to gain confidence and quality with time. Okay, look at the following example with only five targets." He flipped to a new page in his binder:

Date:	March 31, 2014			
Unit Name & Dept.:	BLM, Services			
Employee Name (Recipient):	John Services			
Supervisor (Preparer):	Dennis Supervisor			

#	Report Card Targets	Target Weight %	x Target Grade	= Target Results
1	Sign agreements with 28 new customers			
2	Exceed $21.5 M sales			
3	Develop another approved service			
4	Complete the X software program project before year end			
5	Increase last year's customer satisfaction by 3%			
	TOTALS			

"As you know, I have several lieutenants who oversee other employees. If each lieutenant has five or six targets, I'll end up with a large number of recommended targets," I said.

"Yes. And some of these lieutenants' employees supervise personnel as well. That means that your lieutenants will create report cards for these supervisors and their teams. Imagine that your entire business unit is focused in parallel on dozens or hundreds of targets that are important to you," Chuck said.

"That would be great. What's next?" I asked.

"Second, assign weights to those selected targets," Chuck said. "The weight distribution reflects your emphasis on the relative importance of the targets. Obviously the total equals one hundred percent."

Date:	March 31, 2014
Unit Name & Dept.:	BLM, Services
Employee Name (Recipient):	John Services
Supervisor (Preparer):	Dennis Supervisor

#	Report Card Targets	Target Weight %	x Target Grade	= Target Results
1	Sign agreements with 28 new customers	30%		
2	Exceed $21.5 M sales	20%		
3	Develop another approved service	20%		
4	Complete the X software program project before year end	10%		
5	Increase last year's customer satisfaction by 3%	20%		
	TOTALS	100%		

"Third, develop a grade scale. Come evaluation time, each target will be awarded zero to one hundred points, according to the grade scale that you developed. You can use any scale you want. At the beginning, you will face some challenges in developing the grade scale for each target."

"What do you mean by *grade scale*?" I asked.

"The scale defines how each parameter is judged. The scale reflects you and the types of targets you selected," Chuck said.

"Chuck, this sounds too theoretical for me. Can you give me some examples?" I asked.

"Sure, one type of scale is a simple binary scale. It's called binary because you either grade it one hundred points or zero points.

"Another type of scale allocates points on a subjective scale, such as this one." He showed me a chart:

Subjective Scale	Points
Very effective	100
Effective	75
Somewhat effective	0
Barely effective	0
Not effective	0

"This particular scale gives points for a certain performance. It emphasizes that performance below a certain level is unacceptable. It's up to you how you select the grading scale. There are no rules, except that the scale has to be communicated beforehand to your lieutenants. When we discuss the same process for expectation pages, we'll go through some more detailed examples," Chuck said.

"Fourth, you need to meet with your lieutenants, explain the tool, the selected targets, and grading scales. They have the right to comment and even suggest changes to your ideas. It's your responsibility to listen and keep the negotiation fair.

"Fifth, once the negotiation is complete, you and your lieutenants sign and date the report card. Not only have you undertaken a great business communication process, you're actually getting to know your people better."

"Got it, Chuck. It's not so scary anymore. I'm ready to move to the second tool, the expectation pages."

"Not so fast. There are a few more things.

"*Phase three* is evaluation at the end of the evaluation period—usually the end of the fiscal year, although there may also be a shorter period. It includes gathering results, grading, tabulating results, and reviewing these with your lieutenants.

"After collecting all the performance data, apply the grading scale previously developed and assign the grades for each target." He flipped to the following page:

Date:	March 31, 2014			
Unit Name & Dept.:	BLM, Services			
Employee Name (Recipient):	John Services			
Supervisor (Preparer):	Dennis Supervisor			

#	Report Card Targets	Target Weight %	x Target Grade	= Target Results
1	Sign agreements with 28 new customers	30%	80	
2	Exceed $21.5 M sales	20%	100	
3	Develop another approved service	20%	75	
4	Complete the X software program project before year end	10%	100	
5	Increase last year's customer satisfaction by 3%	20%	100	
	TOTALS	100%	-	

"Then tabulate the last column results for each target and sum the total score. You can see what I mean in this summary table." He showed the following page:

EXHIBIT 17:

REPORT CARD SUMMARY TABLE

Date:	March 31, 2014
Unit Name & Dept.:	BLM, Services
Employee Name (Recipient):	John Services
Supervisor (Preparer):	Dennis Supervisor

#	Expectation Page Targets	Target Weight %	x Target Grade	= Target Results
1	Sign agreements with 28 new customers	30%	80	24
2	Exceed $21.5 M sales	20%	100	20
3	Develop another approved service	20%	75	15
4	Complete the X software program project before year end	10%	100	10
5	Increase last year's customer satisfaction by 3%	20%	100	20
	TOTALS	100%	-	89

Chuck continued: "In this particular case, the unit performance score was eighty-nine. I suggest you review these report card materials, and if you have more questions, don't hesitate to contact me. Next, let's proceed with the second evaluation tool—expectation pages."

- 37 -

EXPECTATION PAGES

"Chuck, I know that these concepts are second nature to you, but if I'm going to implement this successfully, I'll have to ask you a lot of questions," I warned him.

"Please feel free to interrupt and ask all the questions you need."

"Okay. So what's an expectation page?" I asked.

"The expectation page, or EP, is a managerial instrument that establishes periodic communication between a manager, lieutenant, or supervisor and his or her subordinates regarding their *individual performance.*"

"That part is clear. What are the main differences between report cards and expectation pages?"

"While the mechanics for handling either are almost identical, the purpose is different. Report cards measure the achievements of a business cell and reflect more of a team effort. In contrast, expectation pages measure each individual's performance on a personal basis. While you may expect your lieutenant's business cell to have certain achievements, you also expect that same lieutenant to achieve personal accomplishments, such as behavioral changes, project management leadership, new business development, and so on."

"How will the employee know how he or she is doing?" I asked.

"The evaluations based on the expectation pages can take place quarterly, semiannually, or annually. With each evaluation, employees learn your, or your lieutenant's, perception on how well they meet those expectations."

"What's the purpose of using the expectation page tool?"

Chuck responded, "This document summarizes seven purposes and their corresponding benefits. You don't have to take notes; I'll give you a copy before you leave." I looked at the following document:

EXPECTATION PAGES: 7 PURPOSES AND BENEFITS

Purpose #1: Enables the business unit leader to precisely define G&O for each employee
- Corresponding Benefits:
    o Explains everyone's roles and responsibilities and how these roles and responsibilities translate into company success
    o Focuses managers on aligning employees' performance

Purpose #2: Requires a complete work-scope definition for each employee
- Corresponding Benefits:
    o Improves employee performance because they understand what is expected from them and can track their own performance

Purpose #3: Establishes a dialogue between the manager and each employee
- Corresponding Benefits:
    o Clarifies the kind of performance that is expected from the employee
    o Resolves issues that are normally otherwise ignored
    o Addresses critical performance issues

Purpose #4: Establishes periodic employee performance evaluations
- Corresponding Benefits:
    - Improves employee behavior and performance
    - Increases the probability of employee retention
    - Significantly reduces the need for unplanned replacements
    - Removes employee uncertainty
    - Establishes a basis for rewarding, retaining, promoting, and replacing employees
    - Reduces costs

Purpose #5: Identifies training needs for managerial and professional development
- Corresponding Benefits:
    - Leads to better training selections, which may in turn induce better results
    - Reduces the amount of time and dollars wasted on generic training

Purpose #6: Improves Employee Morale
- Corresponding Benefits:
    - Improves efficiency
    - Increases productivity
    - Increases creativity
    - Facilitates recruiting of new employees
    - Lowers turnover
    - Speeds integration of new employees
    - Reduces conflict in the workplace

Purpose #7: Provides a basis for the future development of a reward system
- Corresponding Benefits:
    - Reduces the amount of time required to implement a reward system

"Is it all clear?" Chuck asked.

"I'm very clear on the purposes and benefits of the expectation pages. Now I need to know more about how to implement them," I said.

"Okay, you as the unit manager will conduct a unit meeting to introduce and explain how the tool works. The process is similar to that of report cards. Just like we're doing now, you'll walk through the following three phases.

"*Phase one* is about assigning each employee with a set of personal G&O, or expectation page targets, which will align with those of the business unit and business cell. Recall the project action items we discussed previously?"

"Yes."

"You can use those content and timeliness grades to help you come up with additional expectation targets as needed. Those grades can shed light on improvement areas like behavior, technical training, accuracy, presentation skills, et cetera. Whereas project action items are very short-term based, expectation page targets are longer-term, typically six months to a year out. Additionally, your ongoing interaction with your people will help you identify other relevant targets.

"*Phase two* is the implementation sequence. This includes five steps." He showed me the following card:

EXPECTATION PAGES: 5 STEPS

1. Prepare the tool and target outcomes
2. Assign weights to each target
3. Develop the grading scales
4. Discuss and refine the tool and targets
5. Sign off and launch

"Could you please expand on each of these elements?"

"Absolutely," Chuck answered. "In the first two steps of developing expectation pages for each employee, the manager will create the initial tool, list up to six individual targets, and assign weights to each target." He showed me the following example:

EXPECTATION PAGES: SELECTED TARGETS

Date:	March 31, 2014	
Unit Name & Dept.:	BLM, Sales	
Employee Name (Recipient):	Steve Salesman	
Supervisor (Preparer):	Sally Supervisor	

#	Expectation Page Targets	Target Weight %	x Target Grade	= Target Result
1	Annual sales objective of $1,000,000	30%		
2	New client sales objective of $350,000	25%		
3	Contact 100% of existing customer base every quarter	15%		
4	Sales efforts made at exhibits, meetings, and conferences	10%		
5	Product/services knowledge	15%		
6	Tracking and reporting sales	5%		
	TOTALS	100%		

"After that, develop the details of the grading scale. Here are the details for each target in our example." He handed me the following sheets:

Target 1: Annual sales objective of $1,000,000

Date:	March 31, 2014
Unit Name & Dept.:	BLM, Sales
Employee Name (Recipient):	Steve Salesman
Supervisor (Preparer):	Sally Supervisor

Scoring policy: 90 points for achieving $1,000,000 in sales. Bonus points if sales goal is exceeded by 15% ($1,150,000).

Possible Outcomes	Points
Achieved annual sales greater than $1,150,000	100
Achieved annual sales greater than $1,000,000	90
Achieved annual sales greater than $900,000 but less than $1,000,000	75
Achieved annual sales less than $900,000	0

Target 2: New client sales objective of $350,000

Date:	March 31, 2014
Unit Name & Dept.:	BLM, Sales
Employee Name (Recipient):	Steve Salesman
Supervisor (Preparer):	Sally Supervisor

Scoring policy: 90 points for achieving $350,000 in new sales. Bonus points if sales goal is exceeded by 15%.

Possible Outcomes	Points
Achieved new client sales greater than $402,500	100
Achieved new client sales greater than $350,000	90
Achieved new client sales greater than $250,000 but less than $350,000	75
Achieved new client sales less than $250,000	0

Target 3: Contact 100% of existing customer base every quarter

Date:	March 31, 2014
Unit Name & Dept.:	BLM, Sales
Employee Name (Recipient):	Steve Salesman
Supervisor (Preparer):	Sally Supervisor

Scoring policy: Sales rep will contact all existing customers at least once a month.

Possible Outcomes	Points
Contacted 100% of existing customers	100
Contacted between 90% and 99% of existing customers	85
Contacted between 75% and 89% of existing customers	75
Contacted less than 75% of existing customers	0

Target 4: Sales efforts made at exhibits, meetings, and conferences

Date:	March 31, 2014
Unit Name & Dept.:	BLM, Sales
Employee Name (Recipient):	Steve Salesman
Supervisor (Preparer):	Sally Supervisor

Scoring policy: Sales rep attracts prospects to booth, develops rapport with them, and ascertains sales opportunities.

Possible Outcomes	Points
Excellent	100
Very Good	90
Acceptable	60
Unacceptable	0

Outcome Definitions:

Excellent

Easily attracts prospects to booth, quickly develops rapport with prospects, and quickly ascertains if a sales opportunity exists

Very Good

Attracts prospects to booth with some effort, develops rapport with prospects, and ascertains if a sales opportunity exists

Acceptable

Generally attracts prospects to booth, develops rapport with prospects, and generally can find out if a sales opportunity exists

Unacceptable

Seldom attracts prospects to booth, does not develop rapport with prospects, and seldom discovers a sales opportunity

TARGET 5: PRODUCT/SERVICES KNOWLEDGE

Date:	March 31, 2014
Unit Name & Dept.:	BLM, Sales
Employee Name (Recipient):	Steve Salesman
Supervisor (Preparer):	Sally Supervisor

Possible Outcomes	Points
Highly knowledgeable about product/services	100
Very knowledgeable about product/services	95
Good overall knowledge of product/services	75
Lacks sufficient knowledge of product/services	0

Outcome Definitions:

Highly knowledgeable about product/services:
Knows every aspect of product/services and is always up-to-date on any changes

Very knowledgeable about product/services:
Knows almost every aspect of product/services but has a few gaps in knowledge and is generally up-to-date on changes

Good overall knowledge of product/services:
Knowledgeable in most aspects of the product and services; needs to increase both overall knowledge and stay current on changes

Lacks sufficient knowledge of product/services:
Does not have a good overall knowledge of products/services and is not up-to-date on changes

---

TARGET 6: TRACKING AND REPORTING SALES

Date:	March 31, 2014
Unit Name & Dept.:	BLM, Sales
Employee Name (Recipient):	Steve Salesman
Supervisor (Preparer):	Sally Supervisor

Scoring policy: Sales data is submitted to the sales recording system on the first business day after month-end.

Timeliness \ Quality	Excellent	Very Good	Satisfactory	Unsatisfactory
On time	100	90	60	0
2nd day	80	70	50	0
3–5 days	70	60	40	0
> 5 days	0	0	0	0

"In step four, every manager holds one-on-one meetings with each of his employees. The manager explains the selection of targets and their importance as well as the grading scales. During these discussions, the employee may suggest modifications. If any modifications are required, the employee and manager will have a subsequent meeting to review the modified tool.

"Finally, the manager and the employee sign and date the expectation page and officially launch it."

"Chuck, it seems to me that my business unit managers will have to invest some time in this. As you know, time is a scarce resource," I said.

"I'm glad you brought this issue up. The main reason that time is a scarce resource is because you as well as many of your employees spend time on issues that wouldn't exist at all if you already had such a system in place. This system of report cards and expectation pages minimizes leaving landmines behind."

"Well, when you're right, you're right. I've learned this the hard way. I'm committed to following your suggestions, and I'll start preparing for implementation," I said.

"Okay. *Phase three* deals with the end-of-period evaluation phase. It includes gathering results; grading each target; calculating target results; and discussing findings with the employee."

"Tell me more about the evaluation phase. This is delicate, since I'll need to face each individual and let him or her know what I think about them specifically," I said.

"At the end of the period, the manager gathers the results for the selected targets. The sources for these data may include the accounting department, the human resources department, customer surveys, and so on.

"Once the results are collected, the manager may proceed to grade the employee. Given the employee's final performance for the period under review, and based on the grading scale for each grading target, the manager assigns the score that corresponds to each target.

"Now look at the summary table." He showed me the following summary table:

EXHIBIT 18:

	EXPECTATION PAGES SUMMARY TABLE			
	Date:	March 31, 2014		
	Unit Name & Dept.:	BLM, Sales		
	Employee Name (Recipient):	Steve Salesman		
	Supervisor (Preparer):	Sally Supervisor		

#	Expectation Page Targets	Target Weight %	x Target Grade	= Target Results
1	Annual sales objective of $1,000,000	30%	90	27
2	New client sales objective of $350,000	25%	90	22.5
3	Contacting 100% of existing customer base every quarter	15%	85	12.75
4	Sales efforts made at exhibits, meetings, and conferences	10%	90	9
5	Product/services knowledge	15%	75	11.25
6	Tracking and reporting sales	5%	70	3.5
	TOTALS	100%	-	86

"After grading the employee in the target grade column, the manager tabulates the target results column and totals the final score. See, Dennis, this methodology of grading and score calculating is identical to the report cards.

"The manager and employee meet to review the graded expectation page. They can discuss any issue. Immediately after the evaluation, they begin preparing for the next evaluation cycle and expectation page. It may have minor or substantial changes, depending on the most recent results and other changes to the company's, unit's, or business cell's goals and objectives."

"Chuck, I think I now understand the theory. I'll need to train my lieutenants, and ultimately all the employees."

"Absolutely. Use these examples to practice and train with. As you review the theory, practice with different weights, grading scales, and grades."

- 38 -

Bonus Compensation

"Chuck, now that I more clearly understand the alignment approach, how can you convert its results into establishing a bonus compensation system?" I asked.

"Yes, it's very simple. At year-end or every six months, you, as the business unit leader, will sit with each of the lieutenants and derive his or her individual performance score by combining the results of the report cards and the expectation pages. In accordance with your business beliefs and the business unit's G&O, you can decide to weigh the report card and expectation page results equally, or weigh them differently—for example, give more weight to the report card or more weight to the expectation page. It depends on what you prefer to emphasize. Remember, always share your intentions with your employees," Chuck said.

"Okay. Can you describe an example?"

Chuck took a piece of paper and said, "You decide what is considered an acceptable grade, below which the employee is considered inept to continue the journey. If we use the combined scores from our previous examples—a report card score of eighty-nine and an expectation page score of eighty-six—and you decided to weigh them equally to get to his final grade, the combined score, also called R_i, can be calculated as:

$$R_i = (RC * 50\%) + (EP * 50\%)$$
$$R_i = (50\% * 89) + (50\% * 86) = 87.5$$

"Now, assuming all the individuals reporting to you passed the aptitude threshold and that a certain pool of money is available for distribution among the lieutenants, you, as the business leader, can decide the maximum individual bonus each of the lieutenants can receive.

"Remember that you have to work very hard during the coming year to help each lieutenant achieve satisfactory results. In spite of your efforts, at the end of the period, one or more of your lieutenants may fall short of expectations."

"Chuck, in the example you just described, the calculated score was eighty-seven and a half. How should I proceed to calculate the bonus amount?" I asked.

"One method to calculate the lieutenant's bonus is to multiply the maximum amount allotted for his or her bonus by his performance score."

"Are there any other ways to do it?" I asked.

"There are many approaches, and all are acceptable, provided you feel you're providing a fair solution. The money pool available to you can be distributed according to the weight provided by the individual result." He showed me the following formula:

EXHIBIT 19:

BONUS FORMULA

$$B_i = \textbf{Bonus Pool} * R_i / \Sigma R_j \text{, where}$$

B_i = Individual bonus

Bonus Pool = Total money available to pay out as bonuses

R_i = Individual's RC-EP score

ΣR_j = Sums the results of all participants in the pool (for example, a pool of lieutenants)

"Some business unit managers prefer other methods. For example, if the Ri score is between:

- $0 < Ri < X$, the bonus is zero (0);
- $X < Ri < Y$, the bonus is half of Bi (50%); and
- $Y < Ri < 100$, the bonus is all of Bi (100%).

"You determine what X and Y are as you see fit and fair, and always remember to be as transparent as possible. In summary, you can select any of the three methods presented above. My recommendation is to use the one you feel most comfortable with, as long you feel it's fair. The sense of fairness will help you in the case that some of the lieutenants require a deeper explanation."

This had been a long session. I was tired, but I knew that this would help dramatically in my business communication. Since it applied to all managers and employees, no one was going to feel as if they had been singled out with a specific problem. I liked that.

Chuck was instrumental in implementing the new process. He gave a general presentation on the subject to the unit's employees, and then, together with Richard, he conducted intense training for all the members of the unit. Chuck and Richard provided a theoretical presentation first, complemented by practical exercises. Questions came up, and answers were provided to all. We worked on the process for a few weeks until we reached the first launch day. The process with the lieutenants was a bit slower, since each one of them had to learn, prepare, and go through both tools. I helped them regarding the selection, weighing, and grading scales for each of the employees. We then launched the employees' expectation pages.

At first glance, these events seemed administrative, but the outcome was magical! Things started to change almost immediately: revenue and profitability went up, and expenses went down. It was exactly as Chuck had predicted, but I never imagined that change would be so quick. The unit started to operate like a well-oiled machine. I was happy, proud, and thankful.

- 39 -

COLLAPSE AND RECOVERY

I got an e-mail from Chuck, letting me know that the Society of Practical Business Management had invited him to participate in a panel discussion. This time the topic was "Outsourcing and Its Implications." Since my unit had been a target for outsourcing for so long, I had a keen interest in attending and hearing what he had to say.

Although I had a scheduling conflict, I was determined to make it, and somehow I arrived just in time for Chuck's presentation. When I entered the building, the lobby monitor showed Chuck being introduced. He was well known to the society as an innovator in the area of business management, and the audience gave him a warm reception. This time, many executives were also in attendance. I took a seat and started recording his presentation:

"For those of you who attended my other presentations in this series, this is the final one. For those who missed them and would like transcripts of those presentations, please contact me, and I'll forward you copies.

"The entertainment industry has had—and continues to have—a growing influence on making education less complex and more fun. American students' performance—in particular in math and science, as compared with countries in Europe and Asia—has continued to degrade." He showed the following slide:

EXHIBIT 20:

OVERSIMPLIFYING MATH LESSONS: THEN AND NOW

THEN: A car dealer sells a car for $10,000. The cost of production and other expenses is 4/5 of the selling price. How much is the profit?

NOW: A car dealer sells a car for $10,000. The cost of production and other expenses is $8,000. How much is the profit?

( ) $2,000 ( ) $4,000 ( ) $6,000 ( ) $8,000 ( ) $10,000

"Many students are developing multiple-choice-based decision-making skills, not critical-thinking-based problem-solving skills. By the time they get to management positions and they're facing management problems, some of these individuals are expecting someone to offer them a multiple-choice set of alternative solutions. Real life doesn't usually work like that. You can see how some managers are growing up without sufficient problem-solving skills to lead their businesses.

"With the constant pressure to improve performance, they have learned to optimize profits only by cutting costs. They start with eliminating job perks and eventually evolve to outsourcing. This trend has ballooned to massive overseas outsourcing and has fueled what's come to be known as *globalization.* The short-term rationale for this movement has been this." He showed and read from the following slide:

GLOBALIZATION: SHORT-TERM RATIONALE

a) The United States is a slow-growth market, and American companies should tap into international markets.

b) Expected financial performance can be achieved through cost reductions.

c) Problems and challenges that cannot be solved in-house should be transferred to someone else.

"The long-term results of globalization on American business include the following." He showed the next slide:

GLOBALIZATION: LONG-TERM EFFECTS

a) An irreversible transfer of knowledge to other countries.

b) A massive transfer of wealth.

c) An almost irreversible transfer of jobs.

d) A negative balance of payments due to addictive purchasing of cheaper foreign products and services.

e) New foreign competition.

"This transfer of wealth has accelerated the emerging countries' absorption of knowledge and technology at an unprecedented speed never seen before in the history of mankind. What other countries couldn't achieve in thousands of years, they accomplished in a few decades.

"America has created its own nightmare. Globalization and foreign competition have continued to challenge American businesses to generate profits by cutting costs. Instead of managing a complex situation, some managers have become addicted to outsourcing. When poorly managed, this has created worse side effects. This process can be referred to as a negative cycle of *overoptimization and collapse.*"

Chuck flipped to his next slide and continued: "What is *overoptimization and collapse?* It's how short-term cost cutting reduces immediate risks at the expense of long-term resources, like knowledge, talent, expertise, and creativity. Experienced personnel are replaced by lower-paid, inexperienced, untrained, and ill-guided new managers. The younger generation can't respond to the company's needs. The mentors are gone.

"Key employees are overloaded with demands for higher levels of productivity. They improve efficiency—but at the expense of effectiveness. At this stage, pushing for optimization through continuous improvement programs seems like a noble idea. However, most of these programs yield tactical gains, with limited impact on what's really needed. A temporary gain of one percent in the efficiency rating may not be enough to avoid the collapse of a unit's effectiveness. Continuous improvement is mostly tactical, while achieving effectiveness is strategic. We have witnessed time and again how a small reduction in costs has led to substantial revenue losses and has ultimately reduced profits.

"Many values are lost, and, out of survival, many bad habits are quickly acquired. There's low morale, poor behavior, poor attendance, less productivity, and more sick days. There's no sense of ownership. Nobody is responsible. Nobody has answers. Systems do not work well. Nobody wants to go the extra mile. Going to work in a collapsed unit has become a chore—only to pay personal bills and send kids to college. It lacks meaning. Self-development and self-realization don't matter.

"What follows is lower-quality products, services, and customer service. The lack of respect for customers and vendors lowers customer satisfaction. Customer complaints increase, product recalls increase, more customers leave, and revenues decline. Unfortunately, this revenue loss far outweighs the savings from cost cutting; profits cannot be sustained, and they are doomed to disappear. So in the face of collapse, being penny-wise ends up being pound-foolish."

Chuck paused for the audience to quiet down and then continued: "When it comes to *overoptimization and collapse*, the auto industry is one of the classic, unforgettable, and most damaging stories in recent history. After decades of losing market share, auto execs ended up with a routine: they announced a cost-cutting program, Wall Street analysts applauded, stock prices went up, plants closed, people lost their jobs, foreign companies gained market share, revenues went down, profits disappeared, stock prices fell, and then it was time to repeat the cycle."

Chuck flipped to his next slide and continued: "So what about *recovery*? For those same managers and executives mentioned before, it has meant possibly outsourcing the entire business as a way to wash their hands, look good in the process, and possibly extend their careers. However, it's very hard to outsource a collapsed business. And you can only outsource so much for so long before there's nothing left to outsource. Maybe that's okay for the retiring generation, but what about the younger generations who need to work and feed their families?"

Chuck paused. Again, as with any of Chuck's presentations, you could feel tension in the air. Many of the executives in the audience were living proof of the examples Chuck had presented. They didn't like it.

"Well, if the answer isn't outsourcing, what is it? Simply put, ladies and gentlemen, it's the opportunity to build something new; to work hard and build a unit that lasts; to urgently adopt a new set of values; and to invite tremendous attention from outside resources, such as consultants and specialists. It takes effort to rebuild infrastructure, increase team size, develop capabilities, change the culture, and, overall, establish new quality standards. A well-managed recovery provides new opportunities to build value—first through stability and then through growth.

"Recovering from collapse is similar to turning around a failing business or to growing a successful one. The depth and the intensity required may be different." Chuck showed the next slide:

RECOVERY PHASES

1) Diagnostics

2) Analysis of weaknesses

3) Business architecture

4) Functional organization

5) Detailed organization

6) Transitional organization

7) Sustainable organization

8) Strategic issues

9) Short-term goals and objectives, including

     a.   Short-term strategy

     b.   Projects definition

     c.   Budgeting

     d.   Alignment and metrics

10) Short-term operational management

11) Long-term goals and objectives, including

     a.   Long-term strategy

     b.   Road map

12) Long-term operational management

13) Redistribution of responsibilities

14) Clarification of employee expectations

15) Establishment of the right metrics that lead to results

16) Implementation of the rules for hierarchical alignment

"Once business stability is achieved, long-term planning takes precedence over tactical execution. We have used this approach for decades with amazing results; I hope you will adopt it as well." Chuck paused. "Thank you for your attention. Please, let's open up the floor to questions."

I was late for a family event, so I left as quickly and unobtrusively as I could. I missed the Q&A session, but I figured I already knew many of the questions and their answers. I had enjoyed the presentation—especially because I was connecting the dots. I could see now that BLM went through overoptimization and collapse. My work with Chuck was BLM's collapse recovery, and we were going through all the change-management principles and phases. The big picture made sense.

- 40 -

SELF-EVALUATION #5

When I woke up the following morning, the first thing on my mind was that six months had passed since my last self-evaluation. I wanted to update it with some notes that would help me navigate through the end of the year.

I opened my evaluation folder and started to grade myself.

---

1. Content
Grade: A- (up from B)

The change design dashboard tool has been helpful in clarifying my next moves. It helped me take the time to understand details of BLM that I otherwise would not. I think I'm getting pretty good at this skill.

Managerial Modification: Although one of my lieutenants, S, has moved slowly, I believe she has grasped this concept better than others. I have spent a great deal of time with another lieutenant, M, on managing his function, but I will not know the results for another few months. I am pessimistic regarding how much he will internalize. Y has made progress in cleaning up customer data prior to assigning accounts. She is willing to put in the time to make sure data is correct, but she has not put the same effort into to standardizing sales activities. This is due to lack of confidence.

Challenge: Get my management team to think strategically about job functions and establish enough job description details so employees are clearer about their roles.

2. *Tools*

2.1 Action Items:
Grade: C- (down from B)

This was an item I let slide. Unfortunately, my direct reports and I have not gotten the maximum value out of the action items tool. I will commit to a renewed approach next year.

Managerial Modifications: Use the rating system for action items with employees. Provide regular feedback as part of any discussion of action items.

Challenge: Need to be more disciplined to keep up on this.

2.2 Matrices:
Grade: C (no change)

This is another area where the time to do homework did not materialize. It is hard to develop and maintain this discipline. I have been trained to skip steps to save time. Although cheaper in the short run, this is expensive in the long run after including rework.

Managerial Modification: Perform homework on all BLM-identified weaknesses.

Challenge: Self-discipline.

2.3 Homework
Grade: C (up from C-)

2.4 Other Tools
Grade: C (no change)

I need to make this a more natural part of my management style. I need to be more direct with employees when asking them how they are spending their time.

Managerial Modification: Using these items to help employees think about ways to be more productive and evaluate their progress and their employees' progress. I will work to incorporate the use of this information into periodic performance discussions.

3. Management

3.1 Managing up

3.1.1 Managing requests
Grade: C+ (up from D)

I slipped up on this once or twice. I still react too quickly when summoned, but I'm getting better. I also think the quality of my responses is better. We had a customer council team that addressed complaints, and right before Christmas, they sent me a request regarding a complaints plan for the present year. I took my time, developed a response, cancelled a meeting they had scheduled with me to discuss my response, and the end result was that the customer council manager was thrilled with my timely and effective response.

Managerial Modification: I will apply a twenty-four-hour rule to all e-mail requests from my hierarchy and other departments that create assignments for me. I will attempt to identify the strategic value of the request as it relates to my goals as a manager.

3.1.2 Avoiding/inviting pressure
Grade: B+ (up from B)

I'm doing better at this. I'm learning to keep my mouth shut at the appropriate time (no easy task!). I looked at the commitments we made to Greg in March, and I realized that we fulfilled our promises. This was only because we did not commit to things we could not deliver. This has not been my experience in other years. I typically somewhat overcommit and then cannot live up to my expectations.

3.1.3 Controlling meetings
Grade: A- (up from B)

I think I have gotten a lot better at this skill. I have moved the steering committee into becoming more of an advisory panel. This is a big change from the first meetings of asking/begging for approvals. Two skills I need to improve on are:

1. Being succinct in my communications and able to explain things clearly and quickly.
2. Controlling my emotions and using the skills I've learned to maintain dialogue in crucial conversations.

3.2 Managing down

3.2.1 Evaluating employee performance
Grade: B (no change)

I have spent a great deal of time with my direct reports discussing their performance. I had formal performance discussions with M and R. I let A know that I was disappointed in the IT support we received, and I let S and T know that their inability to deliver on time was unacceptable. I did not have specific performance discussions with D or Y. These discussions are hard for me and take a lot of my time. I think I overrated my performance on this skill in the past. I was probably at more of a C level. I'm glad Chuck helped me launch the alignment program. I know it will help a lot.

3.2.2 Supporting employees and deciding if they can contribute
Grade: B (up from C-)

I actually spent a great deal of time one-on-one with employees on their projects, particularly A, K, S, and M. The results of these efforts are in the end products. For IT and contracts, we have achieved a level of success; for engineering, it is still somewhat unknown. I still need to be more direct in making assignments and following up (see action items) and holding employees accountable.

Managerial Modification: I will work to make initial assignments as "crisp" as possible prior to meeting with the employee. I will set up progress reviews that are very frequent at the beginning of the project and less frequent as the project moves forward. I will set up "jam sessions" with employees to actually do some of the work with them to make sure they understand the assignment. I cannot wait to see the results of the alignment program.

3.2.3 Monitoring employees
Grade: C (no change)

I did not use the action items and other tools to monitor as I should have. Monitoring is necessary over the next year because it is the only way that nonperformers will step up or move on. This will be a major priority.

The November meeting with the engineers was very effective. I planned to conduct a similar meeting with account reps but ran out of time. I need to spend more time in casual conversations with employees. They gladly tell me things that the supervisors reporting to me might not. I learn a lot with employees. The customer visits with the account reps are very valuable. I learn a lot riding with them, and I get to observe their customer interaction skills. I need to make these interviews a higher priority next year.

4. Time Management
Grade: B (up from C+)

This change has been due to necessity. I was managing time better before, but I had less to do. Now I feel like I try desperately to manage time, yet I never seem to have time for all the things I have to do. While I know my time management skills have improved, I still have trouble keeping up. I continue to work on this skill. I am much better than last year. It is difficult for me to conduct one-on-one sessions with employees efficiently and effectively. To be effective often takes a great deal of time. I am not comfortable delegating many meetings because I am not confident of the outcome. I will revisit the engineering meetings in January and see how T is doing.

Managerial Modification: I will set aside one-half to one day per week to work from home or some other quiet spot to concentrate on planning only.

Challenge: Time.

5. Controlling Emotions
Grade: B- (up from C)

Some of the things that we have talked about have helped me greatly.

I now know that my ability to think through an issue and brainstorm a good answer over a day or two is a strength rather than a weakness. I now can capitalize on that strength and use it to my advantage. I still struggle with becoming frustrated with others. Employees don't always place the same importance and urgency on their tasks that I think they should. The overall environment sometimes seems built to frustrate the efforts of even the best employees.

I have learned a lot in the last six months about things I can do differently. I have applied those new skills, and they worked.

Managerial Modification: I need to consciously continue to use these skills so I don't backslide to any bad habits.

6. Decision Making

6.1 Strategic versus tactical items
Grade: B (up from C+)

I am getting better at this. I know in the past few months, I have had a better understanding of which activities are strategic, and this knowledge has helped me to better manage my employees and their tasks. Taking the time to connect action items to goals (or seeing that the action items in many cases do not connect) has helped me place the appropriate level of urgency and importance on what I do. This will help in time management and other areas.

Managerial Modification: Since I currently have only one main goal (customer satisfaction), I will work to determine which of the decisions I am asked to make will impact my primary goal. I will strongly weigh in favor of positively impacting customer satisfaction, even at the risk of sacrificing time or money.

6.2 Action-reaction versus multiple variables
Grade: B- (up from C)

The dashboard tool helped me a lot. I understand how to judge the strategic impact of a particular action. The example on the metrics (tying it back to the goal) was helpful. I also understand the concept of molecular biology to arrive at the correct answer. The funny thing is we usually don't allow time for this work and then end up with the wrong decision, only to cause an additional waste of time and energy far greater than if I had done it right in the first place. I still make what I think is the right decision only to find myself arguing with Chuck later because he has a different "right" decision.

6.3 "Patching decisions" and reversibility
Grade: B (up from C+)

I made some personnel decisions that I would have done differently if I had it to do over. My biggest regret is not sitting in on interviews. This would have given me some basis to compare candidates.

6.4 Defending your own logic
Grade: B (up from C)

I think I have done better here, as evidenced in recent steering committee meetings.

7. Discipline

7.1 Self-discipline
Grade: C (down from C+)

This is a continuing struggle. I sometimes feel like I am one of the few people in my group applying discipline to myself and my work. Because of the quantity of things that need to be done, discipline is necessary. It is not logical, but a part of me wants to rebel against the discipline.

8. Fighting Power
Grade: C (no change)

I felt like giving up a few months ago, because of the new backlog. I'm still struggling with work input versus reward. I'm not very good at asking for what I believe I'm worth. This is something I would like to learn more about next year. I need to focus on the work/exercise/rest cycle. I need to place the same priority on exercise and rest that I do on work. I need to allow my body and mind time to regenerate. This will be a priority for the next quarter.

- 41 -

BUSINESS VALUATION

Friends told me that Chuck's presentation at the Society of Practical Business Management was excellent, in particular the way he handled the Q&A session. I felt a sense of pride. I called Chuck, congratulated him on the presentation, and scheduled our next meeting at his place. His place was our lab. It was the only place I felt really free to ask questions, learn, bounce ideas around, and make thoughtful decisions.

When we met, I briefed Chuck on my last self-evaluation and the dramatic progress we were making. When I first took over BLM, everybody was disorganized. It was like they were little children playing pee-wee football and everyone was chasing after the ball. Now, everybody in my unit knew exactly what was going on and what was expected from them. My unit went from having no report card and expectation page targets at all to many. Every employee had six expectation page targets, and each lieutenant and supervisor had six additional report card targets. Everyone started to play their positions. Now, for the first time, it was more like a professional football team.

After I completed my story, Chuck said, "It's like an owner who wants his horse to win every race. A horse can't race if it's not in peak condition. And a horse can't race without a good jockey. If the owner wants to win, his horse and jockey need to be at their best.

"Originally, the value of your unit was negligible or even worse. It was a liability to the company's reputation and a prime candidate for outsourcing without any profit potential to the company. This has been a long and intense process of healing a unit from an illness that almost killed it and converting it into a profitable, contributing unit. In fact, there are but a few complaints and no negative press articles; on the contrary, you've received many thanks and praise letters.

"When we first started implementing this methodology, we needed to adjust all the nuts and bolts in your organization. You've gone through the phases of diagnostics, team building, operational improvement, monitoring, and control. You're shifting from dealing with numerous managerial adjustments to just a few well-defined issues that will result in modifications and updates to BLM's long-term strategy, short-term strategy, and the road map. Your road map is a work in progress. During this period, the hierarchy has only seen the tip of the iceberg and hasn't perceived major progress.

"As the corrective projects are completed, and BLM starts to become more cohesive and more confident in its capability to perform, it'll be time to focus on a few additional issues that will make the difference between a normal unit and a successful one. In the coming months, we have the opportunity to spin off BLM into a subsidiary that the company can grow or sell. There's a lot of value to the company because BLM will have reached a point of stability; it will have overcome many or most of the previous messes it was encountering. The return on investment on spinning off a subsidiary can be very high, especially if the company decides to sell it. Now that your unit is gaining ground, it's time to plan again."

"Chuck, if they consider the prospects of a spin-off, how will Peter and the other executives judge me? Will they focus only on profitability?"

"They may. But remember, while profitability numbers can be achieved by cutting costs, that's rarely enough to succeed because it's not a sustainable practice. The right approach requires building the right internal stability that can and does foster growth, and that's what increases your business unit value."

"Valuation at the lower levels of the hierarchy is almost a nonexistent concept," I said.

"You're correct. Although revenues and earnings are important, valuation is the best indicator for measuring the performance of a business unit. Understanding this concept and learning how to calculate it will make you a more well-rounded leader. Just like companies do, business units can also measure their annual change in business unit valuation. Do you remember when we introduced the decision-making concept of Q_{DM}? Valuation includes selecting future parameters that shape the Q_{DM} function of the business unit."

"What's the simplest way to do this?" I asked.

"Try using NPV, or net present value, as a valuation tool. It requires decisions regarding the cost of capital, future business growth, new product development, service policies, and so on. Looking only at current profitability does not give you the full story, because it just tells you about the past," he said.

I was taking notes nonstop. With my unit's progress, I was hungry for more success. "What other methods do you suggest using to calculate valuation?"

"Valuation methods vary with the economy's growth, the company's growth, prevailing interest rates, net cash generation, sentiment, and other factors. Many are based on multiples of historical performance. Some methods use multiples of EBTDA— or earnings before taxes, depreciation, and amortization. In fast-growing companies, they may also use multiples of sales. Book value is another way to estimate the value of the business, that is, assets less liabilities. Liquidation valuation reflects how much the business will be worth if it's liquidated. All methods based on multiples rely on comparables, meaning the prices by which similar companies were sold.

"Valuation based on future performance relies mostly on the net present value method, or NPV. Although you can get these results by using an Excel program or even a business calculator, it's important to understand the fundamentals of this calculation."

"What do you mean by the fundamentals?" I asked.

"NPV includes a sequence of cash flows. It inputs the future cash flows of the operation and a discount rate, like the company's cost of capital, and outputs a value. Each cash inflow and outflow is discounted back to its present value, or PV. Then they are summed." Chuck walked over to his white board and wrote:

$$\text{NPV} = \sum_{t=0}^{N} \frac{R_t}{(1+i)^t} \text{ , where}$$

t is the time of each cash flow, most commonly expressed in years;

i is the discount rate, or the rate of return that could be earned on an investment in the financial markets with similar risk; it's also referred to as the opportunity cost of capital;

R_t is the net cash flow or the amount of cash inflow, minus the cash outflow, at time t; and

N is the total number of periods.

"It seems the value of the terms decreases with time," I observed.

"Yes, since the value of the terms decreases as t—the number of periods—grows, the number of periods needed for calculation purposes can be limited; at a future point in time, the additional terms do not add to the final value," he said.

"And how would you select the discount rate?"

"The discount rate is the rate used to discount future cash flows to the present value and is a key variable of this process. In general, a business unit usually doesn't have the capability to borrow money, and therefore the firm's weighted average cost of capital, after tax, is often used. Another related concept is to use the firm's reinvestment rate. The reinvestment rate can be defined as the rate of return for the firm's investments on average," Chuck said.

"Should I use only one fixed rate?"

"You could use a variable discount rate with higher rates applied to cash flows occurring further along the time span to reflect the yield curve premium for long-term debt. An NPV calculated using variable discount rates better reflects the real situation than one calculated from a constant discount rate for the entire investment duration. While using variable rates over time may be a superior methodology, it's seldom used in practice."

"How accurate is this method?"

"The NPV formula is sound, but using such a formula may overprice the valuation because it doesn't explicitly discount for *risk*," he said.

"How could risk be incorporated to make the calculation more accurate?"

"There are several ways to try to incorporate risk in these calculations," Chuck said. "On the one hand, you can reduce the numerator by discounting the net cash terms, or R_t by some factor. On the other hand, you can increase the denominator by using a higher cost of capital. Either way reduces the value of the terms in the equation and the aggregate valuation."

"What factor should I use?"

"Your best bet is to do some sensitivity analysis by trying different values for each of the risk elements. You'll end up with a range of values for the final valuation as a function of risk. Using the discount rate to adjust for risk is often difficult to do in practice, especially internationally, where currency conversion rates may also play a role. Also, different people assess risk differently. For example, an investment bank prices an initial public offering at a certain value per share based on its laundry list of assumptions. However, different

investors use different assumptions, and a few days later, the stock
ends up trading at above or below its original IPO value.

"Using several methods to value the business unit year after year
will add to the problem-finding efforts, helping you make better
decisions. It will also provide a fair way to compare the different
available methods. You could also repeat the effort for every business
cell to better understand how each impacts the business unit. Does
this make sense?"

"It does. I'm sure it'll be more obvious once I start applying it."

We spent the rest of our meeting looking at and valuing the
different business cells. At the end of the day, we wrapped up our
meeting and I headed home, my head spinning with excitement
about these new perspectives.

Time was flying by. I met Chuck the following Wednesday, but this
time we met at the company in the northern conference room. I
could see the river from there. It was a nice view, although my office
was only on the tenth floor.

We were still having problems with the HR department's rules and
regulations. Everybody knew we needed better-quality employees,
but I couldn't get them from elsewhere inside the company, and
there was a hiring freeze on candidates outside the company.

Chuck arrived on time dressed in his suit and tie and looking
very sharp. We both grabbed a cup of water from the cooler and sat.

"Hi, Dennis," he said. "I'd like to share something interesting."

"Go ahead," I said. I knew he had an inside scoop.

"I met with Greg. I told him about the progress we've made,
in spite of the lack of recognition from others. As you know, I've
worked with Greg for many years, and we've developed a deep trust
and mutual respect. I came to him with an idea.

"I asked Greg if he was ready to spin off BLM. He smiled
and asked me if I thought this unit, which a little more than a
year ago was in desperate condition, could stand alone and be

independent and profitable. I told Greg that profitability is up, the team is stronger, the infrastructure is better than ever, there is a sense of purpose, discipline is at its highest in many years, you are working very hard, and you're developing yourself as a leader. Greg said he's seen a similar spin-off situation in the past. He's open to hear you make your case before making a final decision. I told Greg that we would find time in our calendars, and we would meet soon."

Greg was the president, and this meeting could be very important for me. "How soon do you think?" I asked with some hesitation.

"Listen, Dennis, you don't have to sweat too much. We can use the presentation you prepared for the steering committee, update a few numbers, and add a few slides that specifically support the spin-off," Chuck said.

I started doing just that. The date was set. In about three weeks, I had to present the spin-off proposal to the president. I worked with Chuck as usual, exchanging e-mails, PowerPoint slides, tables, and ideas. I started to gain more confidence; we were really making progress.

Although he was invited to the meeting, Peter was unavailable and excused himself. The meeting with Greg took place and we presented the issue of valuation. With all the adjustments we made, and with all the good things that were happening, we were sure that we could finish that year with an EBDTA of $25 million. It was really amazing. Depending on the multiple used, valuation could be in the range of $180 million to $250 million. I marveled to myself, "A quarter of a billion dollars, for something that was considered a worthless liability only two years ago?"

My meeting with Greg and Chuck was very successful. Greg asked Jen, his strategic advisor, to review the numbers to make sure that everything was exactly as presented. Greg was extremely happy. It confirmed his instincts to hire Chuck and made our project very legitimate, particularly considering that two years ago the company almost outsourced the unit's function with zero income.

A few days later, Greg said that he would like us to meet with the company's in-house counsel to explore spinning off a subsidiary. Although it was a great vote of confidence, the timing was bad. The company had recently fired most of its in-house lawyers and transferred their workload to an outside law firm. Because a spin-off required a lot of effort, as well as involving unions in some decisions, it was too embryonic to outsource the legal work. The lead in-house attorney even said that the company could get a better value for the buck by doing the legal work in-house. The reality, however, was that the few remaining in-house lawyers already had more work than they could handle. Without anyone to do the work, this sail lost its wind.

- 42 -

MANAGING IT RIGHT!

Chuck was not planning to give up, but while preparing to meet with Greg again, we received more unexpected news. Greg had suffered a heart attack. He was hospitalized and survived a triple-bypass operation. The rumor of Greg's departure from the company would soon be fact. A few weeks after his recovery, Greg formally announced he was retiring by year-end.

On December fifth, Greg retired from the company for which he had worked for thirty-two years. The company honored Greg with a very large farewell party. Chuck and his wife, Irene, attended. Greg and Chuck had gone through a lot together, and in spite of the many challenges they'd faced, they had always prevailed. They were like warrior brothers.

By Christmastime, Stanley, a long-time division senior VP ended up replacing Greg as president. Although Peter didn't get the president's job as he had hoped, he kept his position as senior VP. During the last quarter of the year, my unit had accomplished a lot, was more stable, and was on track to continue improving. All this reflected well on Peter since BLM was part of his division.

After the New Year, I completed another self-evaluation. I was happy to see all As and Bs. Chuck had let Stanley and Peter know about my progress with BLM and as a manager. It seems I had come a long way and was ready to fly solo. It was perfect timing for the company as well because Stanley wanted Chuck to help out with another business unit.

In March, Chuck's time with BLM was up. I organized a modest party, and everyone from BLM attended. During the event, Chuck spoke highly about me, my qualities, and the results of my leadership efforts. He always made everybody feel like part of a winning team…and we were. Some of my people said a few words, thanking Chuck for his active and decisive participation. This was very uncommon since, in the past, my team had usually come to hate consultants.

Dustin, one of my lieutenants, generally was a quiet man. It was his speech that touched me most. He stood up and started to speak with great determination. "Chuck, this is a great moment to celebrate success, but it's a sad moment for me because you're leaving. We have become accustomed to your challenges, your wisdom, and overall your constant pursuit of fairness."

There was absolute silence in the room. Most were surprised to hear Dustin deliver a speech. He continued: "You have given me and all my colleagues in this group something priceless. You have given us back our pride, not only as employees but as human beings. You gave me back the pride I needed to be a better husband and a better father. You restored my motivation and the feeling of hope. I'm thankful to you, your knowledge and dedication, the patience you had, and the discipline you imposed. Through tremendous efforts, we became a winning group. Lately, I'm proud to walk the corridors, and I'm proud to say I belong to BLM. What a change!"

Without exception, everyone was touched by his words. All the employees, supervisors, and lieutenants stood up and applauded for a long time. While Dustin was delivering his speech, I saw tears in Chuck's eyes. Chuck approached Dustin and shook his hand. He then returned to where I was and gave me a hug. He stayed for a few more minutes, said good-bye to the others, and left. He would be starting with the other business unit the next day.

Months later, Peter called me in for my year-end evaluation. As usual, he started talking about sports. Then he paused. "Dennis," he said, "what you did with BLM has been wonderful for your business unit, for this division, and for the company. It's fitting that you've been selected for excellent performance. Only five percent of the managers in this company are selected for this category. Congratulations!"

"Thank you," I answered. This was very important to me.

"This also comes with a category promotion and a bonus. In addition, BLM was selected as the 'most improved' business unit in the company. It went from being at the bottom of the ratings to the top of the list. Well done!"

"Thank you," I said. I was very happy. We chatted for another few minutes.

It was late in the day. I returned to my office, organized my desk, and left for home. I picked up Cheryl and the girls, and we went out to celebrate.

Over the course of the following year, I had a few encounters with Chuck, and on several occasions he came to my office to visit. As he would walk the corridor toward my office, several of my employees would go out of their way to greet him. He had earned their respect.

A couple of years later, on a Sunday, my family and I were preparing to leave for church. Before leaving, I checked my e-mail and saw one from Chuck letting me know that he picked up another consulting client in Chicago to help with one of its business units. They heard about all the good he had done at my company and wanted Chuck's expertise to help them grow as well. I couldn't stop from answering immediately.

From: Dennis
To: Chuck

Congratulations and good luck with the new client! Next time you're back in the city and have time to get together, please let me know. I will always be grateful for the mentoring and life lessons you provided me. I look back on our two years together as a significant time in my life. The way I approach my work—and for that matter, many aspects of my life—is very different now than it was five years ago. I continue to try and push myself and internalize the things I have learned

If you ever need anything, let me know. I will do whatever I can to help.

Your student,
Dennis

Writing the e-mail was emotional for me. After hitting the "send" button, I shut down the computer and went outside. Cheryl was standing close to the front door. She said, "Dennis, we're waiting for you, and it's getting late. Honey, your eyes are red. What's going on?"

"I'm fine. I just e-mailed Chuck and reflected on his going-away party. Dustin shared the nicest words about how Chuck had changed him. It wasn't just Dustin who changed. Chuck changed us all in the past few years.

"I've gained so much confidence. I love how my employees have trusted me more and more. Initially, it's like they were testing me, but once they started seeing results, they became invigorated, and I've seen them trying harder and harder ever since. This has had positive effects on our customers, vendors, and upper management. Everyone appreciates that I can *manage it right!*"

I knew that life was more than any strategic plan. There were more adventures to come. Cheryl and I hugged. She wiped the tears from my eyes.

THE END

APPENDICES

Appendix 1:

RFM—The Detailed Questionnaire

Section 1: Business Fundamentals

- Define the unit's mission.
- Business definition: What are the unit's distinctive business cells? Be very specific in defining all the different business cells in which the unit is involved.

Section 2: Business Analysis; for each business cell, separately:

- Describe the business.
- Identify and describe the main short-term and long-term goals (descriptive) and objectives (numeric).
- Describe the success criteria (as of today or as defined for the future).
- Describe and detail all the main activities to be deployed by each business and the minimum amount of personnel required to satisfy the "success criteria" previously described.
- New business models: write down processes followed or to be followed (if change is expected) in detail. Flow charts are recommended.
- Identify all potential sources of revenue from each of the business's activities.

- Provide current performance measures for each business (financial and operational).
- Include current performance benchmarks (i.e., versus competitors, industry average, etc.)
- How is the performance audited?

Section 3: Market Analysis

- Market segmentation: for each of the businesses, explain the criteria actually used (or to be used) for segmentation.
- Customer segmentation (by type, size)
- Emphasis on the segmentation used for marketing and sales purposes
- Total market size and market share
- Trends in the industry: include any available market studies.
- Threats and opportunities
- Uniqueness of service/product
- Competition and competitive threats
- Differentiation
- Detailed pricing analysis: include any materials related to price analysis for each service business.

Section 4: Marketing Activities

- Describe in detail all marketing activities deployed in the last six months.
- Describe in detail all marketing activities that have yet to be deployed during this fiscal year.
- Include:
  - Lectures (speaking assignments)
  - Shows
  - Exhibitions
  - Advertising
  - Promotions, etc.

- Provide samples of marketing materials (i.e., sales kits, transcripts of presentations, etc.).
- Explain how customer satisfaction is currently measured.
- Include any existing reports on customer satisfaction.
- Describe the databases available to the business unit to conduct its own analysis and to track business operational parameters.

Section 5: Sales Force and Sales Activities

- Describe in detail the sales cycle.
- Full discussion of sales barriers
- Full discussion of sales potential
- Sales force: size and qualifications, now and in the future
- Number of dedicated full-time sales personnel
- Quotas
- Mechanisms for growth and sales strategy
- Sales territories: How are the territories distributed among the individual salespeople?
- Sales history by individuals (Who sold what? For how much?)
- Do the sales personnel have other responsibilities on top of selling? What are they?
- Sales kit(s) in use today
- Any additional materials in preparation
- Backlog status
- Detailed revenue forecast (sales plan for the current year, month by month)
- Conceptual roadblocks, threats, and opportunities
- Service revenue of the installed base vs. revenue from other sources
- Top customer list and geographic location (concentration)
- Are there any products required by users that the business unit cannot provide? What are they? Provide reasons.

- Is there any flexibility in pricing in the lines of business that are operating in a competitive arena?
- What are the steps to generate a proposal? How do you know it is competitive?
- Is your company losing any customers in any of the businesses under the unit's responsibility?
- What are the trends and the reasons?

Section 6: Financials, Billing, and Forecasting

Include all expenses incurred by the corporation in supporting this business unit. Allocate where appropriate.

P&L:

- Financial results calendar for last year: P&L final year end, quarterly, and monthly
- Actual monthly and quarterly results for present fiscal year
- Two-year forecast
- Itemize revenues and expenses for products and services
- Describe how COGS (cost of goods sold) is calculated
- Cost of signing on a new customer
- Cost of warranty
- Cost of maintenance (including other departments)
- Cost of insurance
- List all sales by business during last calendar year and year to date (YTD). When applicable, differentiate between payments received from clients as cost of development vs. service to be rendered.

Balance Sheet:

- Provide a hypothetical balance sheet as if the business unit was completely independent (emphasize the different types of inventories).

Other Financial Issues:

- Describe the process of credit analysis and where the responsibility resides.
- What kind of financial audits are being conducted?
- Describe any ongoing (or lack of) financial controls.

Billing:

- For each business, describe and specify what portion of the billing is done directly by the business unit and what portion is done by the company's service units.
- What mechanisms are used to identify billing errors, and what is the process followed to correct them?

Forecasting:

- Describe the total market potential (in dollars) or the maximum total potential revenue and its expected growth for every line of business in the business unit.
- What percentage (%) of this potential has been already achieved?

Section 7: Expense Analysis and Capital Equipment

P&L:

For each business and as part of a P&L report as previously described:

- First, detail by business cell and by function (e.g. marketing, sales, administration, customer service, etc.)
- Second, show the expenses broken down by type of expense (e.g., compensation, travel, internal services, external services, etc.)

Balance Sheet:

- Regarding capital investment, present the detailed capital investment budget for the year and the rules by which this equipment is capitalized in the balance sheet.
- Relate in detail to the level of inventories sustained for every business activity. Differentiate.
- How will the capital equipment budget be impacted by the ongoing "outsourcing program"?

Section 8: Organizational Structure and Personnel

- Describe the organization, now and as you envision it at maturity.
- Show the number of employees in each group and subgroup.
- Describe in detail the processes to be followed for every business cell and main activity, including but not limited to:
    - New Business
    - Maintenance
    - Billing
    - Operating system projects
    - Partnership projects
- Include a short (although very specific) description of the main roles and responsibilities of the positions shown in the organizational diagram and their relationship to the processes previously described (include individual deliverables).
- Regarding "transactional positions," indicate the number of daily/monthly transactions and their nature (i.e., customer service, order-taking, etc.).
- List the positions to be hired.
- Explain the compensation methods being used within the business (including managers and sales personnel).
- List the compensation ranges (salaries + benefits) for every role filled or to be filled.

- Explain the level of experience needed to fill the designed jobs.
- What are the training challenges for the designed operational and managerial team?
- Indicate how many individuals are operating outside the business unit (full-timers and part-timers from other departments and outside the company) who contribute to the unit's operations. List them by name.
- Describe in detail the work done by subcontractors, the economic justification for their activity, their quality and responsiveness, and the risk involved.
- Do the same for future outsourcing. Be very specific regarding "the business case" and present a thorough comparison between the current situation versus the "to be" scenario. Include the additional supervisory capabilities required to manage the outsourced activities.
- What is their responsiveness to the unit?
- What will that relationship be in the future organizational design?
- List all reports issued by the unit in the last six months. These may be:
    - Internal
    - Up the hierarchy
    - To other units
    - To vendors/contractors
- Include their frequency and who the recipients are.

Section 9: Technical Support

Present succinctly:

- The role and job descriptions of all the people in this category within the business unit and others in the company or outside who act under the direct control of the unit in the area of technical support.

- Conduct a preliminary evaluation, including the number of individuals needed to operate the businesses in the future.

Section 10: Customer Support

- Describe the mechanisms used to serve your customers in each of the businesses under the business unit's responsibilities.
- What services are provided directly by this business cell, and what services are provided by other sectors of the company?
- Estimate the character and cost of customer support for each of the businesses.
- Specify the warehouse facilities used.

Section 11: Additional Business Information

Gather the following:

- Detailed, recent business plans
- Marketing plans
- Customer service plans
- Any consulting work completed within the last three years
- Is the group involved in any way, shape, or form with the absorption of new technologies?

Section 12: Partnerships and Joint Ventures

- List in detail all contacts, possibilities, and opportunities to establish partnerships and/or joint ventures as well as existing relationships.
- Clearly differentiate between those in progress versus those that may be feasible in the near future.

Section 13: Union Relationships

- Clarify the role that union workers will play in the transition period and the final structure.

Section 14: General Management

- Describe the main managerial tools used in every one of the businesses.

- Describe the main managerial tools needed in every one of the businesses.

- Name and describe the functionality of all the units within the company that have any role in relation to any business for which the business unit is responsible.

- For each business, describe all the contractors actually working for the company and describe the financial and operational relationship, including any related metrics.

- For each business, define the decision-making process at the different levels of your organization:

    a) Hierarchical at the company level (manager and above)

    b) Internal to the business unit (manager and below)

    c) Contractors

Section 15: Executive Time Management

- Describe and detail the "time pie" for each manager and supervisor who has been involved or committed to this business in the last six months (or shorter periods for new hires).

- How will each employee be deployed (from a time-pie perspective) in the future?

Section 16: Miscellaneous

Include any other important materials that were not requested in the previous sections. In particular:

- Any pending litigation

- Situations that could soon be in litigation

- Indicate the most frequent types of complaints, by business cell

- List all complaints, their nature, and any pending resolution

- Safety challenges

- Any impact of legislation that may result in mandatory compliance, along with a plan of action

Section 17: Major Challenges

For each business cell, describe its three to five major challenges.

Appendix 2:

Chuck's Words of Wisdom

Chuck was famous for his memorable words of wisdom. Below is a listing of many that Chuck shared with Dennis during their Wednesday meetings.

On General Managerial Behavior:

When you have a valid solution at hand, apply it and avoid tangential adventures.

The rules that apply to rapid-growth situations don't apply to defensive situations.

Turnaround requirements supersede ordinary project management needs.

For every meeting you attend, define your meeting objectives and the outcomes you seek. Do your homework.

Remember, no customer left behind.

Achieving greatness is rarely easy, so don't expect smooth sailing all the time.

Winning the war is more important than winning every battle.

Success is not cheap.

Objectives give purpose. Metrics show how you're progressing. Results are what you accomplished.

Hope is not a strategy. Believing in and conforming to sound principles is essential.

"It's not so much how busy you are, but why you are busy. The bee is praised. The mosquito is swatted." (Mary O'Connor, Romance author)

"In order to do what really matters to you, you have to first of all know what really matters to you." (Dr. Ed Hallowell, psychiatrist and author)

"For changes to be of any true value, they've got to be lasting and consistent." (Anthony Robbins, author)

On Decision Making:

Don't fix symptoms. Solve the real problem.

Be granular in understanding a problem or issue and in conceptualizing the solution.

Make solutions crisp and clear.

Often the worst thing is to do nothing.

Make a decision, commit to it, and move on. If it's wrong, change it.

Think before asking for opinions.

First impressions are probably wrong. Avoid acting on gut instinct only.

Out of a hundred solutions, ninety-eight might be wrong. Choose wisely.

People don't learn from making mistakes. They learn from finding solutions.

Solve problems the first time so you don't have to keep fixing them.

Effectiveness is sustainable; efficiency is not.

Excellence of decision making = Quality * Quantity.

Don't optimize something that does not work.

Don't build the second floor before the basement.

Don't build the second floor when the first floor is burning.

Hire future bosses, not current employees.

On Implementation:

Ignore distracting critics and focus on the solution.

Without execution, change does not occur.

    a) Attributes for execution: discipline, perseverance, and dedication.

    b) Attributes for inaction: fear of failure, fear of success, laziness, not understanding, lack of prioritization, lack of focus, and lack of a champion.

A collection of action items is not a plan.

Eliminate excuses and things get done.

If no sense of urgency exists, create it.

A crisis requires all of your resources. Not every situation is a crisis.

On Leadership:

"No man will make a great leader who wants to do it all himself, or get all the credit for doing it." (Andrew Carnegie)

Business management is about performance, not baby-sitting.

A manager's success depends on the success of his or her employees.

Nonperformance cannot be tolerated.

Coaches need to define the rules.

"A coach is someone who tells you what you don't want to hear, who has you see what you don't want to see, so you can be who you have always known you could be." (Tom Landry)

A person who doesn't grow cannot teach.

Differentiate between those who can grow and those who cannot.

Without leadership, no one can follow.

Build teamwork at the top, and your people will follow.

Employees need to play positions. This is pro ball, not the pee-wee leagues.

Don't tolerate bad behavior, such as tardiness, poor or late assignments, unresponsiveness, and the like.

Demand quality.

Face personnel issues.

Develop a feedback loop to ensure monitoring and control.

Your inheritance is not your legacy.

"The kind of people I look for to fill top management spots are the eager beavers, the mavericks. These are the guys who try to do more than they are expected to do—they always reach." (Lee Iacocca)

"Ability is what you're capable of doing. Motivation determines what you do. Attitude determines how well you do it." (Lou Holtz)

Management is a delicate balance between discipline and freedom.

On Managing the Hierarchy:

If you invite pressure, you get pressure.

During periods of uncertainty, don't talk about improvements; let the results speak for themselves.

When meeting with the hierarchy, request resources and share successes.

Give upper management an opportunity to help rather than just approve your work.

When you take a punch, remember to step back and assess.

Use paper and pen to evaluate situations.

To be successful, fight for everything you need.

It ain't over til it's over.

On Managing Stress:

Energy is all you have. Spend it wisely.

High stress levels drive poor decisions.

When faced with panic and anxiety regarding an issue or situation, wait one day and think about it.

Define your fear before you face it.

"The gem cannot be polished without friction, nor man perfected without trials." (Chinese proverb)

General:

"Vision without action is a daydream. Action without vision is a nightmare." (Japanese proverb)

"Never allow perfection to become the enemy of the good." (Walter Mondale)

"He who asks is a fool for five minutes, but he who does not ask remains a fool forever." (Chinese proverb)

"The absence of alternatives clears the mind marvelously." (Henry Kissinger)

"The dictionary is the only place that 'success' comes before 'work.'" (Vince Lombardi)

INDEX

About the Authors

Carlos Zorea, PhD, MSc, founder and CEO of Zorea Consulting, is a business management expert with fifty years of experience in corporate management, executive capacities, and executive consulting. His unique and extensive career spans all phases of business, from development to growth. Dr. Zorea's vast business expertise has proven itself over the years in his roles as chief executive officer, chief operating officer, and as chairman or board member of several companies.

Dr. Zorea increases corporate value by working one-on-one with CEOs and presidents of Fortune 500, midsized, and start-up companies to make high-quality decisions using proven tools, methodologies, and processes. Accordingly, these client companies have achieved growth and improved profitability within a short period of time.

Dr. Zorea's educational background includes a master of science in management from Stanford University's Graduate School of Business and an aeronautical engineering doctorate.

Dee Zorea, MAS, has collaborated with Zorea Consulting on business management theory, corporate strategy initiatives, and client service. He brings more than fifteen years of business experience in finance, accounting, and marketing. Dee completed his undergraduate studies at Dartmouth College and his master of accounting science at Northern Illinois University.